PREACHING The Parables

PREACHING

The Parables

JOHN R. BROKHOFF

Cycle C Texts
from Common, Lutheran,
and Roman Catholic
Lectionaries

C.S.S. Publishing Co., Inc.

Lima, Ohio

PREACHING THE PARABLES C

Second Printing 1989

Third Printing 1992

Library of Congress Cataloging-in-Publication Data

Brokhoff, John R.
  Preaching the parables C.

  Bibliography: p.
  1. Jesus Christ—Parables.   2. Bible.   N.T.   Luke—
Homiletical use.   I. Title.
BT375.2.B76   1988   251   88-6047
ISBN 1-55673-063-2

8860 / ISBN 1-55673-063-2

Table of Contents

Proper designations refer to the Common Lectionary.
Pentecost designations refer to the Lutheran Lectionary.
Ordinary Time designations refer to the Roman Catholic Lectionary.

Introduction

It can be said that Luke is a book of parables. This is true to some degree with all the Gospels, for one-third of the material in the Gospels consists of parables. Of the four Gospels, Luke contains more parables than any one of the rest. Forty percent of Luke's material consists of parables compared with thirty-six percent in Matthew and sixteen percent in Mark.

In the Lectionary, Cycle C, there are nineteen parables. For fourteen Sundays in a row, except for two Sundays, a preacher has a parable for a text, from Pentecost 10 to Pentecost 23. It reminds us of Mark's statement: "He did not speak to them without a parable." (Mark 4:34)

An unknown writer tells of another "book of parables":

A church board of a certain congregation was examining a candidate for church membership. One of the questions asked him was, "What part of the Bible do you like the best?" "I like the New Testament best," he replied. "What book in the New Testament?" "The book of parables, sir." "Would you kindly relate one of these parables to this board?" So the uncertain candidate bluffed as follows:

"Once upon a time a man went down from Jerusalem to Jericho, and fell among thieves, and the thorns grew up and choked him. And he went on and met the Queen of Sheba, and she gave that man, sir, a thousand talents of gold and silver and a hundred changes of raiment. And he got in his chariot and drove furiously. And when he was driving along under a tree, his hair caught in a limb and left him hanging there. And he hung there many days and many nights, and ravens brought him food to eat and water to drink. And one night while he was hanging there asleep, his wife, Delilah, came along and cut off his hair, and he dropped and fell on the stony ground; and it began to rain, and it rained forty days and forty nights. And he hid himself in a cave. And he went on and met a man who said, 'Come in and take supper with me.' But he said, 'I can't come for I have married a wife.' And the man went out into the highways and byways and compelled him to come. He went on and came to Jerusalem, and saw Queen Jezebel sitting high up in a window, and she saw him. She laughed and he said, 'Throw her down out of there.' And they threw her down. And he said, 'Throw her down again,' and they threw her down seventy times seven and of the fragments they picked up twelve baskets full. Now whose wife will she be in the day of judgment?"

There was no one who felt qualified to question the candidate further, for each board member had a deep suspicion that his or her own organized Bible knowledge was as sketchy as that of the candidate. The man was voted into the church.

The Four C's Format

In this book we will consider each parable according to four C's: context, content, contemplation, and contact.

1. Context: A parable is not an independent unit, but is related to a subject or problem which Jesus is handling at the time. It is important for us to fully define the setting of the parable, taking note of what precedes and follows it. The parable is also part of the Gospel lesson appointed for a certain Sunday in the church year. How, then, does the parable in the Gospel lesson relate to the theme of the day and to the other lessons? Finally we need to put the parable in the perspective of the entire Scriptures.

2. Content: What does the parable say or teach? What is the general theme and the most important point? Is there more than one idea being expressed? Who are the personnae in the parable, and what does each represent? To be certain that we understand the meaning of the parable, we need to translate it into our own words (precis). To further clarify the most important idea, we should summarize the truth of the parable in one sentence (thesis). Out of this thesis will then emerge a theme which will become the central point of the proposed sermon. More specifically, we should also note words or phrases that need to be examined closely and carefully defined. A theological wordbook would be helpful here.

3. Contemplation Now that we see the parable in perspective and have a grasp of the message of the parable, the time for deeper reflection has come — for thought, listening, meditating, and prayer. How should we understand the parable? What does it mean to me and my people? What is the parable saying to us? Do you have any unique insights into the truth of the parable? Do you see any sermon possibilities?

4. Contact: The time for action has come. We must ask ourselves whether the subject of the parable has any relevance for today's society. Does the parable address a question that the people are asking? Is there a need in the church which this parable would help to fill? It is time, in other words, for the rubber to hit the road. The revelation of the parable must be made relevant to the people who will fill the pews this Sunday. What is its special relationship to them? What are their needs, their questions, and their problems? If you can find no point of significant contact, then it is better to forget the parable! To help make the sermon indigenous to life, illustrative materials are suggested.

What Others Say

After — and only after — going through this four C's process for yourself, you may want to know what others have to say about the particular parable you are using this Sunday. The following books may then be helpful:

Bailey, Kenneth — *Poet and Peasant*. Eerdmanns, 1976.
Buttrick, George — *The Parables of Jesus*. Harper, 1928.
Crossan, John — *In Parables*. Harper and Row, 1985.
Dodd, C. H. — *The Parables of the Kingdom*. Scribners, 1961.
Granskou, David — *Preaching on the Parables*. Fortress, 1972.
Hunter, Archibald — *Interpreting the Parables*. Westminster, 1960.
Jeremias, Joachim — *The Parables of Jesus*. Scribners, 1962.
Jones, G. V. — *The Art and Truth of the Parables*, 1964.
Linnemann, Eta — *Jesus of the Parables*, 1966.
Ogilvie, Lloyd — *Autobiography of God*. Regal, 1979.
Pentecost, J. D. — *The Parables of Jesus*. Zondervan, 1982.
Purdy, John — *Parables at Work*. Westminster, 1985.
Redding, David — *The Parables He Told*. Revell, 1962.
TeSelle, Sallie — *Speaking in Parables*. Fortress, 1975.
Via, Dan — *The Parables*, 1967.

Preaching the Parables

The popularity of Jesus' parables indicates their importance to Jesus and the church. They constitute one-third of Jesus' teachings. Mark claims that "he did not speak to them without a parable." (Mark 4:34) Forty percent of Luke's material consists of parables compared with thirty-six percent in Matthew and sixteen percent in Mark. In the lectionary, Luke (Cycle C) has nineteen parables, Mark (Cycle B) has four with an additional four from John, and Matthew (Cycle A) has thirteen plus one from John. If a preacher confines the selection of his or her text to the Gospel lessons, Cycle C provides the most opportunities to deal with parables. In fact, Cycle C offers a parable for eleven consecutive Sundays (Proper 10, Pentecost 15 to Proper 22, Pentecost 20). Fifteen Sundays of the Pentecost season deal with parables. One may say that Pentecost in Cycle C is a season of parables.

Luke's Parables

Scholars tell us that in Luke there are thirty-seven parables. Nineteen of them are in Cycle C. All but five are found only in Luke. If it were not for Luke, we would not have some of the very best parables, including the Good Samaritan and the Prodigal Son. The five parables in Series C not peculiar to Luke are:

Sunday	Reference	Parable
Advent 1	Mark 13:28-31 (Luke 21:25-36)	Sign of the Fig Tree
Epiphany 8	Matthew 15:14; 7:24-27 (Luke 6:39-49)	Blind Leading the Blind House on a Rock
Pentecost 13 (Proper 15)	Matthew 16:2-3 (Luke 12:49-56)	Weather Signs
Pentecost 14 (Proper 16)	Matthew 7:13-14, 21-23 (Luke 13:22-30)	The Shut Door
Pentecost 17 (Proper 19)	Matthew 18:12-14 (Luke 15:1-10)	The Lost Sheep

Duplication of Themes

One of the problems of preaching on all the parables in Cycle C is the duplication of themes. This calls for a creative handling of the parables involved and allows for treating various aspects of the theme.

Sunday	Reference	Parable
Lostness		
Lent 4	Luke 15:1-3, 11-32	Lost Son
Pentecost 17 (Proper 19)	Luke 15:1-10	Lost Sheep and Coin
Forgiveness		
Lent 4	Luke 15:1-3, 11-32	Prodigal Son
Pentecost 4 (Proper 6)	Luke 7:36-50	Two Debtors
Compassion		
Pentecost 8 (Proper 10)	Luke 10:25-37	Good Samaritan
Pentecost 19 (Proper 21)	Luke 16:19-31	Lazarus and Dives
Prayer		
Pentecost 10 (Proper 12)	Luke 11:1-13	Friend at Midnight
Pentecost 22 (Proper 24)	Luke 18:1-8	Unrighteous Judge
Pentecost 23 (Proper 25)	Luke 18:9-14	Two Men at Prayer
Materialism		
Pentecost 11 (Proper 13)	Luke 12:13-21	Rich Fool

Pentecost 18 (Proper 20)	Luke 16:1-13	Dishonest Steward

End of Age

Advent 1	Luke 21:25-36	Sign of the Fig Tree
Pentecost 12 (Proper 14)	Luke 12:32-40	Watchful Servants
Pentecost 13 (Proper 15)	Luke 12:49-56	Weather Signs
Pentecost 14 (Proper 16)	Luke 13:22-30	The Shut Door

Humility

Pentecost 15 (Proper 17)	Luke 14:1, 7-14	Seats at Table
Pentecost 23 (Proper 25)	Luke 18:9-14	Two Men at Prayer

Sign of the Times

Advent 1	Luke 21:25-36	Sign of the Fig Tree
Pentecost 13 (Proper 15)	Luke 12:49-56	Weather Signs

Classification of Parables

According to A. M. Hunter, the parables of Jesus can be classified into four categories. The nineteen parables in Cycle C could be classified as follows:

Sunday	*Reference*	*Parable*

Parables of the Kingdom

Advent 1	Luke 21:25-36	Sign of the Fig Tree
Pentecost 14 (Proper 16)	Luke 13:22-30	The Shut Door

Parables of Grace

Pentecost 4 (Proper 6)	Luke 7:41-43	Two Debtors
Lent 4 (Proper 12)	Luke 15:11-32	Prodigal Son
Pentecost 15 (Proper 17)	Luke 14:7-14	Seats at Table
Pentecost 17 (Proper 19)	Luke 15:1-10	Lost Sheep and Coin
Pentecost 23 (Proper 25)	Luke 18:9-14	Two Men at Prayer

Parables of People in the Kingdom

Pentecost 8 (Proper 10)	Luke 10:25-37	Good Samaritan
Pentecost 10 (Proper 12)	Luke 11:1-13	Friend at Midnight
Pentecost 16 (Proper 18)	Luke 14:25-33	Count the Cost
Pentecost 18 (Proper 20)	Luke 16:1-13	Dishonest Steward
Pentecost 20 (Proper 22)	Luke 17:5-10	Doing Your Duty
Pentecost 22 (Proper 24)	Luke 18:1-8	Unrighteous Judge

Parables of Crisis

Lent 3	Luke 13:1-9	Barren Fig Tree
Pentecost 11 (Proper 13)	Luke 12:13-21	Rich Fool
Pentecost 12 (Proper 14)	Luke 12:39-40	Watchful Servants

Pentecost 13	Luke 12:49-56	Weather Signs
(Proper 15)		
Pentecost 19	Luke 16:19-31	Lazarus and Dives
(Proper 21)		

Procedure for Preparation

Preaching the parables is different from preaching on regular texts. We are dealing with a simile, or an analogy, or a metaphor, or an allegory, or a story. It is a whole new ball game from preaching on the usual text such as "God so loved the world . . ." Consider the following steps in preparing to preach on a parable.

1. What is the point of the parable? What is the parable saying? What is the Word in this parable? What is the truth or principle or revelation behind and/or within the parable? This calls for exegesis and getting to the historical situation of the parable.

In getting to the answer to the above questions, we need to remember that there are three levels to the parables.

A. *Level of Jesus' parables as he told them to the people of his day.* He used parables to explain what the Kingdom of God was like and what the people were like in the Kingdom. When he was criticized, he defended his style of ministry by telling the "lost" parables in Luke 15. He answered a lawyer's questions, "Who is my neighbor?", by telling the story of the Good Samaritan. When he wanted to teach lessons on persistence in prayer, or forgiveness, or sharing with the needy, or being prepared for the end, he told an appropriate parable.

B. *Level of the oral period.* After Jesus' ascension, his followers recalled and retold his parables. It was the period of the apostolic church. The stories were passed along by word of mouth. Scholars are able to find several developments in the parables of this period.

First, allegory was used. The parables were used to apply or explain conditions that prevailed at the time. Matthew used allegory to explain the parable of the weeds. (Matthew 13:36-43) Mark explained the parable of the sower allegorically. (Mark 4:14-20) These are samples of the early church's adaptation and application of the parable to current conditions. As far as we know, Jesus did not use allegory.

Second, the church added a moral to some of Jesus' original

parables. One of these morals is in Luke 12:21: "This is how it is with those who pile up riches for themselves but are not rich in God's sight."

Third, tag lines were put at the end of a parable. One is "For everyone who makes himself great will be humbled, and everyone who humbles himself will be made great." (Luke 14:11) Another: "Then those who are last will be first, and those who are now first shall be last." (Luke 13:30)

C. *Level of the written period.* For a permanent record the church saw the necessity of gathering and recording the stories Jesus told. Matthew, Mark, and Luke were among those who performed this service. The evangelists made some changes in the parables to make them relevant to their day and its problems. At times the parables were tied down to specific situations. For instance, the parable of the seats of honor was located in the home of a Pharisee where Jesus noticed how some chose chief seats at a banquet. (Luke 14:1, 7)

Sometimes the evangelists put parables together which made the same point. Mark combined the parables dealing with patches and new wine. (Mark 2:21-22)

Again, the evangelists may change the situations and people addressed. Matthew has Jesus give the parable of the lost sheep to the Disciples, but Luke has Jesus tell it to the Pharisees. (Matthew 18:12; Luke 15:1-2)

2. **What does the parable mean?** At this point we have the main point or the truth of the parable, but what does it mean? Do we understand it? How shall we interpret the parable?

For 1500 years the answer was allegory. This method of interpretation was begun by Clement of Alexandria (A. D. 150-215). Some of the greatest church leaders used this method: Origen, Augustine, Gregory the Great, Thomas Acquinas, Richard Trench and others. In the nineteenth century Julicher put a stop to that! He persuaded the church that a parable had only one main point. The details in a parable are not separate points but contribute to the main point.

Julicher's contribution was well taken. New Testament scholars, Dodd, Jeremias, Bullmann, Fuchs, and others, since his time have refined and added to his position.

The preacher of today struggles with these questions: (1) What is the central teaching of the parable? (2) Is there more than one truth? He or she prays for the Holy Spirit to give insight and enlightenment that the answers may be found.

3. Does the parable relate to life here and now? Revelation and relevance are two sides of the same coin. An effective and helpful sermon must have both. Does the parable meet a need people have today? Does the parable deal with an issue of our twentieth to twenty-first centuries?

Jesus did not speak in parables just to tell stories. The parable often resulted from specific situations or needs. The parable was an answer or solution to a question or problem brought to his attention. A review of the parables which we will be preaching on in Cycle C shows us how Jesus told parables to answer specific needs. Jesus told parables —

A. *To teach.* To teach people not to be critical of others. In the Parable of the Blind Leading the Blind (Luke 6:39-49), Jesus was at the time urging the people not to judge others. To criticize others for blindness is like the blind leading the blind. Again, the Parable of the Two Debtors (Luke 7:38—8:3) resulted from a Pharisee's criticizing a prostitute for expressing her gratitude to Jesus. Do people today need a lesson on not being judgmental?

To teach persistence in prayer. In Cycle C there are two parables dealing with persistence. The Parable of the Friend at Midnight (Luke 11:1-13) is related to Jesus' teaching the Disciples how to pray. The lesson is not only in content (the Lord's Prayer) but in method — persistence. The Parable of the Widow and the Judge (Luke 18:1-8) was told "to teach them that they should always pray and never become discouraged." (v.1) Are we today lacking in persistence in prayer?

To teach humility. The parable of chief seats (Luke 14:1, 7-14) came in connection with a dinner party in the home of a Pharisee. (v.1) As the people gathered, Jesus noticed how in pride they chose the best places. Again, Jesus tells a parable (Luke 18:9-14) about two men in the temple at prayer to teach humility. "Jesus also told this parable to people who were sure of their own goodness and despised everybody else." (v.9)

B. *To defend his life-style.* In Cycle C we have the "lost chapter" (Luke 15) that contains three well-known parables: the Lost Sheep, the Lost Coin, and the Lost Son. These were told to answer the Pharisees' criticism that Jesus associated with sinners, tax collectors, and outcasts. By these parables Jesus defended his ministry to sinners. By associating with them he was seeking the lost.

C. *To answer questions.* Jesus used parables to answer questions. The answer was implied in the story. One day a biblical scholar asked him, "Who is my neighbor?" Jesus answered with the Parable of the Good Samaritan. (Luke 10:25-37). Again, while Jesus was on his way to Jerusalem, someone asked him, "Will just a few people be saved?" The answer was the Parable of the Closed Door. (Luke 13:22-30)

D. *To overcome materialism.* Materialism then and now is expressed in covetousness. One day a man asked Jesus to persuade his brother to share their father's inheritance. Jesus recognized his greed and responded with the Parable of the Rich Fool. (Luke 12:13-21)

The parable of Lazarus and Dives (Luke 16:19-31) needs to be seen in the context of the foregoing. When the Pharisees heard Jesus' teachings on possessions, they laughed at him "Because they loved money." (v.14) To overcome this love of money, Jesus tells the story of a rich man and a beggar.

It is obvious, is it not, that every one of the above parables deals with a human need or problem. So, in our preaching, we need to see what our needs are so that the parables can speak relevantly to our congregations.

What Parables Can Teach about Preaching

A study of the parables can teach us to be effective preachers. The parables are not saying that a sermon is to be a parable, but they contain certain elements that should characterize good sermons. Consider what we can learn from them.

1. The value and necessity of homiletical materials. The fact that one-third of Jesus' teachings consists of parables shows us that our sermons need illustrative materials. Without proper illustrations, stories, and anecdotes, the sermon becomes heavy, dull, and uninteresting. Illustrations are necessary to get and hold interest, to teach deep truths, and to uplift and inspire people to lead godly lives. Good illustrations are hard to come by. A preacher is constantly searching for them. To get good homiletical material, preachers need to sharpen their observation ablility and to increase their sensitivity to the meaning of everyday things and events.

2. The use of the secular. Not one of Jesus' parables is "religious." The materials are secular. Though he knew the Scriptures better than anyone, he never quoted his Bible in the parables. He told about worldly things, people, and events. There was a victim of robbers on the Jericho road. A farm manager used dishonest methods to feather his nest. A friend demands bread in the middle of the night. A teenager runs away from home with his pockets full of his inheritance. The blind lead the blind. A fig tells a story.

Why, do you suppose, Jesus did not tell Bible stories or quote the Scriptures? He might have re-told the wonderful stories of Abraham, Samson, Moses, and Daniel. Were the stories too well known by the average person, thus having little impact? Perhaps the reason Jesus used secular accounts was that it was the best way to make contact with the people. He met them where they were and used illustrations with which they could identify.

We can learn from Jesus that our illustrations should come not so often from the Bible, but from life, from people, and from the world. For most people the Bible is foreign and it is another world. Speak about personal experiences, the tales of other people, the life situations, and the happenings in the world, and you will get a hearing. The daily newspaper is one of the best sources for this kind of homiletical material.

3. Vivid language. The parables are told in vivid language, a language that enables us to see the truth. These words put eyes into our ears just as deaf people put ears into their eyes. In the parables we see the characters and sense the situation. By this kind of language we get involved in the problem and participate in the solution. In our use of homiletical material, we need to use imagination. We must see the situation before we can describe it to our people. The words we use to accomplish this are to be simple, plain, monosyllabic Anglo-Saxon words of action. Avoid ecclesiastical jargon. Refuse to use religious language. Put the truth in the people's everyday speech.

4. Brevity. Jesus' parables are amazing in saying so much in so few words. Most of the parables are less than a paragraph. Probably the longest parable is the Prodigal Son because it is a story about two lost sons. Preachers have a tendency to elongate an illustration so that, at times, the illustration is one-third the length of the sermon. Moreover, a lengthy story often overshadows the point of the message being made at the time. Good illustrations are usally short. They quickly come to the point and the punch line is prominent. This is because an illustration does not exist for itself but exists only to elucidate a lesson or a principle.

5. Inductive method. Jesus apparently avoided the deductive method of reasoning in his parables. He preferred the inductive method. He started out with a problem, need, or situation and let his hearers think about the solution or answer. He had them discover the truth for themselves and to come to their own conclusions as to the solution.

He often began with a question, "Can a blind man lead a blind man?" (Luke 6:39) He asked a Pharisee, "Now which of them will love him more?" (Luke 7:42) Before telling the story of the Good Samaritan, Jesus asked the lawyer, "What is written in the law? How do you read?" (Luke 10:26) After telling the parable, he wanted the lawyer to find the answer to his question, "Which of these three, do you think, proved neighbor to the man who fell among robbers?" (Luke 10:36)

Our sermons will be more effective if we use the same method. At the beginning of the sermon, state the problem or raise the issue or ask the question. Ask the people to think about the possible answer. What are their options? What conclusion must we come to? In our day, people do not want to be told what to do or what not to do or what to think. They do not like authoritarian dictation. They want to think for themselves and come to their own decisions. The preacher gives them the options and helps people to think the problem through. He or she so guides the thought that the right conclusion is inevitable.

6. Dialogical approach. In the parable Jesus uses a dialogical method. He does not speak *to* the people but *with* the people. He constantly gets them involved in the subject. He refers to them, asks them questions, refers to their everyday interests, and lets them answer his questions. Consider his dialogical strategy:

Luke 21:29 — "Look at the fig tree . . ."

Luke 7:44 — "Do you see this woman?"

Luke 11:5 — "Which of you who has a friend will go to him at midnight . . . ?

Luke 15:4 — "What man of you, having a hundred sheep . . . ?"

Luke 17:7 — "Will any one of you, who has a servant plowing or keeping sheep . . . ?"

Jesus' dialogical method is for us preachers today. People do not want to be *preached at* but rather they want tc be *talked with*. Preaching is a two-way communication, a dialogue, or conversation. The people in the pews want and need to be involved in the sermon because it is about and for them. We are talking about their lives, needs, and problems. They should be included. And the way to do it is Jesus' way — the way of dialogical preaching.

Advent 1

1. The Sign of the Fig Tree

Luke 21:25-36

²⁵*"And there will be signs in sun and moon and stars, and upon earth distress of nations in perplexity at the roaring of the sea and the waves,* ²⁶*men fainting with fear and with foreboding of what is coming on the world; for the powers of the heavens will be shaken.* ²⁷*And then they will see the Son of man coming in a cloud with power and great glory.* ²⁸*Now when these things begin to take place, look up and raise your heads, because your redemption is drawing near."*

²⁹*And he told them a parable: "Look at the fig tree, and all the trees;* ³⁰*as soon as they come out in leaf, you see for yourselves and know that the summer is already near.* ³¹*So also, when you see these things taking place, you know that the kingdom of God is near.* ³²*Truly, I say to you, this generation will not pass away till all has taken place.* ³³*Heaven and earth will pass away, but my words will not pass away.*

³⁴*"But take heed to yourselves lest your hearts be weighed down with dissipation and drunkenness and cares of this life, and that day come upon you suddenly like a snare;* ³⁵*for it will come upon all who dwell upon the face of the whole earth.* ³⁶*But watch at all times, praying that you may have strength to escape all these things that will take place, and to stand before the Son of Man."*

Are we able to read the signs of the times for what the future will bring? If a groundhog in Pennsylvania sees his shadow, so the superstition goes, we can expect six more weeks of winter. It is said that if you take the seed from a ripe persimmon and split it open, the shape of the pulp inside the seed can determine the type of winter which is ahead. If it is in the shape of a spoon, the winter will be mild. If it is shaped like a fork, the winter will be average. If the pulp resembles a knife, the winter will be severe.

In 1986 there was a nuclear disaster in Chernobyl, Russia. Over 100,000 people had to be evacuated in a nineteen mile danger zone and eighty people died from radiation sickness. The radiation went as far as Lapland where reindeer meat still cannot be eaten because of radiation from Chernobyl. Soviet physicians learned that, in the event of a nuclear war, the medical system would be absolutely helpless. Is this nuclear accident a portent of what will happen to the world when a nuclear outbreak occurs?

What about the end of the world and Christ's return? Is the end coming? If so, will it be soon? Jesus used the same method as we do to tell what is coming. He tells the parable of the budding trees. At springtime do we see the trees; tender branches and the leaves about to appear? Can't we see that summer is close at hand? Look at the world situation. Does it not intimate that the end is coming and Christ is returning?

Context

Context of the Season

Today's parable is a part of the Gospel lesson for Advent 1, Cycle C. This Sunday not only opens the Advent season but also the church year. It is the new year's day of the church. With the beginning of a new church year, we start the story of the teachings and work of Christ. "Advent" means "coming to." Christ comes to the world as an infant to grow to manhood, to die as the Messiah, and to rise to glory with the Father.

There is something unrealistic in our references to Advent in terms of Jesus' coming as though he never came. Advent means that Jesus is coming again. It is a fact that Jesus came to the world around 4 B.C. On the cross he made atonement for our sins. To merely say he is coming is misleading and play-acting as though he never came. The theme of Advent is that Christ is coming again. Accordingly, the First Sunday in Advent deals with the Second Coming at the end of time. If he is coming again, in succeeding Sundays in Advent we deal with the ministry of John the Baptist who calls us to prepare by repenting.

Christ's coming again is a future event. His return will mark the end of the world and the judgment of the nations, resulting in the division of the sheep and the goats.

Christ's coming again can be a present experience also. Spiritually he can come to those who have not yet received him into their hearts. To those who are already believers he can come again in a deeper, fuller measure. In this case, it is a renewed coming in terms of deeper faith, more love, and greater commitment to him. For Advent to make sense, we need to say that Jesus is coming again now and in the future. He comes again here and now spiritually and is received into the heart by faith. He comes again cosmically to judge the nations and to gather his people for life eternal.

Context of the Lectionary

The First Lesson. (Jeremiah 33:14-16) With the fall of Jerusalem in 586 B.C., the nation of Judah ceased to exist and the Babylonian captivity brought to an end David's reign. David was promised that his family would always be in power. What now? Is the promise broken? In this pericope a post-exilic writer claims that this promise will be fulfilled. A son of David will reign over Israel when she returns to Jerusalem from captivity. As the son of David, Jesus fulfilled the promise when he came to rule over the Kingdom. Who is coming? The son of David according to promise.

The Second Lesson. (1 Thessalonians 3:9-13) When Christ returns, what kind of people shall we be? Paul urges his people to be blameless in holy living and to love each other until Christ returns. Here we are given the ethical dimension to the Parousia.

Gospel. (Luke 21:25-36) Jesus speaks of conditions near the time of his return: celestial signs, distress on earth, fear. When will he return? Just as we know summer is near by seeing the leaves about to sprout on trees, we will know the time is close at hand. To be ready for his return, we need to live righteously and to watch and pray.

Psalm. (Psalm 25:1-10) The Psalmist expresses trust in God and prays that those who wait for the Lord will not be put to shame.

The Prayer of the Day. The Prayer begins, "Stir up your power, O Lord, and come."

The Hymn of the Day. "Fling Wide the Door" The Hymn exhorts us to open our hearts and minds to receive the King of Glory.

Bringing it all together. The lections and propers revolve around the theme of Christ's Second Coming.

Context of the Scriptures

Parallel passages Matthew 24:32-35 and Mark 13:28-31 are almost word for word the same. In Luke's account (Luke 21:29-33) we note the following variances. (1) Luke refers not only to the fig tree but to "all the trees." This makes it a universal experience, for not all people are limited to fig trees. (2) Both Matthew and Mark say that when these calamities occur, "You know that he is near." Luke says that "the kingdom of God is near." Of course, Jesus and the Kingdom are one, because not only does Jesus bring the Kingdom but he is the Kingdom.

Various Fig Trees
Matthew 24:32-33; Mark 13:28-29; Luke 24:29-33 — The
budding fig tree
Matthew 21:18-22; Mark 11:12-14 — The cursed fig tree
Luke 13:6-9 — The barren fig tree

The Fig Tree in Other Passages
Genesis 3:7 — Adam and Eve made aprons out of fig leaves.
1 Kings 4:25 — Sitting under one's fig tree was a sign of
prosperity and happiness.
2 Kings 20:7 — A cake of figs cures King Hezekiah's boil.
John 1:48 — Jesus sees Nathanael under a fig tree.
James 3:12 — A fig tree cannot yield olives.
Revelation 6:13 — The stars fall to earth like the fig tree sheds
its winter fruit when shaken by a gale.

Content

Precis of the Pericope

In the heavens there will be chaos involving sun, moon, and stars. At
the same time, on earth, there will be chaos with the roaring of the sea and
raging tides causing people to be scared to death over what is happening.
After this, Jesus will come with great power and glory. In the face of these
things, stand up and look up because your deliverance is at hand.

Then Jesus told them a parable about the fig and all other trees. When
the leaves begin to appear, you know summer is soon to come. Similarly,
when you see the chaos in the heavens and on earth, you know that the
Kingdom of God is about to come. All these things will happen in this generation. Heaven and earth will come to an end, but my words never!

Watch out then that you do not get too involved in feasting, drinking,
and in worrying, so that the end will catch you unaware. For the day will
come to everyone everywhere. So watch and pray for strength to escape these
horrors and to confront Jesus.

Thesis: Understand the signs of the times and take the necessary precau-
tions of repentance and pray for the return of Christ.

Theme: The signs of the times — read them correctly!

Content of the Parable

The parable simply says that, as we know summer is near when we see the leaves coming to the trees, we should recognize the fact that the return of Christ will happen soon. To understand this point we need the rest of the Gospel lesson. What are the approaching leaves? They are the chaos in heaven and on earth. (vv. 25-28). If we see that the end is near and Christ's return is imminent, what can we do about it? The Gospel lesson answers:

V. 28 — Look up and see that deliverance is at hand.

V. 33 — Have a sense of security in Jesus' words.

V. 34-36 — Live responsibly and expectantly for Christ's return.

Key Words

1. "Signs." (v. 25) Signs tell us something — how fast to drive, where to get food, lodging, and gas when traveling. Signs also tell us where to go and give us information: "Open" or "Closed." The strange things that are happening in the sky and on the earth are to tell us something about Christ's return. The coming leaves on the trees constitute a sign that Parousia is near.

2. "Son of man." (vv. 27, 36) Twice in this pericope Jesus refers to himself as the "Son of man." It is a title that means more than just his humanity ("man"), but is a term for "Messiah." The Son of man is also Son of God. Thus, his coming means "redemption" or "salvation." (v. 28) With his coming arrives also the Kingdom of God, for the Kingdom consists of God's people who live under the reign of God. The Son of man will return to deliver his people from the horrible conditions on earth and in the sky.

3. "These things." (vv. 31, 32) When "these things" are seen, they are like the budding trees showing summer is at hand. What are "these things"? They are the strange things happening in the sky and the terror on earth. But, more than these are what Jesus mentions earlier in chapter 21. He tells of the persecution coming to his followers and the destruction of Jerusalem and the temple. Here we see the collapse of the universe, both the heavens and the earth, and the destruction of the religious establishment — the end of the nation (God's people) and of the temple where Yahweh and his people meet.

4. "Near." (v. 28) In this Gospel lesson "near" is used three times. When the trees bud and leaves are about to come, we know, says Jesus, that summer is near. How near is the Parousia? For almost 2000 years we have been preaching that Christ's return is near. Along with Jesus, we do not know the exact day, but it is "near." But, how near is "near"? It may not be as near as we think. In Mark, Jesus says that he will not come until the Gospel is preached to all nations. (13:10) In his second letter Peter explains the delay of Jesus' coming: "The Lord is not slow about his promise as some count slowness, but is forbearing toward you, not wishing that any should perish, but that all should reach repentance." (3:9) "Near" may not be so near, if the Gospel must first be preached to all nations and the world must first come to repentance.

5. "Generation." (v. 32) "This generation will not pass away till all has taken place." Did Jesus mean his own generation or our generation? If he meant his generation, then he was mistaken about the time of his return. Rather, Jesus is referring to this generation which would see the destruction of the temple and Jerusalem and which would suffer persecution for his sake.

6. "Pass away." (v. 33) It may seem that Jesus' statement that heaven and earth but not his words, will "pass away" is out of place. However, it is a statement of comfort and confidence in the midst of the total disruption and disappearance of the heavens and earth. In the midst of chaos and change, Jesus assures us that his words, teachings, and truth will be permanent. His words constitute the rock in sinking sand. It gives us a sense of security and hope for the living of these chaotic times.

7. "Stand." (v. 36) Where do we "stand" in the time of chaos and the return of Christ? Here is the place where we enter the scene. Jesus returns and we confront him. We are to "stand" before him. What kind of people must we be? In today's Second Lesson Paul says we are to be "unblamable in holiness." In the light of Jesus' near and unexpected coming, our lives should be so good and pure that we can "stand" before him. Here we have the ethical dimension of this Gospel lesson.

Contemplation

Preaching Values and Context

It is not wise to separate a parable from its context. In preaching on a parable, we draw from the context. C. H. Dodd reminds us: "We must look first to the particular setting in which the parables were delivered. The task of the interpreter of the parables is to find out, if he can, the setting of a parable in the situation contemplated by the Gospels, and hence, the application which would suggest itself to one who stood in that situation."

1. The worst times are the best time. In the parable Jesus says, "When you see these things take place." (v. 31) What are these worst times? Verses 25-27 give the answer. In the midst of these worst times comes the best time for Christians, the coming again of Christ. (v. 27)

2. The certainty of Jesus' return. When the leaves appear, "summer is already near" (v. 30) and "the kingdom of God is near." (v. 31) The return of Christ will certainly happen. He will come "with power and great glory." (v. 27)

3. The meaning of the times. "You see for yourselves." (v. 30) You see the budding trees. What do they mean? It calls us to be alert and sensitive to what is happening around us. We need to see and understand the handwriting on the wall.

4. The changeless and the changing. The budding trees tell us Christ will soon return. In connection with his coming, there will be turbulence in the sky and terror on earth. The heavens will be shaken. (v. 26) Conditions on earth will involve destruction, despair and dissipation. In the midst of this topsy-turvy world, there is one changeless thing, the words of Jesus. (v. 33) It is the lighthouse during a raging sea. The one thing stable and sure is the Word of God as spoken by Jesus.

5. The quality of life for end times. As the budding trees tell us summer is near (v. 30), the conditions in the world warn us that Christ and the Kingdom are near. (v. 31) Therefore, we are to "take heed to" ourselves. We need to become presentable ("stand," v. 36) to the returned Christ. To be presentable there is need for repentance, a turning away from "dissipation and drunkenness and cares of this life." (v. 34) It calls also for a life of faith that is expressed in watching and praying for strength to escape the calamities. (v. 36) Advent is the time for this preparation. Consequently, Advent is a season of repentance in anticipation of Christ's coming again. If he is to come again on Christmas either cosmically or personally, we need to repent in order to be "blameless in holiness." (1 Thessalonians 3:13)

Homily Hints

1. Take a Look! (21:25-36) In the giving and the circumstances of the parable, Jesus urges us to take a look.
>   A. Look at — "Look at the fig tree" — v. 29.
>   See what and who are coming.
>   B. Look up — "Look up and raise your heads" — v. 28.
>   See your salvation.
>   C. Look in — "Take heed to yourselves" — v. 34.
>   See inside your life and see the need for repentance.

2. Christ is Coming Again! (21:27-31) As the budding trees tell us summer is near, world conditions indicate Christ is coming and the Kingdom of God is near.

    A. The certainty of his coming — v. 27.

    B. The manner of his coming: power and glory — v. 27.

    C. The reason for his coming: redemption — v. 28.

    D. The time of his coming: "near" — v. 31.

3. Do You Believe in Signs? (21:25-36) The parable tells us that when the trees are budding, it is a sign of coming summer. When there is chaos in the heavens and fear on earth, it is a sign of the end and Christ's return. Do we believe in signs and obey them? "Wrong way," "Closed," "Detour," "Bridge out"? When signs are up, we have several options —

    A. See the signs.

        Budding trees — cosmic chaos and earthly turbulence.

    B. Ignore the signs.

        We ignore the signs because we really don't want Christ to come.

    C. Believe the signs.

        Prepare for Christ's coming: repentance and faith.

4. Living during End Times (21:25-36) We may be living in end times. "The distress of nations" (v. 25) is surely today's situation. As the summer of the parable is "near" and the coming of Christ is "near" (v. 31), the end may be just around the corner. How are we to live in these days? Our text says —

    A. Be on the lookout for him: "Watch" — v. 36.

    B. Be secure in your faith — v. 33.

    C. Be responsible in your behavior — v. 34.

    D. Be in prayer for strength — v. 36.

Contact

Problems

1. The lost season. With the beginning of the Advent season and a new church year, a preacher faces questions like these. Shall I insist that my congregation observe Advent and thereby refrain from Christmas hymns, decorations, and parties until Christmas? Shall I follow the Lectionary and preach Advent themes?

Particularly in nonliturgical churches the Advent season is a lost one. It is the one season of the church year that is being ignored in favor of Christmas. In this regard the world is setting the agenda for the church, because the world uses the Advent season to sell articles for Christmas gifts. In many churches Christmas has replaced the Advent season. During Advent many churches sing Christmas carols, hold candlelight services, hear Christmas sermons, and are decorated with a Christmas tree in the chancel. The excuse is, "People are thinking Christmas now and we need to strike while the iron is hot."

For many, Christmas is a secular and cultural event without a touch of spirituality. It is a business bonanza, a materialistic spree, a holiday season for pleasure and/or vacation. The religious meaning of Christmas is largely hidden or lost in secular trappings.

What has happened to the old-fashioned spiritual Christmas? The cause is our disregard of Advent. The church set aside this four-week pre-Christmas season as a time of spiritual preparation for Christ's coming. It is a time of quiet anticipation. If Christ is going to come again into our hearts, there must be repentance. Without repentance, our hearts will be so full of worldly things that there will be "no room in the inn" for Christ to be born again. This spirit of repentance is symbolized by the liturgical color, violet. At the same time, we use the color of blue during Advent to express our hope for his coming again. We stand on tiptoe looking for his coming. We have the joy not of celebration, which is the joy of Christmas, but the joy of anticipation. We express this hope in the blue color of the paraments.

A conscientious observance of Advent will make Christmas a beautiful and meaningful experience. Christ will come again, be born in us again. Christmas will change from a holiday into a holy day of renewed love and peace. In the light of this, can a preacher not preach on Advent themes according to the Lectionary?

2. Is Christ coming or not? Before we can prepare a sermon on today's parable, we must know the answer to the above question. If Christ is not returning, there is no need for a sermon on this subject. On the other hand, some may believe that Christ had already come when the Spirit came on Pentecost and is present in the church today. In this case also, a sermon on the parable is unnecessary.

According to a 1986 survey by the Princeton Religion Research Center, sixty-two percent of Americans believe Jesus will return some day. According to this poll, over one-third of Americans do not believe in the Parousia. If we believe that Jesus will return, preachers have a challenge to persuade people to believe in his coming.

To preach on today's parable demands a belief in the Parousia. Why would one believe it? For one thing, the Bible teaches it. The subject of the Second Coming occurs 1845 times in the Bible, 318 times in the New Testament. Seven out of every ten chapters in the New Testament refer to the Parousia. Moreover, the church has believed in it since the first century, for Sunday after Sunday she confesses in the Apostles' Creed. "From thence he shall come to judge the living and the dead."

3. Is the Second Coming to be taken seriously? Is it possible that church people no longer take the Parousia seriously? In some denominations almost every Sunday the sermon at least refers to it and Gospel hymns and anthems treat the subject. Is it possible we could be crying "Wolf" so often that we are no longer being heard? The church year and lectionary call upon us to deal with the subject at the end and beginning of the church year. We hear the same passage at least once a year, year after year. Since the first century, each generation believed Christ would come in that generation. For instance, Paul wrote: "For salvation is nearer to us now than when we first believed; the night is far gone, the day is at hand." (Romans 13:11, 12) If time after time he did not come, why would anyone be concerned about his coming in our generation?

This is a real problem for the preacher. The fact is that there is always the possibility that today is the day of his return. No one knows the time. We live constantly with the possibility. It calls for living each day in a state of grace in the event that Christ would come today or tomorrow.

Points of Contact

1. Controversy. The Second Coming is a live subject among church people today. In Mark 13:32, Jesus plainly said that only the Father knows the day of the end and the return of Christ. In spite of this, some groups of Christians seem to know more than Jesus or the angels on this matter of date. In the fifteenth century the Taborites, for instance, fixed the date in the middle of February. The Seventh Day Adventists claimed the end would come on October 22, 1844. Jehovah's Witnesses and the Mormons also set a date. In more recent times Fundamentalist leaders use the books of Daniel and Revelation to determine a specific date. In response, the Lutheran Council in the USA in 1986 prepared a statement opposing this date fixing. The statement objects to holding to the view that current history is in a countdown stage toward the imminent end. The paper declared, "To make human measurements out of heavenly visions is simply forced imposition on the text."

2. Popularity. The Second Coming is a popular subject in contemporary society. Many are fascinated by the prospect of the world's destruction. When will it all end? How will it end? We are a society faced with star wars, nuclear war, violence, and terrorism. When the world appears to be hopeless and people are desperate, it becomes interested in last things.

It is a popular subject with Fundamentalists, Pentecostals, and

Charismatics. Often it is the main theme of sermons and songs. The lack of attention given to the Parousia by mainline churches gives the impression they do not believe in it. They do believe in the Parousia, and each year it is the subject for consideration according to the church year and lectionary. But, the doctrine needs to be kept in proper perspective and balance within the total Gospel.

3. Ultimate questions. People in the pews are asking and are concerned with ultimate questions about life and the world. They hear various answers which conflict with each other. They want clear and true answers to questions like these: Whose world is this — God's or Satan's? Will God allow humanity to destroy his world? Because of a possible nuclear holocaust, will there be any people on earth when Christ returns? Will not the wrongs be righted and justice be meted out to those who committed crimes and got away with them on earth? Does history go on endlessly without meaning or consummation? Is it possible that God will use a nuclear destruction as the scene for Jesus' return? All of these questions and more are involved in preaching on the Parable of the Budding Trees.

Illustrative Materials

1. Awareness. Some years ago a botanist was studying the heather bell on the highlands of Scotland. While studying the flower a shepherd came up and asked what he was doing. Rather than try to explain, he invited the shepherd to look at a flower through his microscope. When he saw the glorious beauty of the flower, the shepherd exclaimed, "My God, and I have been tramping on them all my life!"

2. The End? In 1986 a United Nations expert predicted that an all-out nuclear war would kill about four billion people, four fifths of the world population. If the entire world's nuclear arsenal, equivalent to 30 billion tons of TNT were used, one billion people in the northern hemisphere would be killed.

Martin Luther: "If I knew that tomorrow was going to end, I would want all the same to pay my debts and plant my little apple tree today."

3. Anticipation. A preacher was describing the end of the world. "Lightning will crackle," he said, "thunder will boom, rivers will overflow, flames will shoot down from the heavens, and darkness will fall over the world." A small boy turned to his father and asked in a whisper, "Do you think they will let school out early?"

4. Preparation. In July 1984 President Ronald Reagan came to Atlanta to make a speech and to spend the night there. It took 160 hours of preparation for his twenty hour visit. Advance teams of forty people came to make necessary arrangements: 167 hotel rooms, bomb-sniffing dogs, a special chef, Godiva chocolates, a private switchboard, and bullet-proof windows in his suite.

5. Watch. On April 10, 1912 the Titanic left Southampton for New York City on her maiden voyage. The ship was as high as an eleven-story building, 900 feet long, and weighed 46,000 tons. It was considered an unsinkable, perfect ship. The Titanic went full-speed into an iceberg and 1100 people lost their lives when it sank to the bottom. A ship, California, was only ten miles away, but she did not respond to the Titanic's SOS and Mayday because at the time the radio operator was asleep.

---

2. The Blind Leading the Blind

Luke 6:39-49

---

[39]*He also told them a parable: "Can a blind man lead a blind man? Will they not both fall into a pit?* [40]*A disciple is not above his teacher, but every one when he is fully taught will be like his teacher.* [41]*Why do you see the speck that is in your brother's eye, but do not notice the log that is in your own eye?* [42]*Or how can you say to your brother, 'Brother, let me take out the speck that is in your eye,' when you yourself do not see the log that is in your own eye? You hypocrite, first take the log out of your own eye, and then you will see clearly to take out the speck that is in your brother's eye.*

[43]*"For no good tree bears bad fruit, nor again does a bad tree bear good fruit;* [44]*for each tree is known by its own fruit. For figs are not gathered from thorns, nor are grapes picked from a bramble bush.* [45]*The good man out of the good treasure of his heart produces good, and the evil man out of his evil treasure produces evil; for out of the abundance of the heart his mouth speaks.*

[46]*"Why do you call me 'Lord, Lord, and not do what I tell you?* [47]*Every one who comes to me and hears my words and does them, I will show you what he is like:* [48]*he is like a man building a house, who dug deep, and laid the foundation upon rock; and when a flood arose, the stream broke against that house, and could not shake it, because it had been well built.* [49]*But he who hears and does not do them is like a man who built a house on the ground without a foundation; against which the stream broke, and immediately it fell, and the ruin of that house was great."*

On the occasion of the fiftieth reunion of our Muhlenberg College class, my wife and I visited the beautiful Gothic chapel. While we were admiring the art work, a bat was flying back and forth from the east to the west walls. It flew as though it were blind. There is a saying, "Blind as bats." But, they say that bats have eyes, flying only at night by sonar. The bat in the chapel raised a question in our minds — are church people like blind bats? Do they have eyes but see not? Though there is physical sight, is there spiritual blindness?

In today's Gospel lesson there are four parables. The first is the parable of the blind leading the blind. To whom was Jesus talking? The four parables constitute the closing section of the Sermon on the Plain. Jesus was speaking to his Disciples and other Jews. He was not speaking to pagan Romans, to philosophical Greeks, or to worldly people. He was speaking to "church" people. Apparently, some of them were the blind leading the blind. In this chapter we will focus upon the first of these four parables for possible preaching.

Context

Context of the Church Year

Epiphany 8 is the last ordinary Sunday of the Epiphany season. It is followed by the Festival of the Transfiguration. If we use the parable of the blind leading the blind, it harmonizes with the theme of the Epiphany season. One symbol of Epiphany is the five-pointed star. With the Wise Men we in the darkness see the light of the star that leads to the Christ-child. Another symbol of the Epiphany season is a candle which sheds its light into a dark world. The candle is the Christ-candle which is lighted at the birth of Jesus and grows brighter and brighter until it (Christ) shines like the sun (Transfiguration). During Epiphany we see the manifestation or disclosure of the glory of God in Jesus. On Epiphany 8 we are on the threshold of seeing Jesus at the Transfiguration as God's "beloved son." However, Epiphany 8 is observed when the date of Easter is very early, for an Early Easter calls for a long Epiphany season.

Context of the Lectionary

The First Lesson. (Isaiah 55:10-13) This is the famous passage in which we have the promise that God's Word will not return void but will accomplish its purpose. It is a comfort primarily to proclaimers of the Word. The First Lesson is obviously related to the parable of the two houses in today's Gospel lesson: obedience to God's Word (Jesus' teachings) will result in stability and security.

The Second Lesson. (1 Corinthians 15:51-58) This lesson concludes a series of three lessons from 1 Corinthians 15, Epiphany 6-8. It is not related necessarily to the other two lessons. However, we can see a connection with the parable of the blind. If we are not blind, we will see Christ's return at the end of time when he will conquer death.

Gospel. (Luke 6:39-49) This is the third and last in the series on Jesus' Sermon on the Plain, Luke's account of the Sermon on the Mount. (Matthew 5-7) The Gospel lesson contains the Parable of the Two Houses which corresponds to Lesson 1. Obedience to Christ's teachings (God's Word) will result in the security of a house built on rock. The Parable of the Blind is given in the context of judging others — Luke 6:37-38, 41-42. The pericope should begin with verse 37 to get the complete context.

Psalm. (Psalm 92:1-4, 12-15) The Psalm harmonizes with Lesson 1 which says that God's Word is productive. The Psalm expresses the truth that the "righteous flourish like the palm tree . . ." People obedient to God's Word will be productive and blessed with the stability of a house built on a rock foundation.

Context of the Scriptures

1. Parallel passage. (Matthew 15:14) Jesus refers to the Pharisees as "blind guides" who lead the blind into a pit. Since this passage does not appear in the lectionary, this is the only time in three years a lectionary preacher has the opportunity to preach on the parable of the blind leading the blind.

2. Who are the blind?
Matthew 23:16 — Pharisees.
Matthew 7:15 — False prophets.
Luke 6:37-38, 41-42 — Unqualified critics.
Luke 4:23 — "Physician, heal yourself." Sick leaders

3. Who cures blindness?
Psalm 146:8 — Lord — "The Lord opens the eyes of the blind."
Matthew 11:5 — Messiah — "The blind receive their sight."
John 9:1-7 — Jesus — healing a man born blind.

4. Cases of overcoming blindness.
Numbers 10:31 — Moses to Hobab — "You will serve as eyes for us."
Numbers 22:31 — Balaam's eyes are opened — "Then the Lord opened the eyes of Balaam and he saw the angel of the Lord standing in the way."

2 Kings 6:17 — Elisha's servant sees God's troops — "Then Elisha prayed and said, 'O Lord, I pray thee open his eyes that he may see.' "

5. What do you see?

Amos 7:8 — Truth — "Amos, what do you see?"

Isaiah 6:1 — God — "In the year that King Uzziah died, I saw the Lord . . ."

Revelation 4:1 — Heaven — "After this I looked, and lo, in heaven an open door."

Content of the Pericope

Luke brings the Sermon on the Plain to a close with a collection of four parables which were not all necessarily spoken by Jesus at one time.

6:39-40 — Parable of the Blind leading the Blind.

6:41-42 — Parable of the Speck and the Board.

6:43-45 — Parable of the Two Trees.

6:46-49 — Parable of the Two Houses.

Items Worthy of Note

1. Humor. Jesus uses humor in two of the above four parables. The scene of a blind person leading another blind person is comical. We can see the blind leader groping, probing, stumbling, reaching, touching only to see both blind persons falling into a ditch. However, the outcome is not so funny — injury or death. Another use of humor is in the parable of the person trying to take a splinter out of another's eye when a whole board protrudes from his own eye. It is humorous because of the ridiculous contrast and foolishness.

2. Questions. In these parables we can see Jesus' use of the inductive method of teaching. He arouses the people's thinking by asking questions. "Can a blind man lead a blind man?" (v. 39), "Why do you see the speck that is in your brother' eye?" (v. 41), "How can you say to your brother?" (v. 42), and "Why do you call me 'Lord, Lord'?" (v. 46) Questions arouse thinking and encourage listeners to participate in finding answers.

Precis of the Parable

Jesus asked, "Can a blind person lead another blind person? Will they not both fall into a ditch? A student is not greater than a teacher, but when a teacher finishes his teaching, a student will know as much as his teacher."

Thesis: Spiritually blind leaders and followers face a common disaster.

Theme: Can you see?

Content of the Pericope

V. 39 — A physically blind person leading blind people will cause all to fall. Likewise, spiritually blind leaders leading other blind people will end up in disaster.

V. 40 — A student is blind in thinking that he or she knows as much as the teacher. When the student sees as much as the teacher, he or she will be equally informed as the teacher.

Key Words

1. "Blind." (v. 39) Jesus is using blindness in the physical sense. A blind person cannot see, has no vision, and cannot see where he or she is going. It is a tragic condition of perpetual darkness. The parable compares this physical blindness to spiritual blindness: blind leaders taking blind people into disaster. It needs to be seen that both leaders and followers are blind. Both parties need spiritual vision.

2. "Man." (v. 39) "Man" is used generically including male and female. Women are equal to men at least in the possibility of being blind physically and spiritually. A blind female leader can be as harmful as a blind male leader.

3. "Pit." (v. 39) A pit or ditch is a place where one may get injured to the point of death. It also may mean captivity, the inability to get out of a pit unaided. The blind following blind leaders will eventually experience disaster. In the Old Testament "pit" was the "grave" or Sheol (Hades). Upon death a person went to the "pit," which was believed to be a region of shadows, misery, and futility. The worst thing about the "pit" was separation from God and the impossibility of release. While the physically blind may fall into a pit of injury and possible death, spiritual blindness could result in everlasting death in terms of separation from God.

Contemplation

Insights

1. The horror of blindness. Physical blindness is a horrible condition. It means a life of darkness, living day after day in the night. There is no seeing a bright sunrise, a glorious sunset, the beauty of a flower, or the face of a loved one. Blindness can mean also helplessness. In the past blind people could not work, and became beggars. The blind need a cane or a seeing-eye dog to walk. The physically blind face the dangers of falling into a ditch or walking into the path of an oncoming car.

Spiritual blindness is even worse. The spiritually blind are ignorant; they have no knowledge of God. They live in the darkness of sin. Their ultimate fate is death in terms of separation from God. While we have sympathy for the physically blind and are moved to help them, there is a far greater need to be concerned about the spiritually blind, the people who are blind to their sins and their need of Christ to give them sight.

2. Double darkness. It is a case of the blind leading the blind. Both parties are in the same condition. It is not enough to condemn or to be concerned about blind leaders. If the followers were not blind, they would not follow blind leaders. If followers are blind, they need not complain when they fall into a ditch. This parable, therefore, applies to all: leaders and followers, clergy and laity.

3. The seeing blind. It is possible to have 20/20 physical vision but to be otherwise blind. This contrast is seen in the account in John 9 of Jesus' healing a man born blind. After the miracle, the Pharisees confronted Jesus about the blind man's new sight. They asked, "Are we also blind?" Because they were blind to their sin, they had no guilt. The problem preachers face is speaking to people with good eyesight but with little or no spiritual vision. So, why are they spiritually blind? What evidence is there to believe they are blind? What, if any, is the cure for this blindness?

4. Is blindness curable? Physical blindness may be permanent. Eye surgery and laser treatments may not, in some cases, restore sight. It is something one has to live with. On the other hand, every spiritually blind person can have vision. There is hope for a cure. The spiritually blind need not be blind to spiritual realities. They can see the truth about God and themselves. It is the task of the preacher to convince people that vision is possible and to show them how such vision can be a reality.

5. Lessons to be learned.
  A. The lesson of stupidity. It is stupid to follow blind leaders.
  B. The lesson of consequences. There is but one ultimate end to the following of blind leaders: a ditch of disaster and death.
  C. The lesson of need. If we are following blind leaders, it is time to look for leaders with foresight. If we are blind ourselves, it is time to seek a cure for our spiritual blindness.

Homily Hints

1. Are You Blind? (6:39-49; John 9:40) The Pharisees asked Jesus, "Are we also blind?" We may not be physically blind, but we with good eyes are blind to spiritual realities. Tests of blindness —
  A. Do you think you know more than your teachers? 6:30.
  B. Are you blind to your own faults? 6:41-42.
  C. Are you blind to the source of a good life? 6:43-45.
  D. Are you blind by building your house on sand? 6:46-49.

2. Double Indemnity (Luke 6:39; Deuteronomy 27:18) Nobody wins when the blind lead the blind. Both parties suffer the worst consequences — disaster and death.
  A. Blind leaders —
    "Cursed be he who misleads a blind man on the road." — Deuteronomy 27:18.
  B. Blind followers — "Fall into a pit." — v. 39.

3. O Say, Can You See? (6:39) How good is your spiritual sight? Have you had the eyes of your soul examined lately? Do you need to upgrade your spiritual lenses? Ask yourself —
  A. Can you see God's hand in world affairs?
  B. Like Simeon, can you see the Christ in Jesus?
  C. Can you see yourself as a sinner in need of a Savior?
  D. Can you see the possibilities in people?

4. Seeing the Truth. (6:39) Reading the truth in the Bible is good. Hearing the truth in church or classroom may be better. Doing the truth is essential. But, best of all is seeing the truth. A picture, they say, is better than a thousand words.
  A. See the truth of God — "I saw the Lord" — Isaiah 6:9.
  B. See the truth of Christ — "They saw his glory" — Luke 9:32.
  C. See the truth of heaven — "After this I looked . . ." — Revelation 4:1.

5. Blind — How did we get that way? (6:39) We may be spiritually blind and not know it. What causes us to become blind followers of the blind?

    A. Hatred makes us blind — "They know not what they do."

    B. Bigotry makes us blind — Pharisees: "You blind guides" — Matthew 23:16.

    C. Romantic love makes us blind — "Love is blind."

6. Blindness Can Be Cured. (6:39) There is a cure for blindness. Jesus gave sight to the physically blind. The spiritually blind can also be healed.

    A. God the Father heals — "The Lord opens the eyes of the blind." Psalm 146:8

    B. God the Son heals — "The blind receive their sight." — Matthew 11:5.

    C. God the Spirit heals — Acts 9:17-18.

Contact

Problems

1. Infrequent use. The Epiphany season, like Pentecost, is an accordion season. It contracts and expands according to the length of the season. The length of the season depends upon the date of Easter. Epiphany 8 is used only when the Epiphany season is at its longest. Consequently, the Sunday is seldom observed.

2. Which parable? This is probably the only Sunday when a preacher is confronted with four parables in one Gospel lesson. Which of the four shall one preach? The first of the four — the blind leading the blind — is presented here for the following reasons. First, Luke refers to the blind as a parable: "He told them also a parable." Second, the parable of the blind blends with the context of the Gospel lesson and its preceding verses: vv. 37-38, 41-42. Third, the theme of the parable dealing with the blind can be applied to the other three parables. Fourth, the parable of the two houses serves as a conclusion not to the pericope but to the entire Sermon on the Plain. Fifth, the parable of the blind is rarely used as a sermon subject and is therefore a fresh sermon possibility.

3. Two kinds. Blindness is of two kinds: physical and spiritual. Indeed, Jesus healed both kinds. The parable of the blind leading the blind deals with spiritual blindness. It may be a problem for a preacher to confine the sermon to spiritual blindness. It is easier to consider physical blindness which is a reality in our society. We are accustomed to seeing white canes, seeing-eye dogs, and literature in Braille. It is more difficult to recognize or to deal with spiritual blindness.

Points of Contact

1. Going to Jerusalem. Today's parable of the blind leading the blind is related to coming Sundays in the church year. Next Sunday is the Festival of Transfiguration, when the three special Disciples had their eyes opened to see Jesus as the Son of God. Immediately thereafter, Jesus is resolved to go to Jerusalem to suffer and die on a cross. He sets his face like flint to go to Jerusalem to fulfill his messianic mission. Could he be the blind one leading the blind Disciples to fall into the pit of death?

2. Blind leaders. Today's parable is relevant to today's leadership. We have blind leaders who are leading blind people to ultimate destruction. In the political area, we have leaders who may be candidates for being blind leaders: Ghadafi, Khomeini, Ortega, Castro together with other dictators, tyrants, or autocrats. In the religious field we also have candidates: Sun Moon, Hubbard, Madeline Murray O'Hare, and various gurus from India. Who today's blind leaders are depends on our political and religious affiliation. We can agree that leaders who stockpile ever-increasing nuclear war materials are blind in leading us to world disaster. Leaders who are lax in controlling and preventing drug abuse are blind to the people's welfare.

3. Blind followers. We cannot place all the blame on blind leaders. The people following them are also blind. If they had eyes, they would see how foolish it is to follow blind leaders and would avoid the pits ahead. It is not a question of people being like sheep without a shepherd. It is a case of sheep with false shepherds. But, the sheep should not be blind to the spiritual condition of their shepherds. Many people are stupid. They do what everybody else is doing. They see a line and they join it without knowing or inquiring where the line ends. Many of us are gullible and naive. We fall for anything and anybody. In fashion, trends, and morals we often follow the crowd. We join the blind following blind leaders.

Illustrative Materials

1. The Blind Leading the Blind. In the Louvre Museum in Paris there is a painting by Pieter Bruegel the Elder called "The Parable of the Blind." It shows several blind men proceeding in single file across sloping ground that ends in a ditch. The blind leader has already tumbled in. The last man in line has no idea of what is happening. He continues to follow in peaceful unawareness until he meets the same fate.

2. The Power to See. The world's largest telescope is being built on Mauna Kea in Hawaii. It will be powerful enough to see the light of a candle from the moon.

3. Spiritual Vision. Fanny Crosby, writer of 6000 Gospel songs, was blinded by an illness when six weeks of age. One time she told a minister, "Do you know that if at birth I had been able to make one petition, it would have been that I should be born blind?" "Why?" asked the surprised clergyman. "Because when I get to heaven, the first face that shall ever gladden my sight will be that of my Savior!"

4. Seeing the Invisible. Mice made a nest in a certain piano. When they heard music, they decided to investigate. One mouse came back and reported that the music came from various lengths of strings. Another claimed the music came from the hammers. They heard the music but they never saw the "invisible" pianist. Likewise, we hear the music of creation but many do not see the invisible Creator.

5. Blind Leaders. Will we ever forget the tragedy of Jimmy Jones who led his people to Ghana and then ordered them to drink poison? By following a blind leader, over 500 people committed suicide.

In *Jesus and the New Age*, Danker tells of a Roman author:
   Doctor: "You are quite pale."
   Patient: "You look worse. Don't try your remedies on me!"

6. Light to See. The last words of O. Henry: "I'm afraid to go home in the dark."

Goethe on his deathbed: "More light!" They raised the shades in his room to give him more light. Still it wasn't enough. He repeated, "More light!"

John Henry Newman:

Lead kindly light, amid the encircling gloom;
Lead me on.
The night is dark, and I am far from home;
Lead thou me on.
Keep thou my feet;
I do not ask to see
The distant scene;
One step enough for me.

Lent 3

3. The Fruitless Fig Tree

Luke 13:1-9

¹*There were some present at that very time who told him of the Galileans whose blood Pilate had mingled with their sacrifices. ²And he answered them, "Do you think that these Galileans were worse sinners than all the other Galileans, because they suffered thus? ³I tell you, No; but unless you repent you will all likewise perish. ⁴Or those eighteen upon whom the tower in Siloam fell and killed them, do you think that they were worse offenders than all the others who dwelt in Jerusalem? ⁵I tell you, No; but unless you repent you will all likewise perish."*

⁶And he told this parable: "A man had a fig tree planted in his vineyard; and he came seeking fruit on it and found none. ⁷And he said to the vinedresser, 'Lo, three years I have come seeking fruit on this fig tree, and I find none. Cut it down; why should it use up the ground?' ⁸And he answered him, 'Let it alone, sir, this year also, till I dig about it and put on manure. ⁹And if it bears fruit next year, well and good; but if not, you can cut it down.' "

When Americans shoplift to the tune of fifty billion dollars annually, when fifty million people cheat on their income tax returns, when half of our teenagers under age nineteen have pre-marital sex relations and one out of ten gets pregnant, when Americans bet thirty-five to fifty billion dollars on football games annually and bingo is second only to attendance at Mass among the religious activities of American Catholics, we are sure that our country needs to repent.

What about those who do nothing, good or bad? Philadelphia Common Pleas Judge Lisa Richette had her car and purse stolen and was beaten up one Sunday while one hundred people coming out of a nearby theatre watched without helping her. The Judge stopped at a newstand, left her keys in the car and the door open. A man grabbed her purse, jumped into her car, and took off dragging the Judge one hundred feet. Police reported that the fact that scores of people watched the crime without getting involved was not unusual, saying, "People don't do that anymore. They just don't jump in."

Are these one hundred people not as guilty of the crime as the robber? Is not an act of omission as much a sin as a deed of comission? Should they also repent? James wrote, "Whoever knows what is right to do and fails to do it, for him it is sin." (4:17) The Parable of the Fruitless Fig Tree deals with a people's lack of fruitfulness. The tree was given one more year to bring forth the fruit of repentance. In a liturgical prayer of confession we acknowledge our sins of omission: "We have sinned . . . by what we have left undone. We have not loved you with our whole heart; we have not loved our neighbors as ourselves." The Parable of the Barren Fig Tree deals with this problem.

Context

Context of History

Jesus saw the handwriting on the wall concerning his nation's future. He understood the signs of the times. Israel in his day was heading for disaster like two trains about to have a head-on collision. There existed the hatred between Gentile and Jew, between Jew and Samaritan, the growing Israelite opposition to Roman domination, the periodic revolt of zealots, and the religiosity of the professional religious leaders. Only an immediate repentance could save Israel from destruction. The time of judgment had come, but it was delayed to give Israel another chance to repent. In the parable the gardener persuaded the owner to give the barren tree another year to see if it would produce fruit. Apparently, Israel failed to repent, for in A.D. 70 Emperor Titus had Jerusalem destroyed and the Jews scattered. It was the end of the nation.

Context of the Church Year

The Parable of the Fruitless Fig Tree comes in the Gospel for the third Sunday in Lent. Ash Wednesday, a day of repentance, opens the Lenten season which is a season of repentance in preparation for Easter. Through repentance we must die to self and sin in order to rise with Christ in newness of life. The Gospel lesson of Lent 3 deals with "Unless you repent, you will all likewise perish." Thus, the parable which deals with a delay of judgment to give the people another chance to repent is appropriate. The Psalm of the Day (Psalm 103:1-13) reminds us that Yahweh is merciful to forgive those who repent. The Prayer of the Day asks God to make us instruments of redeeming love. The Hymn of the Day focuses upon the Redeemer of the repentant: "Jesus the Very Thought of Thee."

Context of the Lectionary

The First Lesson. (Exodus 3:1-15) Yahweh, concerned over his people in Egyptian slavery, calls Moses to lead the people to freedom in the promised land.

The Second Lesson. (1 Corinthians 10:1-13) Having yielded to temptation, the Israelites committed sins which brought their destruction. We need not follow their example, for God promises to provide an escape when tempted.

Gospel. (Luke 13:1-9) In the Parable of the Fruitless Fig Tree, God's people deserve destruction for being barren, but upon the intercession of the gardener (Christ) the judgment is delayed to give people time to repent.

The relation of the three lessons can be seen in their thematic unity:
1. Theme: When God Cares Enough.
   Lesson 1 — Yahweh's concern for his people in bondage.
   Lesson 2 — God promises to provide an escape from temptations.
   Gospel — God gives sinners another chance to repent.
2. Theme: God provides escapes.
   Lesson 1 — An escape from slavery in Egypt.
   Lesson 2 — An escape during temptations.
   Gospel — An escape from judgment through repentance.

Context of the Gospel Lesson

The parable needs to be understood in the light of the Gospel lesson. It reported to Jesus that a number of Galileans were massacred by Pilate while at worship in the Jerusalem temple. This could have been a trick report involving politics. They may have expected Jesus to be outraged over this tragedy and to condemn Pilate for the atrocity. Then Jesus could have been accused of treason.

However, Jesus sees the report as a religious problem. Since the Jews, particularly the Pharisees, held that suffering and tragedy were the result of sin, Jesus pointed out that the Galileans and also the eighteen upon whom the tower of Siloam fell were not worse sinners than anyone else. Unless those still living repented of their sins, they would also perish. When would this happen? Because of their fruitlessness, like the fig tree, judgment was due now — "cut it down." However, the gardener begs the owner to give the tree another year during which he would cultivate and fertilize the tree. If the tree did not produce by then, he would agree to cut it down. In the parable Jesus teaches that God in his mercy gives people a second chance, another year, to repent. If they do not repent during this extended period, they will experience the same fate as did the Galileans and the men upon whom the tower fell.

Context of the Scriptures

1. Fig tree. Jesus cursed a fig tree because it was barren (Matthew 21:18-20; Mark 11:12-14) This tree is not to be confused with that in the parable. (Luke 13:1-9) The account of the fig tree that was cursed does not appear in the three-year Lectionary. Preachers are spared struggling with that problem. Donald Soper, British Methodist leader, once read that Jesus cursed a barren fig tree. He went to his father for an explanation. His father said he did not believe Jesus did it. Donald replied, "But, it's in the Bible!" His father answered, "I know Jesus better than that!"

2. The Vineyard. (Isaiah 5:1-7) Yahweh calls Israel his vineyard. He planted it and expected grapes. Instead he got wild grapes. In today's parable, the owner (God) did not get even wild grapes; he got nothing.

3. Suffer and sin. The Disciples asked Jesus concerning a man born blind whether the man or his parents caused it by sin. In John 9:3, Jesus states that the blindness was not the result of sin. In today's Gospel lesson, Jesus makes the same point relative to the Galileans and the men killed by the tower's fall.

4. Intercession. The gardener in the parable intercedes for the fig tree and succeeds in getting from the owner another year to produce figs.
> Genesis 18:22-33 — Abraham intercedes for Sodom and Gomorrah.
> Exodus 32:30-32 — Moses intercedes for his idolatrous people.

5. Source of fruit.
> John 15:4-5 — He who abides in Christ bears much fruit.
> Galatians 5:22 — The Spirit produces fruit.
> Matthew 7:18 — A good tree (heart) bears good fruit.

6. Call to be fruitful.
> Genesis 1:28 — "Be fruitful and multiply."
> John 15:8 — God is glorified when his people are fruitful.
> James 1:22 — "Be doers of the Word and not hearers only."
> Matthew 3:8 — "Bear fruit that befits repentance."
> Psalm 1:3 — A tree planted by a river yields fruit in its season.

Content

Content of the Pericope

vv. 1-3 — The Galilean worshippers, killed by Pilate, were no greater sinners than others. Unless all sinners repent, they will experience the same fate.

vv. 4-5 — The eighteen workers whom the tower of Siloam fell upon and killed were not super-sinners. The same will happen to all who do not repent.

vv. 6-9 — Upon the intercession of the gardener, the fig tree is given another year to yield figs. If it fails to produce, it will be cut down.

Content of the Parable

v. 6 — For three years the owner of a vineyard comes to his fig tree for figs but finds none.

v. 7 — The owner orders his gardener to cut down the tree, not only because it is barren, but because it takes up space and saps strength from the rest of the vineyard.

vv. 8-9 — The gardener asks the owner to give the tree another year during which he will cultivate and fertilize it. If then it does not produce, he would agree that it should be cut down.

Precis of the Parable

A man planted a fig tree in his orchard. Year after year for three years he came for figs but there were none to be had. He called in his gardener and ordered, "For three years I have come to this tree for figs, but I never get any. So, cut it down. Why should it take up space in the garden?" But the gardener answered, "Sir, let it live another year. I will cultivate and fertilize the ground around it. If by then it does not produce fruit, I will cut it down. On the other hand, if it produces, all well and good."

Thesis: Because of Christ's intercession, God gives his people another chance to produce the fruit of repentance.

Theme: Your last chance to repent!

Key Words

1. "Planted." (vv. 2, 4) The fig tree was planted by the owner. The tree did not get into the orchard by accident. The tree was not a volunteer as some plants are. It really had no choice in the matter. The owner chose the tree, wanted it, and had high hopes for its being a good tree. Applied to Israel, it could be said that Yahweh chose Israel as his people and planted it in the orchard of the world. On a personal level, one is here because God gave each of us life. We did not choose to be born. God planted us in this place for this time.

2. **"None."** (vv. 6, 7) This is a tragic word. The tree was planted. The owner looked forward to tasty figs. But, for three years he found "None." Why did he expect fruit? It is the nature of a fig tree to have fruit before it has leaves. He probably saw the leaves and expected fruit. It is tragic for one to appear to have fruit but have none — not even one fig! It is tragic also for a life to bear no fruit. The oldest person in the Bible is Methusaleh who lived for 969 years, and then died without any record of any accomplishment. He has been described as a man with "no hits, no runs, and no errors."

3. **"Cut."** (vv. 7, 8) This is a hard word. It is a word of judgment. The consequence of being barren is destruction. The fruitless tree is ordered to be cut down. Then it is usually cast into the fire. It is a frightening picture of death and destruction. Jesus did not mince words when warning what awaits a person whose life adds up to nothing. Is your life only taking up space on earth? Are you only a free-loader, living off the fat of the land without paying your rent? The bare truth is that a person, corporation, church, or nation that does not produce the fruit of repentance is doomed.

4. **"If."** (v. 9) It is a tiny word of only two letters. Can there be a shorter word than "if"? Though small, it has a large significance. In the parable the gardner says, "If it bears" and "If not." It is a difference between life and death, productivity or barrenness. "If" throws the burden upon the tree, upon the person or people. It is our responsibility to produce. Once again we have a choice: life or death — why will you die? Choose life — be fruitful!

Contemplation

The Parable of the Barren Fig Tree lends itself to allegorical interpretation. The owner of the vineyard is God. Israel is the fig tree. Jesus is the gardener who intercedes for the tree. The three years the owner came seeking fruit are the three years of Jesus' public ministry. Failure of Israel to repent in the bonus year resulted in the destruction of Israel as a nation in A.D. 70. If one followed this type of interpretation, the parable would be only a history lesson. The parable has a broader meaning for people of every generation.

Insights

1. **Planted.** The tree was planted. It was not a volunteer as some trees are. It was in the garden not by accident, nor was it placed there by Satan. As a person or a people, we were planted where we are, in this time and place. We are God's property, his people. Therefore, he is concerned about our welfare and has a right to expect fruit from us.

2. **Purpose.** The owner of the vineyard planted the tree for a purpose. It was a fruit tree. Its purpose was to produce figs. The tree's primary purpose was not to be beautiful, cast shade, or provide lumber. It was planted to bear fruit. Each person is planted on earth for a purpose, to bear fruit of good works and service to others. A tree does not eat its own fruit. It is given to all who come for it. Christ came not to be served but to serve, to bear fruit.

3. **Patience.** The owner of the tree had patience in waiting for the tree's fruit. He really waited six years. It took the tree three years for the fruit to be clean, and then each year for three years he came for figs. Finally his patience ran out and he ordered the tree to be removed. Likewise, God gets tired of our moral and spiritual barrenness. Since Adam and Eve, God has put up with humanity, but time is running out.

4. **Plea.** The gardener representing Christ intercedes for the tree. He begs the owner to give it another chance, another year. In the meantime, he will cultivate the soil and fertilize it. He feels sorry for the tree, believes in the tree, and expects the best from the tree. It reminds us of Abraham appealing to God in behalf of Sodom and Gomorrah, of Moses interceding for his rebellious people, and of Jesus praying, "Father, forgive them . . ." His plea is an expression of grace, the grace of forgiveness and forbearance.

5. **Penalty.** "Cut it down" is the command. It is the word of judgment, of penalty. Judgment is sure to come to those who fail to fulfill God's purpose of fruitfulness. In this case, judgment comes not for sins of commission in terms of thought, word, and deed. It is a matter of sins of omission. It is not what we have done wrong, but what good we have failed to do. A barren life is a blighted life.

6. **Pressure.** The tree was given one more year to produce figs. If it failed, it would be destroyed. This puts pressure on us to repent and to produce

the fruit of repentance. Repentance is an urgent matter. The time is short. Produce — or else!

Homily Hints

1. What Do You Have to Show for Your Life? (13:6-9) Every person faces these questions: What good have I done? What did I accomplish with my life? Has my life counted for anything good? In answer to these questions, we need to consider —
- A. We were planted in God's vineyard to produce fruit for him.
- B. We acknowledge our perversity in terms of barrenness.
- C. We face the penalty: "Cut it down."
- D. We experience God's patience: "This year also."

2. Your Last Chance. (13:8-9) In his mercy God gives us one more chance, our last chance, to repent. To repent means to produce godly fruit of character and service. We have one more chance —
- A. To repent.
- B. To let God be God for us.
- C. To commit our lives to Christ.
- D. To love one another.

3. Something Greater than Justice. (13:6-9) In this parable we see the justice and mercy of God, the Law and the Gospel.

Thanks be to God that his mercy supercedes his justice. When a woman went for her portrait, she told the photographer, "Be sure, young man, you do me justice." Brazenly he replied, "Madam, you don't need justice but mercy!"

Sinners of omission need mercy more than justice.
- A. Justice — "Cut it down" v. 7.
- B. Mercy — "Let it alone" — v. 8.

4. How to Become a Fruitful Person. (13:8) The sad fact is that we are barren of good fruit just as the fig tree was. The gardener thought he knew how to get the tree to produce the following year. He was going to dig around the tree to loosen the ground. Then he was going to put manure on it. What can we do to become fruit-bearing people? Consider the following —
- A. Whoever abides in Christ bears fruit — John 15:4-5.
- B. Whoever has the Holy Spirit produces — Galatians 5:22.
- C. Whoever has a good heart produces good fruit — Matthew 7:18.

Contact

What does this parable of the fruitless fig tree have to do with contemporary life? Is there a message in it for us today? At what points does the rubber hit the road?

1. A second chance. People today are interested in getting a second chance at life. The parable tells of the owner, upon the gardener's intercession, who gives the tree another chance to produce before having it cut down. Today many want a second chance after death rather than before death. According to a 1986 Gallup poll, twenty-three percent of the American people believe in re-incarnation, that is, a second chance to live over again on earth. Also, some people think they can repent after death and thereby enter heaven. But in the case of Lazarus and Dives, after death a great gulf separated the two and there was no bridge between heaven and hell. The fig tree without fruit is to be cut down and burned. There is no second chance for that tree to live again on earth or in heaven.

2. Today's greater sin. The parable deals with barrenness and fruitlessness. The tree is condemned not for what it has done, but for what it has not done. It is the sin of omission. In today's society we seem to be more concerned about the sins of commission: murder, rape, theft, etc. Our prisons are overflowing with people who committed sins. Today's parable calls our attention to the even greater sin, the sin of omission. As is often said, evil flourishes in our society because good people do nothing to stop the evil. "Do not withhold good from those to whom it is due, when it is in your power to do it." (Proverbs 3:27)

3. The consequence of non-repentance. In Jesus' day the question was raised whether sin caused the death of the Galileans massacred by Pilate while they worshiped and of the eighteen workers killed by accident when the tower of Siloam fell on them. Today the question is still asked. What about the seven astronauts who perished in The Challenger seventy-three seconds after lift-off? What about those who died in the Amtrak wreck when two trains collided north of Baltimore? Were the more than one hundred who died in the hotel fire in Puerto Rico special sinners? How do you explain the plight of the hostages held in Lebanon? The parable teaches that as these people died, so will fruitless people die if they do not repent. "Cut it down" is the ultimate consequence of non-repentance. If one wants to live, it is urgent to repent now before the year of grace is ended.

4. The demand of fruitfulness. The owner of the fig tree came for fruit. He planted it for that reason. If it was not going to produce, it was of no value to him and he would naturally get rid of it. In today's world there is the same demand for production.

In business, workers must produce or get fired. People doing piece-work get paid according to the amount produced. A salesman working on commission must sell or there is no pay.

In higher education, the slogan is "publish or perish." A vice-president of a college of medicine wrote to his faculty: "There is no merit to be gained in teaching; you are expected to bring thirty to fifty percent of your salary through research projects; if you are unwilling to make this institution internationally famous through research, you are invited to leave."

In the church, congregations must grow or die. A sterile church has little or no influence on society. In the midst of terrific social, moral, and political problems, churches often deal with trivia: bingo, fish fries, bazaars, silver teas, and the like. Rome burns while the church plays. An indifferent church cannot make a different world.

Illustrative Materials

1. Sins of Omission. In a letter to Dear Abby a woman wrote about an acquaintance who took her five-year old son to an emergency room after he had had an accident. The mother said, "I want a white, American doctor, and don't let my son bleed to death while you're looking for one." The letter-writer had said nothing, but she felt that her silence had condoned the woman's sentiments. She asked Abby what she should have said.

———————

Hitler put Pastor Martin Niemoeller in the Dachau concentration camp from 1938 until 1945, when he was released by the Allies. Later he wrote:

> "In Germany the Nazis first came from the communists, and I didn't speak up because I wasn't a communist. Then they came for the Jews, and I didn't speak up because I wasn't a Jew. Then they came for the trade unionists, and I didn't speak up because I wasn't a trade unionist. Then they came for the Catholics, and I didn't speak up because I was a Protestant. Then they came for me, and by that time there was no one left to speak for me."

2. Second Chance. During the Civil War Roswell McIntyre was drafted into the New York cavalry. Because the war was not going well and soldiers were badly needed, he was sent into battle with very little training. In the midst of a battle, he got scared and ran off. He was court-martialed and condemned to be shot for desertion. His mother appealed to President Lincoln, claiming that he was young and inexperienced and needed a second chance. The generals demanded the enforcement of discipline lest this case undermine the discipline of the Army.

Lincoln thought and prayed. Then he wrote his famous statement: "I have observed," he wrote, "that it never does a boy much good to shoot him. This letter will certify that Roswell McIntyre is to be readmitted into the New York cavalry. When he serves out his required enlistment, he will be freed of any charges of desertion." Lincoln wrote this letter in his own handwriting.

That letter is on display in the Library of Congress. Beside it is this note of explanation: "This letter was taken from the body of Roswell McIntyre who died at the battle of Little Five Forks, Virginia."

3. Non-productivity. An Atlanta woman died at the age of one hundred. Her obituary had the following headline: "Mrs. Butzon, one hundred, knitted mittens for WW II soldiers." What can one say for one who lived one hundred years? Is knitting gloves for soldiers the best one can do with one's life? It is a little better than zero.

A man named Whalstrom purchased an old bombsight. He took it apart and put it back together adding some extra parts. Neighbors became interested and brought parts to him. Over ten years he added wheels, cogs, belts, lights, and bolts. He ended up with a machine called "Whalstrom's Wonder." When he turned the machine on, 3000 parts began to move, bells rang, lights flashed, and wheels pulled wheels. What did the machine do or produce? It did not do anything — it just ran!

4. Purpose in life. The fig tree was planted for a purpose. Purpose gives aim to life.

It is said that fifty percent of people do not pay any attention to where they are going. Forty percent will go in any direction. Ten percent know what they want and go for it.

The bishop of Exeter, England, was traveling by train to perform a confirmation ceremony. He misplaced his ticket and was unable to produce it when requested by the conductor. "It's quite all right, my lord, we know who you are," said the conductor. "That's all very well," answered the bishop, "but, without the ticket, how am I going to know where I am going?"

Lent 4

4. The Prodigal Sons

Luke 15:1-3, 11-32

¹Now the tax collectors and sinners were all drawing near to
him. ²And the Pharisees and the scribes murmured, saying, "This
man receives sinners and eats with them."

³So he told them this parable . . . ¹¹"There was a man who
had two sons; ¹²and the younger of them said to his father, 'Father,
give me the share of property that falls to me.' And he divided
his living between them. ¹³Not many days later, the younger son
gathered all he had and took his journey into a far country, and
there he squandered his property in loose living. ¹⁴And when he
had spent everything, a great famine arose in that country, and
he began to be in want. ¹⁵So he went and joined himself to one
of the citizens of that country, who sent him into his fields to feed
swine. ¹⁶And he would gladly have fed on the pods that the swine
ate; and no one gave him anything. ¹⁷But when he came to himself he said, 'How many of my father's hired servants have bread
enough and to spare, but I perish here with hunger! ¹⁸I will arise
and go to my father, and I will say to him, "Father, I have sinned
against heaven and before you; ¹⁹I am no longer worthy to be called
your son; treat me as one of your hired servants." ' ²⁰And he arose
and came to his father. But while he was yet at a distance, his father
saw him and had compassion, and ran and embraced him and
kissed him. ²¹And the son said to him, 'Father, I have sinned against
heaven and before you; I am no longer worthy to be called your
son.' ²² But the father said to his servants, 'Bring quickly the best
robe, and put it on him; and put a ring on his hand, and shoes
on his feet; ²³and bring the fatted calf and kill it, and let us eat
and make merry; ²⁴for this my son was dead, and is alive again;
he was lost, and is found.' And they began to make merry.

²⁵"Now his elder son was in the field; and as he came and drew
near to the house, he heard music and dancing. ²⁶And he called

one of his servants and asked what this meant. [27]*And he said to him, 'Your brother has come, and your father has killed the fatted calf, because he has received him safe and sound.'* [28]*But he was angry and refused to go in. His father came out and entreated him,* [29]*but he answered his father, 'Lo, these many years I have served you, and I never disobeyed your command; yet you never gave me a kid, that I might make merry with my friends.* [30]*But when this son of yours came, who had devoured your living with harlots, you killed for him the fatted calf!'* [31]*And he said to him, 'Son, you are always with me, and all that is mine is yours.* [32]*It was fitting to make merry and be glad, for this your brother was dead, and is alive; he was lost, and is found.'* "*

The Parable of the Prodigal Son is the greatest parable. This is the opinion of Lloyd Ogilvie. Others would agree. George Murray says, "The most divinely tender and most humanly touching story ever told on our earth." Robert Bridges claimed, "An absolutely flawless piece of work." G. B Caird in his commentary on Luke writes, "Best known and best loved of all the parables of Jesus." To one who is to preach on the parable, it is a challenge to do it justice.

While we may be unanimous in our opinion that the parable is the greatest, we may not agree about the name, "The Prodigal Son." How it got its name, who gave it, or when it was given, I, for one, do not know, but it is universally and traditionally called "The Prodigal Son." Disagreeing with this name, Jeremiah entitles it "Parable of the Father's Love." Danker focuses on the elder son, "The Parable of the Reluctant Brother." Thielicke emphasizes the father, "The Waiting Father," and the Good News Bible refers to it as "The Lost Son."

The objection to the name, "The Prodigal Son," is twofold. On the one hand, "Prodigal" is misleading. It refers to "Prodigal" in terms of wastefulness. While this is a fact, the younger son's predominant trait is not his wasting his inheritance but his repentance and return home. On the other hand, we may object to the title because it covers only one of the three characters in the parable. There were two bad sons — one far away and one at home. Both needed to repent and return to the father. For some, the father is the central character — the waiting, longing, forgiving, and appealing father. We admit that our title for this chapter, "The Prodigal Sons" is also inadequate because the father is not included. Perhaps we should call it "The Parable of a Good Father and his Two Bad Sons." The parable deals with all three persons: the attitude of the father toward his wayward sons and their responses to this attitude.

Context

The Parable in the Context of the Church Year

The Prodigal Son parable is the Gospel lesson for the Fourth Sunday in Lent. Lent 4 is only two Sundays before Passion Sunday, the opening of Holy Week, culminating in the cross on Good Friday. What does this parable have to do with the suffering and death of the Christ?

Last Sunday (Lent 3) we heard Jesus' call to repent lest all perish. This was appropriate for Lent because it is a season of repentance. On Lent 4 we consider our need to repent as seen in the two sons, what is involved in repentance according to the example of the younger son, the consequence of not repenting as seen in the elder brother, and the love of the father who makes repentance worthwhile and possible. In this Lenten season of repentance it is fitting to consider the One to whom we return for forgiveness.

Context of the Lectionary

The First Lesson. (Joshua 5:9-12) The Israelites celebrated their entrance into the Promised Land by renewing the covenant through circumcision and observing the Passover.

The Second Lesson. (2 Corinthians 5:16-21) In Christ God reconciled the world, and the church was given the ministry of reconciliation.

Gospel. (Luke 15:1-3, 11-32 — Parable of the Prodigal Son) God in Christ loves sinners.

Psalm. (Psalm 34:1-8) Praise the Lord who answers prayer and delivers us out of trouble.

Unifying Theme — A Merciful God Delivers from Sin

The First Lesson. Delivered from Egyptian bondage, the Israelites arrive in the Promised Land.

The Second Lesson. Through Jesus, the world was reconciled to God and the church is charged with continuing the ministry of reconciliation.

Gospel. As a loving father, God welcomes and forgives sinners.

Psalm. We praise the Lord for delivering us from fears and troubles.

Prayer of the Day. The prayer is addressed to a God of mercy for forgiveness and cleansing from sin.

In the light of the Lessons and Propers for Lent 4, it can easily be seen that the parable harmonizes with the overall theme of deliverance. The Israelites were delivered from bondage in Egypt. In Christ God reconciled sinners to himself, and the church continues the message of reconciliation of sinners to a merciful God. In the parable, God is seen as a loving, forgiving, and welcoming father who restores a sinner to sonship. The Psalm praises Yahweh for deliverance from fear and trouble. In the prayer we beg for forgiveness and cleansing.

Context of the Gospel Lesson

The Gospel lesson assigned for Lent 4 consists of two parts. The first part (vv. 1-2) gives the occasion and reason for the parable. In Luke 15, often known as the "Lost Chapter" — lost sheep, coin, and son — there are three parables. In today's Gospel, only the third parable is given.

The introductory verses give the key to an understanding of the parable, and also indicate how it may be preached. "Tax collectors and sinners" gathered around Jesus to hear him teach. This aroused the anger of the Pharisees and scribes who criticized him for associating and eating with the sinners. To them Jesus' association with sinners implied Jesus' approval of their life-styles. How could a godly man who claimed to be a prophet approve sin? To justify his attitude and action related to sinners Jesus tells the story of a father with two sons. Obviously, the father represents God, the younger son the sinners, and the elder son the Pharisees. By this story Jesus is explaining God's attitude toward sinners, and that his own attitude toward sinners is the same. For this truth to be communicated today to our people, it is necessary to deal with the entire pericope. To deal only with the father, younger, or older son would miss the point of the parable.

Context of Related Scriptures

1. Warnings against association with sinners.
Psalm 1:1 — "Blessed is the man who walks not in the counsel of the wicked, nor stands in the way of sinners . . ."

Proverbs 4:14 — "Do not enter the path of the wicked, and do not walk in the way of evil men."

2 Corinthians 6:17 — "Therefore come out from them, and be separate from them, says the Lord, and touch nothing unclean."

2. God's attitude toward sinners.

Psalm 103:13 — "As a father pities his children, so the Lord pities those who fear him."

Jeremiah 31:20 — "Therefore my heart yearns for him; I will surely have mercy on him says the Lord."

Luke 5:32 — "I have not come to call the righteous, but sinners to repentance."

Luke 14:15-24 — The parable of the great banquet: the poor, maimed, blind, and lame are invited.

Luke 19:10 — "For the Son of man came to seek and to save the lost."

Content

Content of the Pericope

vv. 1-2 — Religious leaders criticize Jesus for associating and eating with sinners.

vv. 11-24 — A father's younger son leaves home, squanders his inheritance, repents, and returns to his father who forgives him.

vv. 25-32 — Upon learning of his brother's return, the older son complains to his father about his ill-treatment, criticizes his brother, and refuses to join in the homecoming celebration.

Precis of the Parable

Religious leaders saw Jesus surrounded by traitorous tax collectors and others well-known for their sins. They seemed to be having a good time — talking, laughing, and eating together. The professional religious leaders were incensed at Jesus' association with these sinners, and began to criticize him. It appeared to them that Jesus was approving their wicked way of life. To justify his position, Jesus told them a story.

A man had two sons. The younger one asked for his part of his inheritance. He sold the property and with the cash left home for a distant land. With the money he gathered friends with whom he "lived it up." Soon his money was all gone, but nobody would give him any. A famine occurred, and he was about to starve. He took a job tending pigs and was so hungry that he wished he could eat what was given to the pigs. Then he began to reflect on his condition. He realized that his father's employees were better off than he. He decided to go home, admit his mistake, and beg his father to let him be one of his servants. As the lad approached the farm, his father ran down the road to meet him, embraced, and kissed him. His father interrupted the son's confession of sin and ordered his servants to bring his son a robe, a ring, and shoes. Furthermore, the father ordered a feast to be prepared that they might celebrate the son's homecoming. He explained by saying that his son was lost and is found, was dead but alive again.

While the festivities were in progress, the older son was returning from work in the fields. When he heard the singing and dancing, he asked a servant what was going on. The servant explained that his father was celebrating the return of his brother. He was so angry that he refused to enter the house to join in the celebration. His father came out and begged him to come in. The elder son bitterly complained that, though he worked hard and never disobeyed his father, he had never been given a party where he could have a good time with his friends. Besides that, he condemned his brother for squandering his inheritance on prostitutes. And after this wicked behavior, he comes home and is given a party! His father answers him by assuring him that he and his father are always together, and that what he has is also his son's. He again explains his action: your brother was lost but is found, was dead but is now alive.

Thesis: God's gracious attitude toward sinners.

Theme: Our heavenly Father loves sinners.

Key Words in the Parable

1. "Sons." (v. 11) A certain father had two sons. Because they were sons, they were entitled to receive their father's inheritance. As sons they had a legal right to receive the father's property. Moreover, they were always his sons. Though the younger one squandered his money, lived in sin, and disgraced his father and himself, he was still his son. The father never disowned him. He was a lost son far away. In spite of the bad spirit of the older son, the father still owned him as a son. He was a lost child also, even if he stayed at home. God is faithful in keeping us as sons regardless of our disobedience. He never disowns his children.

2. "Share." (v. 12) The younger son asked his father for his "share" of his inheritance. He could not wait until his father's death. He wanted to enjoy life now. It was a possibility in those days for the father to give his inheritance before he died. If he did so, he kept the property until he died but he could not sell or give it to another. In dividing an inheritance the oldest son received twice as much as another son. (Deuteronomy 21:17) Thus, the younger son's share was one third of his father's total possesions.

3. "Squandered." (v. 13) Probably from this word the parable got its name, "prodigal," for it means wasteful or extravagant or lavish. In this sense of the word, all three persons in the parable were "prodigal." The young son was prodigal in spending his money. The father was prodigal in lavishing his love on his sons. The older brother was prodigal in being extravagant in his complaints and criticism.

4. "Heaven." (vv. 18, 21) The young man confessed to his father, "I have sinned against heaven and before you." "Heaven" is where God is; to sin against heaven is to sin against God. How did he sin against heaven? Did he not sin only against his father by leaving home and wasting his money? The truth is that when we sin against a human, at the same time we sin against God. The Decalogue was written on two tablets: three on one tablet concerning our duties to God and seven on the other tablet dealing with our responsibilities toward our fellow human beings. To sin against a human is to sin against God. Note the order: "I have sinned against heaven and before you." Sin against God comes first. It is a greater sin than one against a human.

5. "Dead." (vv. 24, 32) How could the father say his younger son was "dead" when he was away from home? He was physically alive but spiritually dead. He came to a dead end. He was penniless, friendless, and foodless. He realized he was about to "perish." He was bankrupt in all the good things of life. He was dead to life, virtue, and security. He was at the point of no return. The youth hit rock bottom and there was no other way to go than to go up. Today's society is filled with living dead people who need to repent and live.

6. "Alive." (vv. 24, 32) Out of death came life for the Prodigal. With his return, he had life with his father in his home where there were love, food, and security. However, life has its problems even after forgiveness and reinstatement in the family of God. The younger son had to live with the consequences of his sin: loss of inheritance, the shame of his error, and living with a brother who hated him. The same can be said of the older brother. He, too, was alive in his father's house, but his life tragically had to be lived with jealousy, selfishness, and pride. He, too, had to live with the rewards of his sin.

Contemplation

This parable can be preached either in part, according to each of the three characters, or as a whole. If a sermon is based on a segment of the parable, the entire text will not be used and Jesus' reason for telling the parable will not be presented. The basic issue is: What shall our attitude be toward sinners — judge, condemn, criticize, isolate, or ignore them? On the other hand, are we to welcome them, understand them, and receive them into fellowship? By virtue of the fact that publicans and prostitutes came to Jesus and listened to him, they repented. How do we feel about this? Do we condemn or rejoice? It is obvious that Jesus is speaking of sinners when he tells of the younger son. God is like the father who welcomes, forgives, and celebrates the return of the wayward boy. The elder son represents the religious leaders who refuse to join in the celebration of the Prodigal's return. Like the Pharisees, he is selfish, jealous, and self-righteous. If God is like the father in the parable, then God rejoices when sinners repent. How Jesus treats sinners is how God feels about them. To get this message across, the whole parable needs to be used.

Insights

1. **Sinful sons.** In the parable a man had two sons. The one was guilty of sins of the flesh and the other sins of the spirit. They were and remained sons. The father had every right to disown them, but he kept them as sons regardless of their lives. The father is a type of our heavenly Father: he is ever faithful. He will never disown nor cast us away because we sin. Unless we repent, we are lost sons of God.

2. **Two in one?** There are two sons. One left to live loosely; the other stayed at home and sinned by his attitude and speech. Could it be that both children live in us? We commit sins of the flesh by loose living, and our "spiritual" sins are seen in our pride, jealousy, and bad spirit. If so, both sons in the parable apply to us.

3. **Like father, unlike sons.** When we consider the father and his two sons, which of the three is worthy of our emulation? Most certainly we do not want to follow the example of the younger man. Nor do we want to be a grouch or a kill-joy like the older son. The father is our ideal, role model, and example. We strive to be like him even if we are only children.

4. **Grace goes hunting.** In the cases of both sons, the father goes out to his sinful children. When the Prodigal was in a far country, his father went out of the house and looked down the road hoping to see his boy come home. And when he did, he did not wait for the slow-moving, bedraggled lad to come to him, but he ran down to meet and embrace him. Likewise, when the party was in progress, the father left the party to go outside to beg his older son to come in and join the celebration. God is exactly like

this. We call it the grace of God, the God who seeks us, longs for us, pleads with us to return to him.

5. Love before repentance. In the parable we see that the father loved his sons before they repented. Even while the one son was living riotously, the father waited and prayed for his son's return. When the Prodigal arrived home and began his speech of confession, the father interrupted him by ordering servants to bring robe, ring, and sandals, and to prepare a banquet. In like manner, in spite of the elder brother's insulting language and his hatred of his brother, the father assured him that they would always have each other and what was his was also the son's. Even before we repent, God loves us. He does not say that, if we shape up, he will then forgive. Paul wrote, "While we were yet sinners, Christ died for us." (Romans 5:8) In the case of Zaccheus, Christ showed his love by going to his home for fellowship, and later Zaccheus repented. We repent after we experience the kindness of the Lord.

Homily Hints

1. How Should Good People Feel about Bad People? (15:1-3, 11-32) Is it wrong to be friends with notorious sinners? Would you have them for dinner? Would friendship with sinners corrupt good morals? What would the neighbors think if you went out with sinners? If sinners came to church, would they be warmly received? In this parable we see the depths to which a sinner can go and two opposing reactions to the sinner.
  A. The depth of sin — the younger son.
  B. The reaction of "good" people — elder son.
  C. The attitude of God — the father.

2. A Father's Two Sons. (15:1-3, 11-32) The parable begins, "A man had two sons." It is customary to contrast these two sons. One runs off and wastes his father's money. The other is a "good" boy who stays home and works on the farm. We may overlook how much they were alike: same father, same training, same home.
  A. Sinful sons — both are "bad" boys.
    1. Younger son — sins of the flesh.
    2. Older son — sins of the spirit.
  B. Beloved sons — both are loved by their father.
    1. Younger son — forgiven, reinstated as a son.
    2. Elder son — "You are always with me, and all that is mine is yours" — v. 31.
  C. Saved sons — both are members of God's family.

1. Younger son — "He was lost and is found" — v. 24.
2. Older son — "You are always with me" — v. 31.

3. Who is the Prodigal? (15:1-3, 11-32) In the parable, who is the Prodigal? It is common practice to point to the younger man. If we consider the definition of "prodigal," all three characters in the parable could be considered prodigals. "Prodigal" means extravagant, and lavish. Consider each person as a prodigal:

    A. Prodigal younger son — squandered his possessions to the point of being penniless.

    B. Prodigal elder son — lavish in his self-righteousness, complaints, and hatred.

    C. Prodigal father — his extravagant love for both sons.

4. A Story with Morals. (15:1-3, 11-32) A story is supposed to stand on its own feet, and to attach a moral tends to detract from the story. In this parable, there is a marvelous story about a father and two sons. No moral is attached. But upon reflection, certain truths come to mind.

    A. All need repentance — both sons are sinners.

    B. What repentance means — younger son's model —

        1. "Came to himself."

        2. "I have sinned."

        3. "I will arise and go to my father."

    C. Consequence of non-repentance — elder son refuses to join the party.

        1. Life of misery because of pride, hatred, and jealousy.

    D. Reason and reward for repentance — the father's love, forgiveness, and acceptance.

Contact

The Church of the Elder Son

To whom is the sermon addressed? If it is addressed to non-Christians who may be on skid row or in dens of iniquity, the younger son in the parable would apply to such sinners. However, most probably the preacher will be speaking to a worship assembly of God's people in a church. For the most part, unlike the Prodigal, they have not run away from home, have not demanded their inheritance before their father's death, did not spend their last penny on loose living. Surely church people have not had the experience of tending swine as an occupation, nor have they ever been at the point of starvation. The younger son does not represent the average church member.

On the other hand, we church people are like the older son, who is a prodigal in his own way. Like him, we never left home. We were faithful to our parents and obeyed them. We have been thrifty, worked hard, and lived a respectable life. We represent the good, law-abiding, dependable people. To such as us the elder son speaks, for we are prone to repeat his mistakes. It is easy to be proud of ourselves in that we are not like the "sinners." We can be self-righteous when we review our faithfulness to God and our upright lives. After all, we have gone to church all our lives, paid our tithes, worked in the church, and tried to live right. Our problem is in dealing with those who have been unfaithful, squandered their possessions, and lived like the devil. Then they were given a feast and a party. Why? We were never recognized with a party because we were good. We can be jealous and hurt. In fact, we may even hate those who get a party!

The parable is directed to church people, just as Jesus told the parable to help the religious leaders of his day to understand why he, as God's representative, was friendly with notorious sinners. Like the Prodigal, the sinners, in coming to him, were returning to the Father. Because of their repentance, it was fitting to dine with them and to rejoice that the lost were now found.

Where is the Gospel?

Is it possible to preach the Gospel by preaching on the parable of the Prodigal Son? There is no reference to Christ nor to the cross. A Christian preacher is ordained to preach the Gospel in every sermon. Paul confessed, "We preach Christ crucified." (1 Corinthians 1:23) According to the parable, God the Father receives the repentant with forgiveness, joy, and restoration as a son. If this is so, where is the need for Christ and the cross to become reconciled to God?

We need to remember that the parable is only one small slice of the Word. Each passage needs to be interpreted in the light of the Bible's total teaching. In the parable we see only one side of God — his wonderful love and mercy. But, there is another side not mentioned — the justice and holiness of God. Because God's justice was satisfied and the Law was fulfilled for us by Christ's sacrifice on the cross, we can be forgiven and accepted as sons and daughters of God.

Moreover, the cross demonstrates the forgiving mercy of God far better than a story of a farmer and his two sons. We can believe the account of the love of the waiting father because of the supreme love shown on the cross. In the parable the love of God is given in words; on the cross we see God's love in deed.

Did he or Did he not?

The parable is open-ended. The father leaves the party and goes to his older son to beg him to come to the party for his returned brother. The father reasons with him, explains why a party was in order, and assures his son that he is not neglected nor unappreciated. He assures his son of his constant presence, and reminds him that all he has belongs to his son. There the parable ends. Did the older son go in or not? Did the Pharisees and scribes change their attitude toward sinners?

Whether the elder son did or did not go into the party, he was not "lost" or "dead" like his brother was. He was at home and had all that his father could give him — himself and his property. If he did not go to the party, as he most probably did not, he was a "lost" child of God. He was a good man in the worst sense of the word. He did the right thing for the wrong reasons. He had just enough religion to make him miserable. There was no joy in his religion or his life. He lived in his own prison of hatred, jealousy, and self-righteousness. Church members can be like that. They are loyal members of the household of God, but they are miserable in their spirit. People in the church are also in need of repentance.

Illustrative Materials

Scared to go home? A letter to Ann Landers from a run-away girl:

> "I ran away from home six months ago because I thought I wanted the freedom to do as I pleased without anyone bossing me around or asking me questions. After three weeks, I had my fill of freedom and wanted to go home, but I was afraid to because I had been so rotten to my mother. Since I've been out on the streets, I've been into cocaine abuse, beaten up, raped, and have come close to being killed. I'm off drugs now and want to go home, but I'm afraid my folks won't take me back."

Welcome home! A girl wrote to Ann Landers:

> "After a few weeks I was fed up with running and dying to see my Mom and Dad and my brothers, but I was scared to go home because I had caused them so much trouble. I was sure they never wanted to see me again. One day I decided to take a chance and show up at the front door. I rang that old familiar doorbell at 6 a.m. When Mom saw me standing there, she grabbed me in her arms and started to cry, 'My baby is home at last!' She woke

up Dad and my brothers, and they were so glad to see me they cried, too. I just couldn't believe it."

The Harmful Good People. Maxwell Perkins, the famous book editor, once wrote:

"One of my deepest convictions is that the terrible harms that are done in this world are not done by deliberately evil people, who are not numerous and are soon found out. They are done by the good — by those who are so sure that God is with them. Nothing can stop them, for they are certain that they are right."

A Rejected Son. Doug Zauderer of Atlanta told his father twelve years ago that he was gay. He was urged to get hormone treatments and counseling. Visits with his parents became increasingly tense. Then three years ago, his parents told him he was no longer welcome in their home and his brother stopped speaking to him. Doug remarked, "After they told me I was not wanted anymore, I didn't have to confront their hostility." (See Psalm 27:10.)

A Father's Love. Arnold Prater tells about the time when, as a senior in high school, he played football. His school was playing their bitter rival. The ball came sailing to him, but somehow it hit his chest. The opposing team took possession of it and later made a touchdown making the score 14-7 in the rival's favor. He was ashamed and humiliated because he felt he had let all his teammates down. He was so ashamed that he waited in the locker room until everyone had gone home. In the gathering darkness he saw a figure: his father was waiting for him. He put his arms around Arnold and said, "Just thought I'd wait and walk home with you." Together through the darkness they walked home.

Proper 6 • Pentecost 4 • Ordinary Time 11

Common   Lutheran   Roman Catholic

---

5. Two Men in Debt

Luke 7:36-50

---

[36]One of the Pharisees asked him to eat with him, and he went into the Pharisee's house, and sat at the table. [37]And behold, a woman of the city, who was a sinner, when she learned that he was sitting at table in the Pharisee's house, brought an alabaster flask of ointment, [38]and standing behind him at his feet, weeping, she began to wet his feet with her tears, and wiped them with the hair of her head, and kissed his feet, and anointed them with ointment. [39]Now when the Pharisee who had invited him saw it, he said to himself, "If this man were a prophet, he would have known who and what sort of woman this is who is touching him, for she is a sinner." [40]And Jesus answering said to him, "Simon, I have something to say to you." And he answered, "What is it, Teacher?" [41]"A certain creditor had two debtors; one owed five hundred denarii, and the other fifty. [42]When they could not pay, he forgave them both. Now which of them will love him more?" [43]Simon answered, "The one, I suppose, to whom he forgave more." And he said to him, "You have judged rightly." [44]Then turning toward the woman he said to Simon, "Do you see this woman? I entered your house, you gave me no water for my feet, but she has wet my feet with her tears and wiped them with her hair. [45]You gave me no kiss, but from the time I came in she has not ceased to kiss my feet. [46]You did not anoint my head with oil, but she has anointed my feet with ointment. [47]Therefore I tell you, her sins, which are many, are forgiven, for she loved much; but he who is forgiven little, loves little." [48]And he said to her, "Your sins are forgiven." [49]Then those who were at table with him began to say among themselves, "Who is this, who even forgives sins?" [50]And he said to the woman, "Your faith has saved you; go in peace."

Recently a business man appeared before a federal bankruptcy court in Tampa asking for protection from his creditors to whom he owed $6,100,000 with assets of only $208,810. In another case, a man borrowed ten dollars from a friend to pay for a dinner. Suppose the creditor, in each case, cancelled the debt. Which of the two, do you think, would be more grateful and appreciative?

Jesus tells a parable of a similar situation. A certain man had two debtors. One owed him 500 silver coins and the other fifty. If the creditor forgave the debts of both, which one would love him more? Simon, a Pharisee, answered correctly when he said the one forgiven the most would love the most. Did Simon love less because he needed less forgiveness? If so, did Jesus have a case against him? By commending the prostitute for her demonstration of love, was Jesus encouraging sin so that forgiveness would result in love?

Context

Context of the Church Season

In the cycle C lectionary, today's parable is the first of fifteen in the Pentecost season. The Lessons and liturgical propers do not appear in thematic form. Each Lesson is given in semi-in-course fashion. The First lesson for this Sunday (Pentecost 4) is the second in a series dealing with Elijah and Elisha. The Second lesson is the third in a series of six from Galatians. The Gospel lessons during Pentecost cover the teachings and works of Christ according to Luke.

Consequently, no theme embracing the Lessons and propers is intended. Each Lesson can be treated independently except as each appears in a series. In the Pentecost season, the Psalm of the Day harmonizes with the First lesson. The Prayer and Hymn of the Day are appropriate for the Gospel lesson.

Context of the Lectionary

The First Lesson. (1 Kings 19:1-8) Threatened by Queen Jezebel, Elijah flees to the wilderness where, while on his way to Mount Sinai (Horeb), he is fed by an angel. Jezebel threatened to kill Elijah because on Mount Carmel he killed 450 of her prophets.

The Second Lesson. (Galatians 2:15-21) Paul writes that Christians are justified not by the works of the law but by faith in Christ. This statement grew out of his conflict with Peter, who compromised the Gospel with Judaizers.

Gospel. (Luke 7:36—8:3) Luke 7:36-50 tells of a prostitute's demonstration of love while Jesus dined at a Pharisee's house. The parable of the two debtors is an indigenous part of the episode. Luke 8:1-3 gives an account of women who followed and ministered to the needs of Jesus and his disciples.

Context of the Gospel Lesson

The parable of the two debtors must be seen in the context of the account of Jesus' visit in a Pharisee's home. The occasion is Jesus' having dinner in Simon's home. A prostitute enters and showers affection on Jesus. This offends the Pharisee. He does not say anything, but Jesus reads his mind. Simon concludes that Jesus is not a prophet, who would know that the woman was a sinner. To answer this unspoken criticism, Jesus tells a story about a creditor who cancelled the debts of two, one owing 500 and the other fifty denarii. Which of the two would love the creditor more? Simon answers correctly that the one forgiven more would love more. Then Jesus illustrates the point of the parable by contrasting what little Simon had done for him with what the prostitute had done to express her love and gratitude. After the conversation with Simon, Jesus assures the woman of her forgiveness. The other guests remarked, "Who is this that can forgive sins?"

Context of the Scriptures

Today's Gospel lesson is related to the foregoing in Luke 7:29-35. Luke reports that the people, especially tax collectors, listened to Jesus' preaching. The tax collectors also heard John and were baptized by him, but the Pharisees rejected both their preaching and refused John's baptism. Jesus points out that the Pharisees did not respond to John the Baptizer's funeral songs, nor to Jesus' wedding music. Yet, a Pharisee, Simon, invited Jesus to his home for dinner.

In Matthew 26:6-13 and Mark 14:3-9, while at Bethany in the house of Simon, a nameless woman pours precious perfume on Jesus' head. He commends her act as preparation for his death.

In yet another version of the story (John 12:1-8) Jesus visits the home of Mary, Martha, and Lazarus in Bethany, six days before the Passover. While at dinner, Mary pours expensive perfume on Jesus' feet and wipes his feet with her hair. Judas Iscariot objected to the waste of money which he said should have been given to the poor.

Deuteronomy 23:18 states that the Lord hates temple prostitutes.

Content

Content of the Pericope

    vv. 36-39 — The setting of the Parable of the Two Debtors.
    vv. 40-43 — Jesus answers Simon's criticism with a parable.
    vv. 44-46 — Jesus applies the parable to Simon and the woman.
    vv. 47-50 — Responses to the anointing — Jesus's response:
    assurance of forgiveness.
    The woman's response: faith.
    The guests' response: "Who is this?"

Precis of the Parable

Jesus was the dinner guest of a Pharisee, Simon. When Jesus was at the table, a prostitute came with a bottle of perfume, washed his feet with her tears, dried them with her hair, and poured the perfume on them. When Simon saw this, he was shocked and said to himself, "If Jesus were a prophet, he would know she is a prostitute and would not allow her to touch him." Knowing Simon's thoughts, Jesus told him about a creditor who forgave a man owing him 500 silver coins and another owing fifty pieces. He asked Simon which of the two loved the creditor more. Correctly, Simon answered, "The man who was forgiven more." Then, Jesus asked Simon to consider the woman's behavior in contrast to his lack of courtesy. She had washed his feet with tears, but Simon had provided no water for him to wash his feet. Simon had given Jesus no welcome kiss, but the woman had repeatedly kissed his feet. Simon had offered no olive oil for Jesus' head, but the woman had poured perfume on his feet. Jesus explained that she loved so much because she was forgiven so very much. Then he assured the woman that her sins were forgiven. Her faith saved her, and he sent her away in peace. The other guests, observing and hearing what Jesus said and did, asked, "Who is this that can forgive sins?"

Thesis: Forgiveness of sin results in love.

Theme: Love according to forgiveness.

Key Words in the Parable

    1. "Eat." (v. 36) It is an honor and a pleasure when we are invited to a home for dinner. It is usually a very pleasant experience of fellowship and animated conversation. In the case of Simon's dinner party, it turned out to be a disaster. This invitation shows that Jesus did not only eat with publicans and sinners, but also with elite Pharisees. Though Jesus was honored by the invitation, his host failed to offer the customary courtesies at his guest's arrival: a welcoming kiss, water for washing the dust off feet, and olive oil for anointing the head. The lack of these common courtesies indicates that Simon did not invite Jesus for dinner in token of friendship.

2. "Woman." (v. 37) A woman of the city, a "sinner," probably a prostitute, has no name. Some have suggested that she was Mary Magdalene or Mary of Bethany, but no one knows who she was. When a celebrated rabbi was entertained in the courtyard of a home, visitors were permitted to slip in and sit against a wall to hear the table talk. This woman felt compelled to express her love for Jesus who had forgiven her. She felt unworthy to kiss his face, but kissed his feet repeatedly. Her tears washed his feet. Though it was a disgrace for a woman to let down her hair in the presence of men, she let down her hair to dry his feet. Then she poured precious perfume on them. In her actions she expressed not only her sense of unworthiness, but also her tender devotion to Jesus.

3. "Himself." (v. 39) When Simon saw the prostitute touching Jesus with kisses, tears, and perfume, he was horrified. A godly man, he held, would not allow a woman of this kind to touch him and thereby defile him. In his own mind, he explained the situation, concluding that Jesus could not be a prophet, a man of God, or he would have recognized her as a woman of the streets. Though Simon said nothing, Jesus read his mind. He knew what Simon was thinking. Simon apparently considered himself a pious and righteous man. He was not a sinner like the woman. This account reminds us that Christ knows what is in our hearts and minds. We need not talk to reveal what we think. With the Psalmist we can say, "Search me, O God, and know my heart!" (Psalm 139:23)

4. "Sinner." (vv. 37, 39) A sinner is one who commits sin. But who is a sinner? Simon called the prostitute a sinner. Jesus considered Simon a sinner also. What is sin? The Greek word for sin is *amartia,* meaning "missing the mark." It is not measuring up to what God requires of us. Sin is a basic condition of rebellion against God. The self opposes God. It is I *versus* God. The center of sin is I; the center of pride is I. The basic sin-condition expresses itself in two kinds of sin. One is external sins: child abuse, adultery, prostitution, drunkenness, murder, rape, etc. This type of sin is represented by the woman. The other type is internal: deceit, hypocrisy, greed, egotism, pride, hatred, jealousy, etc. People with this kind of sin do not consider themselves sinners. These people are respectable, law-abiding, and do not get in trouble with the police. Simon is this latter type of sinner. His problem is the lack of consciousness of his sins. Without this awareness, he does not feel a need for forgiveness. But since he does not receive forgiveness, he has no love for God or man.

5. "Forgiven." (vv. 42, 47) In the parable, the creditor forgave the two men their debts. To forgive a debt is to cancel it. What is the difference between forgiving a monetary debt and forgiving sins? According to the *Revised Standard Version*, Jesus has us pray in the Lord's Prayer, "Forgive us our debts . . ." — a debt owed to God. Like the creditor, God cancels our debts outright. The account is settled: "Paid in full." There is no installment paying of the debt. In his mercy, God for Jesus' sake completely and entirely wipes out our debts to him. No wonder forgiven people express their thanks in works of love and devotion!

Contemplation

Insights

1. Faith and forgiveness. Are we forgiven because we love or believe? "Her sins, which are many, are forgiven, for she loved much." (v. 47) These words of Jesus may lead us to think that the more we love, the more we will be forgiven. However, the *Good News Bible* corrects this impression: "The great love she has shown proves that her many sins have been forgiven." (v. 47) If love brought forgiveness, it would become a matter of works of love to merit forgiveness. Rather, forgiveness is a gift of God in Christ. Faith makes forgiveness a personal experience. Forgiveness motivates us to love out of gratitude. Thus, Jesus said to the woman, "Your faith has saved you." She was saved because her faith accepted forgiveness, and forgiveness put her in right relations with God.

2. Love and forgiveness. According to Jesus, the more we are forgiven, the more we will love. Does this mean that we should sin more to be forgiven more and thus love more? Paul raised the same question, "Are we to continue in sin that grace may abound?" (Romans 6:1) Paul hastened to answer, "By no means!" When we are forgiven, we will so love God for his mercy that, henceforth, we will do all we can to please him by living according to his will. Gratitude is the power to motivate us to live godly lives. Even though love of God will keep us from future sinning, we will still owe him 500 pieces of silver. A human being can never love enough to be sin-free.

3. The Sin of no sin. Simon and the woman were both sinners. Only Jesus had no sin. Of the two sinners Simon did not acknowledge his sin because he did not realize he was sinning, as did the prostitute. She was guilty of sins of the flesh. She knew it, confessed it, and was forgiven. Proof of her forgiveness were her acts of affection for Jesus, who forgave her. Simon asked for no forgiveness because he did not feel he had done anything wrong. He was blind to his sin of self-righteousness in judging the woman as a sinner. He sinned in not being courteous to Jesus as his guest. His sin was in misunderstanding and in his lack of appreciation for Jesus as a prophet. If one has no sin, there is no need for forgiveness. The problem with Simon was his unwillingness to see himself as a sinner. If one has sin and does not acknowledge it, one cannot be forgiven. The sin of no sin cannot be forgiven until there is a confession of sin.

4. Our creditor. In the discussion of the parable and the setting of Simon and the prostitute we must not overlook the creditor in the parable. Where can we find a creditor who would cancel our debts both small and great? He asked for no installment payments from the debtors. It was an outright cancellation of the debts. Only God could be this kind of creditor! Out of love and mercy, God forgives all without any strings attached. The cancellation of debts was a pure act of grace. In the Lord's Prayer, we plead, "Forgive us our debts." Each sin is a debt owed to God, for we cannot sin against ourselves or others without, at the same time, sinning against God. When the Prodigal returned, he confessed, "I have sinned against God and against you." God came first! Since sin is a debt owed to God, only he can forgive the debt. As God's Son, Jesus forgave the woman.

Homily Hints

1. Be Glad You Are a Sinner! (7:42-50) If we were not sinners, we would not know Christ as Savior. Nor would we ever taste the sweet mercy of our God. This is not to encourage sin but to acknowledge rather than deny our sin. A sinner —
    A. Receives forgiveness — vv. 42, 47.
    B. Is motivated to love — vv. 42-43, 47.
    C. Lives in peace with God — v. 50.

2. Who is a Sinner? (7:36-50) In today's Gospel lesson there is disagreement over who is a sinner. Simon does not think he is a sinner. The woman admits she is a sinner. Simon is not sure that Jesus is not a sinner like the woman, for if he were not, he would not have allowed her to touch him. In the parable, both men were debtors or sinners. Consider —
    A. What is sin — only sins of the flesh (prostitution)?
    B. Who are the good people — Simon?
    C. Are all people sinners — the two debtors?

3. Who Loves the Most? (7:41-47) The woman in the pericope loves Jesus extravagantly, in contrast to the miserly love of Simon. The man owing 500 denarii loved the creditor more than the other man who owed only fifty coins. The one who loves the most is the one who —
   A. Sins the most (Prostitute).
   B. Is forgiven the most (Greater debtor).
   C. Loves the most out of gratitude — vv. 44-47.

4. Spiritual Bankruptcy. (7:41-43) In recent years a growing practice is to file for bankruptcy to protect one's assets from creditors. But there is a far wider spiritual bankruptcy in terms of our debt to God. Consider the human bankruptcy —
   A. Our universal indebtedness — both men, like all people, are debtors.
   B. Our total indebtedness — both men "could not pay."
   C. Our permanent indebtedness — we are sinners until death.

5. The Incredible Creditor. (7:41-43, 48) In the parable there is an incredible creditor who cancels completely the debts whether small or large. A denarius is equivalent to a day's wages. Who could find a creditor like him in today's world? Indeed, God in Christ is this kind of creditor who forgives (cancels) our debts owed to him. What does it mean for him to forgive our debts?
   A. He loves debtors — he is concerned about their welfare.
   B. He cancels debts — he knows they cannot pay the debts.
   C. He absorbs the debts — he assumes the loss.

6. A Sinner Without Knowing It. (7:40-50) The trouble with Simon was that he was as great a sinner as the prostitute but did not know it. If he had known it, he probably would have sought forgiveness and expressed his gratitude in works of love for Jesus. King David also sinned by committing adultery and murder, but did not realize his sin until Nathan said, "You are the man." A consciousness of sin leads to forgiveness and forgiveness to love. How then can we know we are sinners?
   A. Examine your life in the light of the Decalogue.
   B. Compare your life with the ideal, Jesus.
   C. Listen to your conscience.
   D. Let the Holy Spirit convict you.

7. Debts upon Debts. (7:41-43) America is the largest debtor nation in the world. National, corporate, and personal debts amount to trillions of dollars. But, this is really small change compared to what we owe God. Ask these questions —

A. How much do we owe — fifty or 500?
B. To whom do we owe this?
   God is our creditor; all sin is against God.
C. When will the debt be paid?
   Like the men in the parable, we are unable ever to pay.
   On the cross Christ paid the debt for us.

Contact

Points of Contact

1. Which sinner are we? Today's parable consists of two sinners, but only one realized her sin. Which of the two are we? We who gather to worship God are, for the most part, unlike the prostitute. Christian people are not in the business of selling sex through prostitution. Church people, generally speaking, are not guilty of sins of the flesh. Rather, we are represented by the Pharisee. We are the "good" people who are respectable and go to church, say our prayers, try to tithe, and obey the laws of state and church. But we have our secret, "Christian" sins of the spirit: pride, self-righteousness, and judgment of other "sinners." In preaching on this parable, we confront a group of polite Pharisees who need to hear the parable of the two debtors.

Yet, the two sinners may not be so clear and definite as black and white. They may not be contained in water-tight compartments. In each of us there may be both sinners, the Pharisee and the prostitute. As Paul Hovey said, "I am neither good nor bad, I am both. I am neither spiritual nor sensual, I am both. I am neither generous nor selfish, I am both. I am neither honest nor dishonest, I am both. I am neither saint nor sinner, I am both."

2. Sin in Order to Be Forgiven? The outcome of the parable is love for the one who forgives us. The point is that the more we are forgiven, the more out of gratitude we will love. In the minds of some listeners, we may be saying that we need to get out and "sin boldly," as Luther said, in order to receive more forgiveness. Out of forgiveness comes love for the creditor. As preachers, we will be careful not to suggest this permissiveness to sin in order to love. It does not work that way. If we love because God has forgiven us, we, out of love, will love his law and delight in obeying his will. But even if love will keep us from willful sinning, we will always be in need of forgiveness, for a Christian until death is both a saint and a sinner.

3. Handle with Care. In preaching to people who may be like the Pharisee and the prostitute, we need to emulate Jesus' method. He could have been rough on the woman by withdrawing from her touches, and on the Pharisee for his holier-than-thou attitude. Yet, he deals tenderly with the woman, does not excuse her sin or ignore it, but assures her of forgiveness and sends her away in peace. In dealing with the Pharisee, Jesus might have told him off, scolded him, condemned him for his bad attitude and failure to extend customary courtesies. Instead, he used an indirect and tactful approach to teach and lead the Pharisee to a self-understanding of his sin. He tells a story of two debtors that matches the situation at hand and lets Simon see himself in the story. Probably he never forgot the lesson he learned, and it is hoped that he changed his attitude toward other sinners. As we preach to people like Simon or the woman, we will want to be as careful and understanding of sinners as Jesus was.

4. A Sinner — Who Me? The point of the parable and its context is that, because we do not love, we are not forgiven. We are not forgiven because we fail to realize our need of forgiveness. In our time, sin has been minimized. We call sin other things such as "mistakes" or "maladjustment" or "indiscretion." Some things are no longer called or considered sins: adultery, living together without marriage, pre-marital sex, pornography, gambling, etc. Even the church has become lax in considering sin to be of first importance. Some churches do not consider sin important enough to be confessed. The confession of sins is either omitted or made optional in the order of worship. This was the problem of the Pharisee: he had no realization of his sin. If there is no sin, there is no need of forgiveness. If there is no need of forgiveness, there is no need of a Savior or a cross. It is an ironic paradox that our sin-saturated society has little or no awareness of sin.

Illustrative Materials

1. Self-righteousness. A woman came to Albert Day to talk about joining the church. As she was giving her reasons for wanting to belong to the fellowship, with great assurance she said, "I have always done what was right."

A pastor was rejoicing with a man who was recovering from a serious illness. The man had been a member of his church for sixty years. His response to the pastor's congratulations: "Yes, I guess I've been a pretty good boy, haven't I?"

In the *Peanuts* comic strip, Lucy is leaning against the piano while "Beethoven" is playing. She says to him, "I have examined my life and found it to be without a flaw. Therefore, I'm going to hold a ceremony and present myself with a medal. I will then give a very moving acceptance speech . . . After that I'll greet myself in the receiving line. When you are perfect, you have to do everything yourself.''

2. Confession. The grandson of Ernest Renan knocked on the door of a rectory one day. A priest opened the door. "Come out," the young skeptic said, "I want to talk to you about a problem." The priest replied, "No, come in. I want to talk to you about your sins."

In 1945 a group of German theologians drew up the Stuttgart Declaration of Guilt:

> "We are all the more grateful for this visit as we know ourselves to be one with our people in a great company of suffering and in a great solidarity of guilt. Through us endless suffering has been brought to many peoples and countries. True, we have struggled for many years in the name of Jesus Christ against a spirit which found terrible expression in the National Socialist regime of violence, but we accuse ourselves for not witnessing more courageously, for not praying more faithfully, for not believing more joyously, and for not loving more ardently."

3. A Kiss. Andor Foldes, a renowned concert pianist, tells of a personal crisis when he was sixteen resulting from a difference with his music teacher. Later, Liszt's last surviving pupil, Emil von Sauer, asked Foldes to play for him. He played numbers from Bach, Beethoven, and Schumann. Then Sauer rose and kissed him on the forehead. He said, "My son, when I was your age, I became a student of Liszt. He kissed me on the forehead after my first lesson saying, 'Take good care of this kiss — it comes from Beethoven who gave it to me after hearing me play.' I have waited for years to pass on this sacred heritage, but now feel you deserve it."

4. Solution to Sin. When Karl Barth visited America, a group of professors from Union Seminary in New York met with him for conversation. One asked "the Baseler lion" what he would say if he met Adolf Hitler. Barth replied, "Jesus Christ died for your sins."

5. Quotable. Reinhold Niebuhr: "Much evil is done by good people who do not know they are not good."
Bishop Fulton Sheen: "The tragedy is not that people are sinners but that they are sinners and refuse to admit it."

C. S. Lewis: "Christianity has no message for those who do not realize they are sinners."

6. Debts. According to *Time Magazine* March 9, 1987, the United States is the world's largest debtor nation, owing $200 billion.

The nation's debt is $2.1 trillion.

Our corporate debt totals $1.2 trillion.

Personal debt, including consumer and mortgage debt, amounts to $2.2 trillion.

The debts of the third world nations amount to $1 trillion.

6. The Good Samaritan

Luke 10:25-37

^{25}And behold, a lawyer stood up to put him to the test, saying, "Teacher, what shall I do to inherit eternal life?" ^{26}He said to him, "What is written in the law? How do you read?" ^{27}And he answered, "You shall love the Lord your God with all your heart, and with all your soul, and with all your strength, and with all your mind; and your neighbor as yourself." ^{28}And he said to him, "You have answered right; do this, and you will live."

^{29}But he, desiring to justify himself, said to Jesus, "And who is my neighbor?" ^{30}Jesus replied, "A man was going down from Jerusalem to Jericho, and he fell among robbers, who stripped him and beat him, and departed, leaving him half dead. ^{31}Now by chance a priest was going down that road; and when he saw him he passed by on the other side. ^{32}So likewise a Levite, when he came to the place and saw him, passed by on the other side. ^{33}But a Samaritan, as he journeyed, came to where he was; and when he saw him, he had compassion, ^{34}and went to him and bound up his wounds, pouring on oil and wine; then he set him on his own beast and brought him to an inn, and took care of him. ^{35}And the next day he took out two denarii and gave them to the innkeeper, saying, 'Take care of him; and whatever more you spend, I will repay you when I come back.' ^{36}Which of these three, do you think, proved neighbor to the man who fell among the robbers?" ^{37}He said, "The one who showed mercy on him." And Jesus said to him, "Go and do likewise."

For years I wanted a boat. Our townhouse on Clearwater Bay had a boat slip but there was no boat for it. Finally, after years of saving, we bought a twenty-one foot boat with a 210 horse power motor. It was only the second time that I had taken the boat out. After going a couple miles down the Intracoastal Waterway, I turned around to come back home. Just as

I was headed home, the motor mysteriously stopped. When I turned on the starter, the engine would not turn over, as though the battery were dead. This had never happened to me before; what was I to do? I called the Coast Guard on the ship-to-shore radio and asked for help, whereupon I was advised to put down the anchor and wait for a commercial boat to tow me home at the rate of seventy dollars per hour. While I waited, a Good Samaritan and his wife came along in their boat. He yelled, "Need some help?" I told him I could not get the motor to start. He threw me a line and towed me to my dock. He refused to take any money for his gas and trouble. All he said was, "Pass it along." Like the Good Samaritan, I did not learn his name or address. He gave his time, inconvenience, and fuel to get me out of trouble, though he did not know me or my profession. To him it was enough that I was a fellow human being in need of help.

Something like this happened in Jesus' day under different circumstances, but the same principles are involved. Jesus told about it, and we know the story as the Parable of the Good Samaritan, which is the subject for an upcoming sermon.

Context

The Parable in the Context of the Lectionary

The First Lesson. (2 Kings 2:1, 6-14) This is the first lesson in a series of four on the life and ministry of Elisha. Elisha follows Elijah to the Jordan River where Elijah ascended on a chariot of fire. Elisha puts on Elijah's cloak and is endowed with the power of Elijah's spirit.

The Second Lesson. (2 Colossians 1:1-14) Similar to the First Lesson, this lesson is the first in a series of four on the book of Colossians. Paul assures the church of his thanksgiving to God for their faith, love, and hope in the Gospel, and of his prayers for their strengthening in faith and love so that they may be well-pleasing to God.

Gospel. (Luke 10:25-37) The Gospel lesson is one of three lessons from Luke 10. During Pentecost the lectionary presents a semi-in-course reading of Luke. Today's Gospel gives us the Parable of the Good Samaritan. It is a part of Luke's special section: Luke 9:51-19:27.

Context of the Gospel Lesson

The Parable of the Good Samaritan is placed within the context of a lawyer, or scribe, coming to Jesus with a question on how to receive eternal life. Jesus asks him how he reads the Scriptures, and the scribe quotes the laws concerning love to God and neighbor. Jesus commends him for giving the correct answer and challenges him to obey these laws so that he might live. Apparently, this is too simple an answer for the lawyer and thus he asks who one's neighbor is. In answer, Jesus tells the story of a man who fell among robbers and was assisted by a Samaritan. The lawyer answers his own question: "The one who showed mercy on him." Again, Jesus challenges the lawyer to follow the good example of the Samaritan.

The parable must be understood in the light of its context. It answers the question, "Who is the neighbor one is to love as oneself?" The central question is how to inherit eternal life. The parable deals only with a part of the answer: love one's neighbor and live. In this context we learn the lawyer's motives for his questions: (1) to test Jesus (v. 25), and (2) to justify himself. (v. 29) Both Jesus and the scribe are in agreement on the two greatest commandments and on the fact that obedience to these laws results in eternal life. This leaves the problem of defining the neighbor — does the neighbor include every person? The parable deals with this question.

Context of Related Scriptures

>Deuteronomy 6:5 — Love God.
>Leviticus 19:18 — Love neighbor.
>John 4:9 — Jews and Samaritans.
>1 Chronicles 23:24-32 — The work of Levites.

Sources of eternal life —

Matthew 19:16-22 — "Follow me."
John 3:16 — Believers have eternal life.
John 6:68 — "You have the words of eternal life."
John 17:3 — This is eternal life, to know thee.
Romans 6:23 — "The free gift of God is eternal life in Christ Jesus our Lord."

Content

Content of the Pericope

>v. 25 — A lawyer's question.
>v. 26 — Jesus' counter-question.
>vv. 27-28 — The questions answered.
>v. 29 — The lawyer's follow-up question.
>vv. 30-35 — The situation given in a story.
>vv. 36-37a — The lawyer's answer.
>v. 37b — Jesus' admonition.

Precis of the Pericope

A Bible scholar intended to trap Jesus with the question, "What shall I do to inherit eternal life?" Since he was a Bible expert, Jesus asked him what the Bible said and how he would interpret it. He quoted the Bible by saying that one should love God with one's whole being and one's neighbor as oneself. Jesus commended him for his right answer and said, "Do this, and you will live."

The scribe was not content to let the matter drop, and so wanting to justify himself and his question, he asked another, "If I am to love my neighbor, who is my neighbor?" In reply, Jesus told about a man who was on his way from Jerusalem to Jericho. He was attacked by thieves who stole his clothes and beat him up so badly that they left him half dead. Later a priest came along, saw the victim, but went on his way. A little later a Levite came along, saw the man, but hurried on without helping. Then came a Samaritan who saw the injured man, stopped, poured oil and wine on his wounds, put him on his animal, and took him to an inn where he personally took care of him. The next day he asked the innkeeper to care for the injured man, and paid him for his trouble. If there were more expense, he promised to reimburse the innkeeper when he came back. Then Jesus asked the teacher which of the three men was neighbor to the victim. He answered, "The one who was kind to him." In response Jesus urged him to go and do likewise.

Thesis: Love of neighbor is helping anyone in need.

Theme: Without asking questions, love serves.

Key Words

1. **"Lawyer."** (v. 25) Luke uses the term "lawyer" rather than "scribe" for the sake of his Gentile readers who probably would not understand the Hebrew word. The lawyer was a teacher of the Mosaic law, a Bible scholar and expert. Because he was a Bible student, Jesus asked him what the Bible taught about eternal life.

2. **"Test."** (v. 25) The lawyer did not really want an answer to his question. He knew the teachings of the Bible. He wanted to trap Jesus by asking a very difficult question, for the Jews had 613 laws. Knowing that the scribe knew the answer, Jesus answered his question by asking a question. The scribe's answer was correct and Jesus told him to obey it that he might have eternal life.

3. "Neighbor." (v. 29) We know we are to love God and neighbor. But, what is the scope of the term "neighbor?" Are there any limits? The Jews of Jesus' day limited the concept of "neighbor" to fellow-Jews. Does "neighbor" include Gentiles or sinners or enemies? In the parable Jesus does not really answer the question, but asks whether we are good neighbors. The command is to love, and love does not define, but discovers, the neighbor. Love is compassion for anyone in need, regardless of a person's race, nationality, geographical location, or creed. Love alone answers the question. The key is compassion.

4. "Man." (v. 30) Who is this "man" lying half dead by the side of the Jericho road? He is given no name and we do not know his religion. If he were a Samaritan, we can understand why the priest and Levite passed him by, for Jews had no relations with Samaritans. If he were a Jew, the priest and Levite broke the law of loving one's neighbor and the Samaritan might have ignored the wounded Jew. It is significant that the injured one is just a "man." He could be any and every person in need of assistance, in need of a good neighbor.

5. "Jericho." (v. 30) Jericho is located seventeen miles northeast of Jerusalem in the Jordan valley, which is 3500 fee lower than Jerusalem. Between the two towns, there was a rocky wasteland, a desert infested with bandits. The road went through an isolated and uninhabited area. For protection travelers usually went in groups.

6. "Priest, Levite." (vv. 30, 31) Priests were divided into twenty-four orders and were required to serve in the temple for one week twice a year. Probably the priest and Levite in the parable were returning home to Jericho upon completion of their rounds of duty.

The Levites constituted one of three orders of the priesthood. A Levite was an assistant priest. Levites were charged with the responsibility of arranging for the sacrifices and of maintaining the places for the temple services. They were in charge of the vestments, sacrificial equipment, and all other arrangements connnected with temple services and sacrifices.

7. "Samaritan." (v. 33) The Jews considered the Samaritans a despised race. In 722 B.C., the Assyrians conquered the ten northern tribes and took many into captivity. The remaining Jews intermarried with the incoming Assyrians. When Ezra led the Jews from Babylonian captivity in 536 B.C., the Samaritans offered to help them rebuild the temple. They were rejected. Consequently, the Samaritans built their own temple on Mount Gerizim. Hostility between Jews and Samaritans was increased between A.D. 6 and 9, when Samaritans defiled the temple by strewing the courts with the bones of dead men.

Contemplation

Insights

1. What love does. "What is love?" is the question usually asked. A better question is, "What does love do?" In the parable note the emphasis on doing: "What must I do to inherit eternal life?", "This do and you shall live," "Go and do thou likewise." Jesus takes the subject out of the theoretical and makes it practical.

The priest and Levite committed the sin of omission. They failed to do something for a wounded man. These religious leaders had religiosity rather than true religion. Their religion was confined to the temple: prayers, sacrifices, chants, and ceremony. True Christian religion is enacted love on the streets of the world. To the church's shame, some people outside the church can be more helpful and caring than those within the church. The priest and Levite were "church" people and the Samaritan was an outsider. Jesus asks, "What do you more than others?" Like the priest and the Levite, Christians are likely to enter to worship, but fail to leave to serve. Once I preached in a small church in Virginia. Above the dossal which hung behind the altar was an electric sign in red letters — "EXIT." At first I found it to be distracting to worship, but it proved to be a reminder to exit to the world for service.

2. Dodging the issue. A theological question can be used as a cop-out in order to avoid the implications or application of a truth. In the parable the lawyer got his answer to the question of how one could receive eternal life. Then Jesus urged him to obey the law of loving God and neighbor that he would have life. That should have settled the matter, but the lawyer did not like the doing of the law. He looked for a loophole. He thought he had one in the definition of "neighbor," because he knew that it was a controversial subject without a unanimous opinion. A similar experience occurred when Jesus had a conversation with a Samaritan woman at a well. When Jesus let her know that he knew she had been married five times and was then living with a man not her husband, she quickly asked where the proper place was to worship the Lord. We are good at putting up theological smoke screens when we do not want to conform to the truth or law.

3. Asking the right questions. "Who is my neighbor?" is the wrong question. A better question is "Am I a good neighbor?" Love answers who a neighbor is. Love does not define but discovers a neighbor. It looks not for discussion but for opportunity to love. Love means compassion and kindness to those who need it. Therefore, the real question is whether we have love for the neighbor. If so, we will see the neighbor in need of loving care.

4. Seeing with your heart. According to the parable, the priest, the Levite, and the Samaritan saw a man lying in blood, close to death. They saw his bloody head, his torn clothes, his bruises, and his exhaustion. The first two men saw the situation and continued on their ways home. The Samaritan saw with his heart; he had "compassion." He sympathized and felt the man's pain. Compassion is a sign of love. It drives one to lend assistance. When we drive through "Buttermilk Bottom," we see the poverty and filth, but without compassion we will pass by and try to forget what we saw. We can see the pitiful hungry children of Africa on television, but without love we will give nothing to the Hunger Appeal. Mother Theresa saw the horrible plight of the poor and homeless dying on the streets of Calcutta, but because of compassion, she organized an order of nuns to help the helpless.

5. Surrogate Samaritans. As there is more than one way to kill a cat, there is more than one way to be a good Samaritan. One can secure surrogate Samaritans. In the parable, the Samaritan did what he could for the injured Jew. He gave him first aid and took him to a motel. Apparently, he had to move on to Jericho to meet another appointment. He could not stay and nurse the man back to health. So, he arranged with the motel manager to look after the injured one on his behalf. He paid for the room and meals, and assured the manager that if the expense was more, he would repay him on his way back to Jerusalem.

We can be good Samaritans through other people and/or institutions. We can donate funds to help the poor, to educate the illiterate, and to evangelize the world through missions. When we give to the church or to any reputable charity organization, we make of them our surrogate Samaritans. We pay others to do what we cannot do.

6. Costly love. It costs to be a Good Samaritan. The cost may be facing danger of being hurt or killed. For the Samaritan in the parable, it cost much to rescue the wounded man. There was material cost: oil, wine, room, meals, and money for care provided by the innkeeper. Also, it was costly in inconvenience — he had to go out of his way to get to the inn. It cost him time — time to stop at an inn, make arrangements for room, meals, and care. Instead of riding, he put the stricken man on his animal and he endured a long walk to the inn.

To help someone is usually costly whether it is in time, inconvenience, or money. But, love never counts the cost. Love is only concerned that the needy person get help or rescue.

Homily Hints

1. Now You Know! (10:25-37) Often when a person says,

"I didn't know what," another replies, "Now you know!" The Bible teacher came to Jesus with questions. By the end of the conversation, Jesus could have said to him, "Now you know!" Through the parable, now we know —
  A. How to receive eternal life — v. 28.
  B. What God requires of us — v. 27.
  C. Who is our neighbor — vv. 29-37.

2. Because He Cared, He Didn't Care. (10:29-37) The Samaritan had compassion. He cared for the beaten man. Yet, his love made him not care —
  A. He did not care that the man was a hated Jew.
  B. He did not care that it cost him to help.
  C. He did not care that he received neither reward nor recognition.

3. Are You a Good Neighbor? (10:29-37) This is the vital question. It is not "Who is my neighbor?" but "Am I a good neighbor?" To be a good neighbor one must answer these questions —
  A. Am I needed to help?
  B. Am I able to help?
  C. Am I willing to help out of compassion?

4. At Your Service. (10:29-37) At service stations, drug stores, supermarkets we have "self-service." Sometimes if we are willing to pay more, we may ask for "full service." The Samaritan gave the stricken Jew full service —
  A. Personal service — he did not dial 911 but gave personal care.
  B. Practical service — he had his own first aid: oil, wine, bandages.
  C. Persistent service — he made arrangements for the man's care after he went on his way.

5. How to be a Good Neighbor. (10:25-37) We may want to be a good neighbor, but not know how to become one. Our text tells us how —
  A. Not by law — the lawyer knew the laws of love — v. 27. (Alaska and Minnesota have laws requiring a person to be a good Samaritan.)
  B. Not by knowledge — the priest and Levite knew the condition of the man — vv. 31-32.
  C. By compassion — love helps — v. 33.

6. Love is a Verb. (10:29-37) Love is a verb: "Love one another . . ." When Jesus asked Peter after the Resurrection if he loved him, Peter assured Jesus that he did. Then Jesus said, "Feed my sheep." Love calls for action, caring, helping, serving.

A. What love is not —
1. a noun only: peace, salvation, kindness.
2. an adjective only: beautiful, inspiring, kind.
B. What love is — a verb of: caring, helping, giving, serving.

7. Don't Get Me Involved! (10:25-37) Today people do not want to get involved in a situation. People can watch and do nothing when a person screams for help. Some are spectators to crimes making no attempt to stop them. Some refuse to testify in court for fear of retaliation. Others do not want to get involved in the legal system. In the parable, the priest and Levite did not want to get involved, for they "passed by on the other side." A Christian is compelled by love to follow the example of the Samaritan and get involved in helping the needy.

Do get involved because —
A. The law of love commands it — v. 27.
B. The victim needs you — v. 30.
C. The example of the Samaritan inspires you — v. 33.

Contact

1. Where is the Gospel? Can one preach the Gospel, the good news of redemption through the cross, and preach on the parable of the Good Samaritan? Is the parable teaching only humanism, philanthropy, and the golden rule? The parable is telling us to come to the aid of any and all needy neighbors. Does one have to be a Christian to help the abused and suffering? The Samaritan was not a true Jew. Are we saying that all we need to do is to be "humans?" Secular groups go about supporting charitable causes. Rock groups raise millions to feed the hungry abroad. Shriners give children free hospital care. A civic organization gives eye care and glasses to the needy.

If we preach on the parable, are we not promoting works righteousness? In the parable, a lawyer asks how to receive eternal life. It is the same as asking how to be saved or how to get right with God. Jesus approved the lawyer's choice of Bible texts: love God and neighbor. If one loves neighbor, like the Good Samaritan did, one is supposed to reap eternal life or salvation. Is this salvation by works? Is this the Gospel, the message that reconciliation with God is a matter of grace received by faith?

How then can we preach the Gospel from this parable? To do this we were called and ordained. The Gospel can be preached by use of the parable if we go to the source of our philanthropy. First, we are to love God. If we accept the love of God which put us in right relations with him, we will in turn love our neighbor. Does God really love us? Look at the cross! Do we really love God? Look at our ministry to our neighbors! Moreover, practical help to the needy, the injured, the poor, and others has its source in our devotion to Christ. In the afflicted, Christians see the face of Jesus. What we do for the oppressed we do for Jesus. "Inasmuch as you have done it unto one of the least of these my brethren, you have done it unto me." The secret of Mother Theresa's great labor of love for the world's most unfortunate is that she feels that by caring for the sick and dying she is ministering to Christ. Certainly non-Christians or non-religious people can be helpful to suffering humanity. There can be natural human sympathy for hurting people. But how much more Christians should help the needy because of their love for God! Eternal life, however, does not come through aiding people in distress but through love of God and neighbor. The Gospel is in God's love for us and, in turn, this love makes us want to help the bruised and battered people of the world.

2. **A Violent Society.** A point of contact between the parable and modern society is the incidence of violence. Robbers attack a man with so much violence that he is almost dead. That is "nothing" compared to the violence seen today on television, and in movies, newspapers, magazines, books, and in daily life. International terrorists take hostages and blow up buildings killing many people. One and one-half million women in America are raped annually. A child is sexually abused every two minutes. Murder in our cities is a daily affair. Our violent society gives us innumerable opportunities to be good Samaritans.

3. **Involvement.** The parable speaks to us today because of our lack of involvement with social issues and conditions. The priest and Levite refused to get involved in the messy affair of a victim of robbery. Our media report repeatedly on cases of bystanders who refuse to help people in trouble. They pass by on the other side of people being attacked. We may not want to be inconvenienced by going to the rescue. Maybe we are afraid of getting hurt by trying to help. Regardless of the reason, many of us prefer to be only spectators. The tragedy is that evil gets away with murder because good people do nothing.

Illustrative Materials

1. **Non-involvement.** A fourteen-year-old girl went for a dip in a fountain at a popular local park one summer day and was brutally assaulted by two youths who ripped off her shorts and repeatedly raped her for forty minutes. At least three adults stood by and watched as the girl screamed for help.

2. **Cost of Involvement.** A man in Florida felt sorry for a hitchhiker.

He was beaten with an iron pipe, his wrists were tied, then he was covered with a pile of branches. He received head injuries, bruises, and cuts. The hitchhiker stole his cash, wristwatch, checks, and car.

A nurse left home early one Sunday morning to go to work at a nearby hospital. On the way she picked up a young man whose car had broken down. Later detectives learned that he had stabbed this mother of four, dumped her body, and then set fire to her car.

3. A True Neighbor.

"The ultimate measure of a man is not where he stands in moments of comfort and convenience, but where he stands at times of challenge and controversy. The true neighbor will risk his position, his prestige, and even his life for the welfare of others. In dangerous valleys and hazardous pathways, he will lift some bruised and beaten brother to a higher and more noble life."

— Martin Luther King, Jr.

4. Love of Neighbor.

A man sat in an inn one night and watched as peasants drank and talked. As the night wore on and the alcohol loosened lips, one man leaned over to his trusted pal and asked, "Tell me, my friend, do you love me?" The other replied, "Of course I love you." The first man responded, "You say that you love me, but you do not even know what hurts me. And only if you understand what most pains me would you be able to truly love me."

5. Compassion.

Bishop Gerald Kennedy once asked a native of Liberia how it was that President Tubman had been re-elected president for so many terms. He replied, "We have a saying here that if a little boy out in the bushes stubs his toe, President Tubman says, 'ouch!' "

6. A Modern Samaritan.

One time a person by letter told Ann Landers of a Good Samaritan on a subway:

"Recently I sat across from a man on the New York subway. His coat was tattered and torn, held together with pins and string. His trousers were in no better shape. He had holes in his shoes and he wore no socks. The poor fellow looked as if he hadn't had a bath in weeks.

"I tried not to stare, looking left, right, up and down, but I couldn't keep my eyes off him. I never saw anyone who was so down and out.

"Just before my stop, as the train came to a halt, a neatly dressed, elderly woman walked the length of the car to the door next to where I was seated, although there were doors down at the other end where she had come from. She handed the pathetic stranger a dollar bill and said, with great dignity, 'I believe you dropped this.' The startled old man reached out, took the dollar, and said, 'Thank you.' "

Proper 12 • Pentecost 10 • Ordinary Time 17
Common   Lutheran   Roman Catholic

---

7. A Midnight Friend

Luke 11:1-13

---

¹He was praying in a certain place, and when he ceased, one of his disciples said to him, "Lord, teach us to pray, as John taught his disciples." ²And he said to them, "When you pray, say:

"Father, hallowed be thy name. Thy kingdom come. ³Give us each day our daily bread; ⁴and forgive us our sins, for we ourselves forgive every one who is indebted to us; and lead us not into temptation."

⁵And he said to them, "Which of you who has a friend will go to him at midnight and say to him, 'Friend, lend me three loaves; ⁶for a friend of mine has arrived on a journey, and I have nothing to set before him'; ⁷and he will answer from within, 'Do not bother me; the door is now shut, and my children are with me in bed; I cannot get up and give you anything'? ⁸I tell you, though he will not get up and give him anything because he is his friend, yet because of his importunity he will rise and give him whatever he needs. ⁹And I tell you, Ask, and it will be given you; seek, and you will find; knock, and it will be opened to you. ¹⁰For every one who asks receives, and he who seeks finds, and to him who knocks it will be opened. ¹¹What father among you, if his son asks for a fish, will instead of a fish give him a serpent; ¹²or if he asks for an egg, will give him a scorpion? ¹³If you then, who are evil, know how to give good gifts to your children, how much more will the heavenly Father give the Holy Spirit to those who ask him?"

We Americans pray, but we may not know how to pray. According to a 1986 Gallup poll, eighty-seven percent of American adults pray, fifty percent use prayer for petitions, and seventy percent claim their prayers are answered. Although we are not allowed to pray in public schools, we manage to pray elsewhere.

But, do we know how to pray as we ought? Are our prayers getting through to God? Do they produce results? When we pray, are we really speaking to God or to ourselves? According to today's Gospel lesson, the Disciples felt, after listening to Jesus' prayers, that they needed him to teach them how to pray. Even Saint Paul admitted that he did not know how to pray as he ought — "We do not know how to pray as we ought." (Romans 8:26)

In response to the Disciples' request, Jesus gives a lesson in prayer. The Parable of the Friend at Midnight teaches one aspect of prayer: persistence. Do you have a friend, Jesus asks in the parable, to whom you could go at midnight and borrow some food for an unexpected guest? Your friend says, "No way can I get up to give you bread. The house is closed up for the night and the whole family is asleep." Yet, you keep pounding on the door, keep calling his name, and repeat your request for food. Finally, your friend yields and gets up. He doesn't help you out because you are friends, but because of your incessant banging on his door and crying out loud. If persistent appeals get an unwilling friend to give what you need, how much more will a willing God answer your persistent petitions?

Context

Context of the Church Year

The Parable of a Friend at Midnight is a part of the Gospel for the Tenth Sunday after Pentecost (Proper 12). It is the first in a series of eleven consecutive parables (Pentecost 10 to 20). In Series C, the Pentecost season is a season of parables.

Context of the Lectionary

The First Lesson. (2 Kings 5:1-15ab) This lesson is the next to the last of ten lessons on the work of Elijah and Elisha. Upon the recommendation of a Jewish slave girl, Namaan, a Syrian general afflicted with leprosy, is sent to Elisha to be cured. After dipping himself seven times in the Jordan River, Namaan returns to Syria a cured man and convinced that Yahweh is the only true God.

The Second Lesson. (Colossians 2:6-15) The Second lesson is next to the last in a series of four from the book of Colossians. In this lesson Paul urges his people to live in Christ, in whom dwells the fullness of God. In baptism we were buried with Christ to sin and we rose with him in newness of life.

Gospel (Luke 11:1-13) The lectionary continues its march through Luke.

Today's Gospel lesson is the only one from chapter 11. In this selection Jesus teaches his Disciples about prayer.

Context of the Gospel Lesson

The Parable of the Friend at Midnight comes at a midsection in Jesus' discourse on prayer. Prior to this discourse, Jesus was at the home of Mary and Martha (10:38-42) for dinner. While dinner was being prepared by Martha, Mary listened to Jesus and was criticized for it by Martha. Now we see Jesus praying, and his prayers are so impressive that the Disciples ask him to teach them to pray. After giving them a model prayer, he tells the Parable of the Friend at Midnight. After the parable, Jesus assures the Disciples that God answers prayer.

Context of Related Scriptures

> Matthew 6:9-13 — The Lord's Prayer.
> Matthew 7:7-11 — The good things God gives through prayer.
> Genesis 18:20-32 — Abraham persists in praying for Sodom.
> Genesis 32:22-32 — Jacob wrestles with an angel until daybreak.
> Matthew 15:21-28 — A Canaanite mother refuses to take no for an answer.
> Judges 16:4-22 — Delilah persists in learning the secret of Samson's strength.
> Matthew 26:36-46 — In Gethsemane Jesus repeatedly prays to know God's will.
> Luke 18:1-8 — A twin parable: the widow and the judge.

Content

Content of the Pericope

> v. 1 — Hearing Jesus pray, the Disciples ask Jesus to teach them how to pray.
> vv. 2-4 — The content of prayer: the Lord's Prayer.
> vv. 5-8 — The method of prayer: persistence — Parable of the Friend at Midnight.
> vv. 9-13 — The benefits of prayer.

Precis of the Parable

One day the Disciples observed Jesus praying. They were so impressed that they, too, wanted to pray like he did. They asked him to teach them as John had taught his disciples to pray. In response, Jesus gave them a prayer now known as the Lord's Prayer. Then he asked them to think of a friend to whom they could go at midnight and ask for three loaves of bread. You knock on his door and call his name. You say, "A friend of mine has come and I have no food to give him." Your friend replies, "Go away! Don't bother me! My house is closed up for the night and my family is asleep. I am sorry but I cannot get up and give you bread." Though he will not get up because of friendship, he does get up because of your persistent knocking and calling, and he gives you food. In the same way, Jesus continued, we are to ask, seek, and knock, and we will receive good things from the heavenly Father. As an earthly father gives good gifts to his children, God the Father will even give himself in the Spirit to those who pray.

Thesis: God answers persistent prayer.

Theme: No end to praying!

Key Words

1. **"Teach."** (v. 1) Jesus' example of praying caused the Disciples to want to learn to pray like him. They heard him pray and they were impressed. They asked him to teach them how to pray as John the Baptizer had taught his followers. Prayer does not come naturally nor instinctively. It is an art and discipline that needs to be learned. A Christian is permanently enrolled in the school of prayer with Jesus as the teacher. In this school, prayer is more than words; it is example. In today's Gospel lesson Jesus teaches his men and us what to pray, how to pray, and why to pray.

2. **"Midnight."** (v. 5) At midnight comes the cry! Of all times, none could be worse. It is the darkest hour. The town is asleep. It is a time when one least wants to be disturbed. It is a time when one would least expect a caller. In the Parable of the Wise and Foolish Women, the bridegroom came at midnight. A need arises, a call comes often in our darkest hour.

3. **"Three."** (v. 5) The caller begs for "Three loaves" of bread. Why three? Can beggars be choosers? Wouldn't two do, or even one? At least one would be better than nothing. In Jesus' day, three loaves of bread were considered the amount needed for one day. We are to live one day at a time. God provides food one day at a time. In the wilderness manna came one day at a time, fresh every day. In the Lord's Prayer we ask, "Give us this day our daily bread." We need not ask for more, for we trust in God's continued providence.

4. "Nothing." (v. 6) The caller gave as his reason for waking his friend the fact that he had "nothing" in his house to feed his traveling guest. Having "nothing" revealed his need. It was a desperate need. The traveler was hungry and he could not wait until morning. Besides that, the caller had the duty of hospitality. If he did not prove to be hospitable, his shame and disgrace would be known throughout the village. His need was so desperate that he used desperate methods of waking his friend at midnight. It made him urgent and persistent.

5. "Bother." (v. 7) The sleeping friend was bothered by the insistent and persistent calling in the middle of the night. He had a right to ask not to be bothered. He was sound asleep. It was an ungodly hour. The house was locked up for the night. His family in the one-room house was fast asleep. To get up and get the bread would awaken the kids who would not be able to go back to sleep. It meant the ruination of a night's rest. Some commentators call this a humorous situation. Surely it was no joke for the sleeping family. If it were a joke, it was a bad and cruel joke!

6. "Importunity." (v. 8) The word in Greek means "shamelessness." The man's constant begging, knocking, yelling, and pleading were aggravating, obnoxious, and troublesome. It was a shameless way to act in the middle of the night just for the sake of three loaves of bread. It was so shameless that it moved the friend to get up and get the bread in order to get some peace and quiet. He did not disturb his family on the basis of friendship, but on the basis of this shameful aggravation.

7. "Receives." (v. 10) In the follow-up of the parable Jesus assures the Disciples that God answers prayers. Ask of God and you will receive. And what you receive is only good. Our heavenly Father is as good as an earthly father who would not give hurtful things to his children. But, God is even better than that! He gives himself, the Holy Spirit, to those who ask for him. If he gives only good things, we can therefore understand why God does not answer those prayers that would not be for our welfare. How good of God to be good to us!

Contemplation

Insights

1. Persistence Pays. Persistence is a law of life. It always pays off. For two years a sister of an American held hostage in Lebanon ding-donged our governmental officials to remember her brother and other hostages. She eventually succeeded in getting their interest and concern. Persistence works in getting an education; dropouts lose out. In becoming a success in one's work, persistence pays off. It is the faithful plodder rather than the brilliant flash-in-the-pan who is the one, like the legend of the turtle and the hare, that ultimately wins the race. In religion the one faithful unto death gets the crown of life. Persistence brings success also to our prayers; this is illustrated in today's parable. Never give up — "to hell with the torpedoes!"

2. God Needs no Coaxing. Our persistence may be seen as manipulating God to do our bidding. We are not to persist in our prayers in order to overcome God's supposed reluctance to help us or answer our petitions. For one thing, he is more eager to answer our prayers than we are to offer them, because he loves us so.

Moreover, God does not need our perseverance in prayer because he hears us the first time we ask. When we pray, we are not telling him something he does not already know. He knows our needs even before we pray. "Your Father already knows what you need before you ask him." (Matthew 6:8) Why then bother to pray? Because God cannot give us help without our wanting it. He does not force us to receive his blessings.

God does not need our persistence, furthermore, because he gives only what is good for us. His good gifts do not come to us because we insist. Because of his love, he gives only that which is for our welfare.

3. Persistence is for People. It is we and not God who need to persist in our prayers. Persistence indicates the depth of our need of that for which we pray. The need is so great that we plead and beg even with tears. In the parable the man needed food for his guest. Without it, he would be condemned for inhospitality.

Our persistence also indicates the depth of our faith. If we pray once or twice and do not get an answer and stop praying, it indicates that we do not really believe that God hears or cares about us.

Persistence on our part shows, too, that we are ever open to receiving the answer to our prayer. Because of circumstances, a prayer may not be able to be answered at the moment. It may take months or even years for the prayer to be answered. If we are not constant in our prayers, we will not be receptive to the answer.

4. No Answer. It happens often that no one answers the phone. Usually then we hang up and remark, "No answer." Prayer is like phoning God and there may be times when we get no answer. Persistence in prayer indicates that previous petitions are not answered, and so we keep on praying in the hope that the prayer will some day be answered. In today's culture, we demand instant response. We go to fast-food restaurants. We drink instant coffee or tea. We use a microwave rather than a conventional oven, because instead of waiting hours we are willing to wait only a few minutes. If God answered immediately, we might receive wrong answers. His delay in answering helps us to realize that what we pray for is not necessarily what we need. Furthermore, his delay, as indicated by our persistence, keeps us from thinking of God as an instant dispensing machine of blessings. It keeps us from seeing prayer as a button we press and out pops a blessing!

5. How Much More. God does better than a friend who gives because he is aggravated by insistent requests. The parable compares human and divine giving. In terms of motivation, God does better than a friend. The friend gets up and gives bread, not because of friendship, but because he wants to stop the repeated knocking and appealing for help. God gives because of friendship, for a Christian is a friend of God. Moreover, God does more than a human father does for his children. He would not give a stone in place of a loaf of bread. If a human father is so kind, how much more God gives only good things to his children. No human can outdo God when it comes to helping and loving his children.

Homily Hints

1. Continuing Education in Prayer. (11:1-13) Continuing education is a "must" for those in various professions. In the school of prayer, there are continuing education courses, because we never learn all we need to know about prayer. In today's Gospel lesson Jesus conducts a course on prayer —
    A. Learn by example — v. 1.
    B. What to pray — the Lord's Prayer — vv. 2-4.
    C. How to pray — persistence — vv. 5-8.
    D. Benefits of prayer — vv. 9-13.

2. Why Persist? (11:1-13) It is easy to become weary in prayer as well as in well-doing. Why must we keep on asking God over and over, again and again? Is this not vain repetition?
    A. We persist not for God's benefit.
        1. God is more ready to give than we are to pray.
        2. God knows our needs even before we pray.
        3. God gives only good gifts — vv. 10-13.
    B. We persist for our benefit.
        1. Reveals the degree of our need — vv. 5-6
        2. Indicates the depth of our faith.
        3. Keeps us open to receive.

3. How Great is Your Need? (11:5-8) Because we have need, we pray for the fulfillment of that need. If the need is not pressing and it does not really matter, we may pray once and forget it. Persistence in prayer depends on how great is our need. In the parable, the man came out at midnight, called, and knocked repeatedly until he got bread. His need was so great that he could not take no for an answer. One's persistence shows the depth of one's need —

    A. Need for protection — Jacob's wrestling all night.

    B. Need to know God's will — Jesus in Gethsemane.

    C. Need for healing — the Canaanite mother.

    D. Need for relief — Paul and his thorn.

4. God Answers Prayer. (11:1-13) According to the parable, a friend may get help from another friend if he persists in asking. In like manner, only more so, God hears and answers the prayers of his children. A human may be good, but God is better. A human can give bread, but God has better gifts. God answers prayer, because —

    A. God's motivation is better — v. 8.

    B. God's gifts are better — vv. 11-13.

5. Better Next Time! (11:9-10) We are not to pray repeatedly in the same way with the same fervor. We are not to be like a broken record that keeps playing the same notes *ad infinitum* until someone moves the needle to the next groove. Rather, each time we pray for the same thing we are to increase in intensity: ask — seek — knock. How then shall we pray?

    A. Ask — and you will receive. If not —

    B. Seek — and you will find. If not —

    C. Knock — and it will be opened to you.

Contact

Points of Contact

1. In Luke we have twin parables: The Midnight Friend and the Unjust Judge. The first falls on Pentecost 10 and ten Sundays later we deal with the other parable. Both deal with the principle of persistence in prayer. In the Midnight Friend parable we deal with prayer in general. The Unjust Judge parable is focused solely upon persistence.

Preachers will be wise to note what lies ahead, lest on Pentecost 10 "everything" about persistence be said, leaving little for Pentecost 20. In the light of this duplication, what can be done?

One option is to switch to the First or Second lesson rather than use the Gospel. But to do so would deprive the congregation of a message from the Parable.

Another option is to preach on both parables. With the Midnight Friend parable the comprehensive subject of prayer could be considered with the parable being one point of the sermon. Ten Sundays later the sermon could deal solely with persistence in prayer.

2. The parable today deals with only one aspect of prayer — persistence. The danger is to emphasize this aspect to the neglect of other vital components of prayer: adoration, confession, thanksgiving, supplication, and submission. Are preachers in danger of giving a slanted view of prayer in dealing only with persistence?

3. Is persistence a contradiction? In Matthew 6:8 Jesus said, "Your father knows what you need before you ask him." If so, why pray for our needs? If God knows our needs, is there any sense in persisting in prayer for the same blessing? Though he knows, is God reluctant to help us and therefore by repeated requests we beg and coax him to respond? Does God withhold his help until a certain amount of persistence is expended?

4. As preachers we must acknowledge the tendency of many to give up praying for a blessing after only a few tries. Contrast this with Augustine's mother who prayed for her son's conversion over the course of thirty-two years! Most of us quit praying for the same need and thereby reveal our lack of faith and our misunderstanding of God. Basically, when we give up, we show that we don't really care about our petition, and we express doubt in God's ever answering the prayer. The idea of prayer as struggle is foreign to many. We want things to be quick and easy. We forget Jacob's wrestling all night in prayer with an angel and how Jacob refused to let the angel go unless he was blessed. Consider also the bloody sweat in Gethsemane; three times Jesus prayed the same prayer asking to know God's will concerning the cross. Time after time Paul begged to have the thorn removed from his body. Prayer can be agony as we plead over and over for God to provide an answer to our problem or need.

Illustrative Materials

1. Example. Jesus set an example in prayer. In Benjamin Franklin's day, the streets of Philadelphia were dark and dangerous. The cost of lighting the streets was too costly. Franklin set an example by hanging a lantern on a long bracket in front of his home. Every evening he lighted the lamp and polished the glass. Soon neighbors also wanted a lantern like his. Eventually the whole city was illuminated by homeowners who followed Franklin's example.

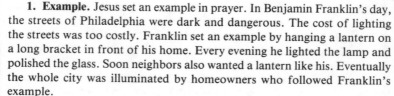

2. Prayer as Struggle. In 1546 Luther's good friend, Frederick Myconius, became deathly sick. He himself expected to die in a short time. One night he wrote with a trembling hand a fond farewell to Luther whom he loved very much. When Luther received the letter, he immediately sent back a message:

> "I command thee in the name of God to live because I still have need of thee in the work of reforming the church. The Lord will never let me hear that thou art dead, but will permit thee to survive me. For this I am praying, this is my will, and may my will be done, because I seek only to glorify the name of God."

3. Constant in Prayer. Anton Rubinstein, a famous Russian pianist of the last century, said, "If I omit practice one day, I notice it; if I omit it for two days, my friends notice it; if I omit it for three days, the public notices it."

4. Value in Plodding. When William Carey went to India as a missionary, troubles gathered around him. Death took one of his children. His wife became insane. For years he labored without one native convert. When he was an old man, a nephew spoke to him about writing his life story. Referring to his biographer, he said, "If he gives me credit for being a plodder, he will describe me justly. Anything beyond this would be too much. I can plod. I can persevere in any definite pursuit. To this, I owe everything."

5. Secret of Success. The late columnist Sydney Harris tells about the time he gave a talk on creative writing to a group of amateur writers. During the question-and-answer period following the address, someone asked, "Mr. Harris, what do you do when you don't feel like writing?" "I write," he answered. "That's the difference between an amateur and a professional."

6. Ready when God Is. Often God cannot answer our prayers at the time, because he needs the cooperation of another person to answer our prayers. One night a married couple went to see a movie. When they returned home, the wife noticed that she had lost her diamond engagement ring. She called the theatre and asked the manager to look for her ring. He made a search for it, but it took him some time. She grew tired of waiting. Finally he found the ring and was excited to tell her the good news. When he picked up the phone to exclaim, "I found your ring!" there was only a dial tone. Since he did not know her name or phone number, he was unable to return the diamond to her. In prayer we may get tired of waiting for God to answer our prayers. When the time comes for the answer, we may not be waiting or listening.

Proper 13 • Pentecost 11 • Ordinary Time 18

Common   Lutheran   Roman Catholic

8. The Rich Fool

Luke 12:13-21

[13]One of the multitude said to him, "Teacher, bid my brother divide the inheritance with me." [14]But he said to him, "Man, who made me a judge or divider over you?" [15]And he said to them, "Take heed, and beware of covetousness; for a man's life does not consist in the abundance of his possessions." [16]And he told them a parable, saying, "The land of a rich man brought forth plentifully; [17]and he thought to himself, 'What shall I do, for I have nowhere to store my crops?' [18]And he said, 'I will do this: I will pull down my barns, and build larger ones; and there I will store all my grain and my goods. [19]And I will say to my soul, Soul, you have ample goods laid up for many years; take your ease, eat, drink, be merry.' [20]But God said to him, 'Fool! This night your soul is required of you; and the things you have prepared, whose will they be'? [21]So is he who lays up treasure for himself, and is not rich toward God."

On the editorial page of a large city newspaper there was a cartoon showing men in the left bottom corner with uplifted faces and arms outstretched to the sky crying, "Almighty God." In the upper right hand corner was a dollar bill coming out of the sky. The men were labelled: Falwell, Roberts, Bakker, Swaggart, and Robertson. The cartoon was a reaction to the scandals involving television evangelists, who were being depicted as men whose almighty God was the almighty dollar.

There was some justification for this critical cartoon. Through persistent begging, receipts of two billion dollars are taken in every year. Some of the television evangelists enjoy $100,000 salaries, drive Rolls Royce and Mercedes Benz cars, live in homes like palaces, and own jet planes. Except for Billy Graham, they do not open their financial books for review. The secular press, with some apparent justification, is accusing them of being more interested in bucks than in Bibles.

This money madness is not limited to television evangelists, but is also characteristic of the world, including Christians. The average man on the street thinks that quality of life consists in the abundance of things possessed; the more possessions, the more life. For many, money is the goal and motivation for life. We think money is the solution to every problem. To get it we are willing to do almost anything. As Saint Paul said, "The love of money is the root of all evils." (1 Timothy 6:10) To get things, we steal, in terms of shoplifting, fifty billion dollars per year. The same amount is spent on cocaine which causes drug dealers to flaunt the law by selling the drug at an enormous profit. To get more money women and men engage in prostitution. Pornography is big business with annual sales of eight billion dollars per year. Some Americans are willing to sell their souls for a few thousand bucks. United States Navy man, Jerry Whitworth, sold military secrets to Russia for $325,000. Greed is behind Wall Street scandals involving financial leaders, who gained millions from inside information on the stock market. Money drives people to rob, cheat, steal, and even murder.

Our entire society is saturated with materialism. We have a "thing" culture fed by advertisements and commercials. The average home has three television sets, and television is watched daily at an average of six to seven hours by each of us. By the time children reach the age of eighteen, they are exposed to 350,000 television commercials. What are these ads saying? They say that pleasure comes through more consumption of things. They are told that they deserve to be good to themselves by having things and by indulging in leisurely pursuits. They tell us that each person is Number One, that power comes from possessions, and that we can have fun without guilt. Believing that television influences behavior, advertisers spend two billion dollars annually on commercials. With this daily impact for six to seven hours, how can the church, with only one hour per week, counteract this false teaching that life consists in the abundance of things possessed? What a challenge to a preacher!

Today's parable, the Rich Fool, deals with this problem. The world has always been too much with us, in Jesus' day as well as in ours. Behind the worldliness and materialism lies covetousness or greed. While Jesus was teaching, a man asked Jesus to persuade his older brother to share with him the brother's inheritance. The younger brother wanted money and possessions inherited by the older brother. Jesus saw this request as an expression of covetousness. As a warning against it, he told the story about a rich man who lost his soul by accumulating wealth. On a church's outdoor bulletin board was this true but tragic message:

Save money,
Lose soul,
Bad bargain.

Context

Context of Luke 12

Luke 12 contains more parables than any other chapter in Luke. In addition to the Parable of the Rich Fool, during the next two Sundays we will be dealing with the Parable of the Watchful Servants (12:32-42) and the Parable of the Weather Signs. (12:49-56)

The Parable of the Rich Fool is the first of three parables in Luke 12. Preceding the parable, Jesus warns against the hypocrisy of the Pharisees (vv. 1-3), urges the crowd to fear God rather than those who can kill only the body (vv. 4-7), and explains the unpardonable sin (vv. 8-12). In the crowd is a man who asks Jesus to persuade his older brother to share an inheritance, and Jesus responds with the Parable of the Rich Fool. (vv. 13-21) The subject of material and spiritual riches continues through verse 34, and verses 22-34 should be included in the unit involving the Rich Fool.

Context of the Lectionary

The First Lesson. (2 Kings 13:14-20a) This is the last in the series concerning Elijah and Elisha. While Elisha is near death, King Joash of Israel consults Elisha regarding the threat of Syria to Israel. Elisha assures him that Yahweh will give Israel the victory.

The Second Lesson. (Colossians 3:1-11) This lesson is also the last in a series, that of the four lessons from Colossians. Because a Christian died with Christ and now lives with the risen Christ, he or she puts off the old nature of sin and puts on the new nature of life in Christ.

Gospel. (Luke 12:13-21) As a warning against greed, Jesus tells a story of a rich farmer who had to build bigger barns in order to accomodate his abundance, and who, in the process of amassing a fortune, lost his soul.

Psalm of the Day. (Psalm 28) It is a prayer for God to hear and answer prayer.

Prayer of the Day. "Give us such wisdom by your Spirit that our possessions may not be a curse in our lives but an instrument for blessing."

Hymn of the Day. "Son of God, Eternal Savior."

"Yours the gold and yours the silver,
Yours the wealth of land and sea;
We but stewards of your bounty
Held in solemn trust will be."

Context of the Gospel Lesson

Among the thousands listening to Jesus teach was a young man who asked Jesus to order his older brother to share the inheritance received from their father. Jesus refused the request, explaining that he was not a civil judge commissioned to decide such matters. To settle such disputes was not his calling or responsibility. But, in this youth's request, Jesus recognized the sin of covetousness, or greed. He used the occasion to teach the people a lesson against greed, telling the story of a rich fool who in amassing wealth lost his soul. According to Jesus, life does not consist in the abundance of things possessed. One who is materially, but not spiritually, rich will experience the same fate.

Context of Related Scriptures

> Deuteronomy 28:1-8 — God promised material blessings to the obedient.
> Psalm 141:1 — A fool says there is no God.
> Ecclesiastes 2:18-26 — The foolishness of wealth in having to leave it behind at death.
> Luke 4:4 — A person does not live by bread alone.
> Luke 18:18-25 — Riches can keep one from discipleship.
> Luke 19:1-9 — A rich man gets salvation.

Content

Content of the Pericope

> vv. 13-14 — Jesus refuses a request to order a division of an inheritance.
> vv. 15 — Jesus warns people against greed.
> vv. 16-20 — The Parable of the Rich Fool.
> v. 21 — Jesus gives the lesson of the parable.

Precis of the Parable

A crowd of people was listening to Jesus' teachings. Out of the crowd came a man who said to Jesus, "Teacher, persuade my brother to divide the inheritance from our father." Jesus replied, "Who am I to be a judge to order a division of the property between the two of you?" Then he turned to the crowd and said, "Beware of every kind of greed, for life does not consist in the abundance of things possessed." Then he told them about a rich man whose land produced bountifully. He began to think, "I don't have a place to store all these products. What shall I do? I know, I will tear down my barns and build bigger ones. Then I will say to myself, 'You are a lucky man. You have enough wealth to provide for yourself for many years. So, why not take life easy and enjoy it?' '' But God said to him, "You fool! This very night you will die and then who will get all of your possessions?" So Jesus concluded, "This is how it is with people who have material but not spiritual riches.''

Thesis: Life consists of spiritual possessions.

Theme: Get rich toward God!

Key Words in the Parable

1. "Judge." (v. 14) In this case Jesus refuses to do a person a favor! He gives a flat and frank "No" to the man. Is there any other time in the record when Jesus refused to help? The young man asked him to persuade his brother to share the inheritance. In those days the eldest son received the father's inheritance. Jesus refused because he was not a judge, nor a divider of property. This was not within his sphere of work or authority. This was a secular matter to be handled by the courts. Jesus was concerned primarily with moral and spiritual problems.

2. "What." (v. 17) The Rich Fool had a nice problem which many would love to have. What shall he do with his surplus of grain when his barns were already full? Usually our problem is a bare cupboard, insufficient funds, hunger, and poverty. This man has the problem of knowing what to do with his affluence. What might he have done? Thank God for the good harvest? Donate the surplus to needy people? Give it to the Hunger Appeal? His solution was selfish. He would hoard all and build bigger barns to house the surplus.

3. "Covetousness." (v. 15) The *Good News Bible* translates "covetousness" as "greed," which is probably better understood in our time. Covetousness is a desire to have what others have. A younger brother asks for a part of his older brother's inheritance. Jesus was wise enough to see that behind the lad's request was greed for his brother's possessions. Greed is important and serious enough for Yahweh to have included it in the Decalogue: "Thou shalt not covet . . .''

4. "I" and "My." (vv. 17-19) "I" and "my" are used eleven times by the Rich Fool. These words were used when "he thought to himself." That was his problem. He was thinking only about himself. He was self-centered. He gave himself credit for all he had: "my crops . . . my barns . . . my grain . . . my goods." Apparently, he never gave it a thought that all he had came from God. He never thought of sharing his abundance with the poor. He was so wrapped up in himself that when he physically died that very night, his soul also died.

5. "Fool." (v. 20) In the biblical sense a "fool" was one who denied that God exists. The rich farmer was called a fool by Jesus because he failed to consider or involve God in his life and work. He was interested only in accumulating resources for the future. He forgot about his soul. A person is a fool to spend his or her time and energy amassing wealth which must at last be left and then leave it all to one who may not appreciate it. This man was a fool, not only because he left God out of his life, but because he did not know when he had enough. He was already rich when the new harvest came in and his barns were already full. This is typical of a greedy person; their theme song is "more, more, more."

6. "Soul." (vv. 19, 20) A human, created from the dust of the earth (Genesis 2:7), is a material being, a body. In the act of creation he was also given a soul through God's breathing into Adam's body. The soul is the spirit or personality of an individual. Because a person is a soul, he or she has the capacity to be related to and to be in communication with God, the Spirit. The real person is the soul which is contained in a physical body on earth and a spiritual body in heaven. In the parable the rich farmer addresses himself as "soul." (v. 19) God also refers to him as a "soul." (v. 20) The soul then is the whole person including body, mind, and spirit. What does it mean then when God says, "This night your soul is required of you?" Does it not mean that God is calling us, our souls, to himself through physical death? If we neglect the soul, what good are our physical assets, which we must leave behind? Each person must ask, "Is it well with my soul?"

Contemplation

Insights

1. The Foolishness of Fools. In the parable God calls the rich farmer a "Fool." Yet, in Deuteronomy 28:1-8 Yahweh promises material blessings to those who obey him. It would seem then that wealth is a sign of God's reward for obedience. This concept could lead a person to the pursuit of wealth, for the more possessions she has, the greater seems her favor with God. But, in the case of the Rich Fool, the pursuit of wealth was primary to the neglect of his soul. It is foolish for anyone to behave this way because —

> A. It leads to greed. One never gets enough money and is never satisfied with what one has.

B. It creates work-a-holism. One works to exhaustion in order to accumulate physical resources. There is no time for anything else. It is all work and no play.

C. When death comes, one must give up all the material accumulation. It is probably left to those who do not appreciate the labor and sacrifice that went into the amassing of it. There are no pockets in a shroud.

2. Choose Your Wealth. In today's parable we have an example of a man who was rich in material possessions, but, as Jesus said, he was "not rich toward God." (v. 21) Every person faces a choice: to accumulate physical or spiritual resources. There is a wealth of the world — crops, goods, and bigger barns. But to confine wealth to material possessions is to become a fool. There is also a wealth of God. There is available the treasures of heaven, the riches of grace. To be rich toward God is to believe in him, to love him, and to be one with him by faith. To receive the grace of God is to have spiritual wealth. The difference in having these two kinds of wealth is that one must work for and earn the wealth of the world, whereas one is given the wealth of God in return for faith in Christ, who became poor that we might become rich. Thus, each of us faces a fateful decision: to which shall we devote our lives?

3. Money Madness. We do not have to be wealthy to be money mad. In the parable the Rich Fool was already rich when he decided to build bigger barns and retire to enjoy his affluence. We can be poor and yet be money mad. Indeed, poverty is a curse. We do need to work hard and save our money in order to provide for the necessities of life. We do not want to see ourselves in a soup kitchen line, or sleeping on a park bench, or becoming a recipient of public welfare. We want enough money to live comfortably. We do need money to live, but it can lead to madness when the only thing to live for is to get and accumulate financial resources.

The average person does not expect ever to get rich, or ever to reach the point of becoming the Rich Fool who has more than he knows what to do with. Nevertheless, we can in our poverty be money-mad by being stingy, chintzy, and pinch-penny. We will not take a vacation because it costs too much. We will not buy a present or send flowers because we say we cannot afford it.

The problem is how to keep money in proper perspective. Yes, we need money to live; we must have it. We must earn and save it for future needs. But, when is enough enough? How can we keep this madness from domineering all of life to the point that we lose our souls in the pursuit of money? How can we keep our possessions from possessing us?

4. No Need for God. The Rich Fool had no need for God, because he had plenty of possessions. He addressed himself, "Soul, you have ample goods laid up." He had "goods" but not God, for Jesus said he was "not rich toward God." If you have all the money you need, why do you need God? God may just as well be dead, because we are getting along quite well without him. We don't need God for flood control; we have dams. We don't need God to heal us, for we have miracle drugs. We don't need God for inner peace, for we have psychiatrists. We don't need God for food, because we have mechanized farms and hybrid seeds. For the Rich Fool, God is absent. He does not acknowledge God as the giver of his crops, but takes all the credit for his wealth. His life is revealed to be a fool's paradise when his soul is required of him.

Homily Hints

1. Don't Be a Fool! (12:16-21) In the parable God calls the rich man a "Fool." What constitutes a fool? Would God call you a fool? A fool is one who —
    A. Leaves God out of one's life — "I," "My" — vv. 17-19.
    B. Leaves all to others — v. 20.
    C. Neglects to accumulate spiritual riches — v. 21.

2. If You were to Die Tonight. (12:20) If you were to die tonight, as the Rich Fool did, would you be sure you were going to heaven? To the surprise of the wealthy man, God demanded, "This night your soul is required of you." Do you have the spiritual resources —
    A. To face the Judgment?
    B. To be accepted by God?
    C. To be ushered into heaven?

3. Greed: for Gold or God? (12:13-21) Jesus recognized greed in the young man who asked Jesus to persuade his brother to share a part of the inheritance. Similar greed for wealth was illustrated in the Parable of the Rich Fool. It is human to be selfish and greedy. Are we greedy for gold or for God? Do we really need God today?
    A. Greed for gold — vv. 13-15.
        1. Consequence: death.
    B. Greed for God — v. 21.
        1. Consequence: life.

4. What Shall I Do? (12:16-21) What a problem to have! A problem of having so much that you do not know what to do with it. This was the problem of the Rich Fool. He had more crops than he had barns. He asked himself, "What shall I do?" Some are asking, "What shall I do with my money?" What is a good sound investment? Put it in a bank? Invest it in the stock market? What can we do with our material assets? Some options —

    A. Spend it — "Eat, drink, and be merry" — v. 19.
    B. Save it — "Build larger ones" — v. 18.
    C. Share it — be "rich toward God" — v. 21.

    5. The Story of a Rich Fool. (12:16-21) Jesus told a story of a man who is like some of us. All are subject to the same fault. In hearing the story we learn about —

    A. His virtue — he worked for his wealth.
    B. His problem — what to do with his wealth — v. 17.
    C. His mistake — made no provision for his soul — vv. 20, 21.

Contact

Points of Contact

    1. For the rich only? Can the average church member identify with the rich man of the parable? "A rich fool — that lets me out! I am not rich and I never expect to be or want to be!" says Mr. Average. But, one does not have to be rich to be greedy for materialistic assets. We can desire and love things rather than God or people or values. Our desire for more and more money is expressed in gambling in hopes of getting rich quick. We are ever ready to make a fast buck. We may be workaholics, struggling for a larger income. Wives may leave home and children to earn a second income and have a larger home, a second car, and new furniture. Our craze for money expresses itself in living beyond our incomes by going into debt. This parable is vitally relevant and carries an important message for all who have a materialistic mind, and for those who put primary emphasis on possessions as the means of obtaining the good life.

    2. A possible duplication of subject matter. Today's parable and an upcoming parable, Lazarus and Dives, deal with material possessions. The latter comes eight Sundays from today, on Pentecost 19 (Proper 21). To avoid duplication and/or repetition, we need to keep both parables in mind. The two parables could be presented with different emphases:

    Pentecost 11 — Wealth without spirituality.
    Pentecost 19 — Wealth without sharing.

    3. What is the basic problem? The problem in today's parable is not wealth but the pursuit of material values. We do not have to be rich to be money-mad. Though we have little, we may be greedy, always wanting more.

Yet, it is no sin to be rich. Jesus did not ask rich people to become poor in order to be his followers. Some of his rich followers were Matthew, Zaccheus, and Joseph of Arimathea. Only when wealth was valued more than the Kingdom did Jesus urge one to sell all and give to the poor. It is also important how we get our money. Is money the main interest and goal of life for which we sacrifice everything else, even God and our souls? The desire for money is normal because we have to have it in order to pay bills for the necessities of life. But, the desire must be kept in control lest material possessions become the sole reason for living. How far should a Christian go in accumulating financial resources? Can we keep heavenly and earthly treasures in proper balance?

4. **Questions people ask.**
   A. Can a true Christian be wealthy?
   B. Can a rich person enter heaven?
   C. Is poverty a virtue?
   D. Does it matter how one gets wealth?

5. **A question for preachers.** How can this parable be made positive? The parable gives an example of greed. We see a foolish man losing his soul over wealth. It tells us what kind of person we should not be — covetous. Where is the Gospel in this parable? How can we preach the Gospel of redemption if we use the parable as a text?

Illustrative Materials

1. **Gain and Loss.** In A.D. 800 Charlemagne was crowned by Pope Leo III as king of the Holy Roman Empire. He became the most powerful ruler Europe had yet seen. When he died, his sarcophagus showed him seated on his throne, dressed in royal robes. On his knee was an open Bible and one finger pointed to the verse: "What is a man profited, if he shall gain the whole world and lose his soul?"

2. **Dying to Get Rich.** The Treasure Salvors, Incorporated tried to raise the treasure from a ship which sank in a 1622 hurricane forty miles west of Key West. A tugboat was converted into a salvage ship, and with it they tried to recover one hundred million dollars from the sunken ship. One night while the ship was at anchor, a storm rolled the ship on its side and three people including the captain were trapped below the decks. They drowned trying to get rich.

3. **This Night.** While on a teaching-preaching mission in Florida, my wife and I were invited to a luncheon in a fabulous home located along the

Intracoastal Waterway. In the course of table talk, we were told that the home had cost over $500,000. Within a year of the family's moving in, the husband-owner died suddenly of a heart attack.

4. Buy Happiness? In *Esquire* magazine a cartoon showed a lovely twenty-eight-year-old woman with this caption: "I'm young, healthy, live in a condo by the sea, drive an expensive foreign-made sports car, eat out as often as I like, date all the right men, enjoy a three-day weekend, and my roller skates cost $180. I guess you could say . . . I'm unhappy."

5. Can't Take it with You. A certain man knew he was dying. He asked his wife to take out a stone from the fireplace where she would find a jar of money. He asked her to place it on the sill of the attic window so that, as he left, he could grab it on his way up. She did as she was told and found a large jar of one hundred-dollar bills which she did not know he had. She put the jar on the attic window sill. A few days after the funeral, she thought she would check to see if he had taken the jar when he had supposedly ascended. She found the jar of money still where she put it and then she remarked, "I knew all along that I should have put it on the basement window!"

Proper 14 • **Pentecost 12** • **Ordinary Time 19**

Common   Lutheran   Roman Catholic

---

9. Watching Servants

Luke 12:32-40

---

32 *"Fear not, little flock, for it is your Father's good pleasure to give you the kingdom.* 33 *Sell your possessions, and give alms; provide yourselves with purses that do not grow old, with a treasure in the heavens that does not fail, where no thief approaches and no moth destroys.* 34 *For where your treasure is, there will your heart be also.*

35 *"Let your loins be girded and your lamps burning,* 36 *and be like men who are waiting for their master to come home from the marriage feast, so that they may open to him at once when he comes and knocks.* 37 *Blessed are those servants whom the master finds awake when he comes; truly, I say to you, he will gird himself and have them sit at table, and he will come and serve them.* 38 *If he comes in the second watch, or in the third, and finds them so, blessed are those servants!* 39 *But know this, that if the householder had known at what hour the thief was coming, he would have been awake and would not have left his house to be broken into.* 40 *You also must be ready; for the Son of man is coming at an hour you do not expect."*

It is hard to tell when you will get back home after a wedding reception. The wedding service was at five o'clock. After the service there was a period of waiting for the wedding pictures to be taken. Then the party and guests went to a restaurant for dinner. It took a while for all to arrive, to be seated, and for the meal to be served. At the conclusion of the meal, there was toast after toast. A five-piece band began to assemble. After some time elasped, the music started, the tables had to be taken down and dishes taken to the kitchen. The band played on and on, and almost every male wanted a dance with the bride. The drinks flowed, and nobody seemed anxious to go home. No one felt that he or she could leave because the bride had not thrown her bouquet to the bridesmaids. It was past midnight before many got home.

There is usually no adjournment time for a wedding reception. Because of this, no one can say, "I will be home at a certain hour."

Today's parable of the waiting and watching servants deals with a similar wedding feast. It concerns a wealthy man who had servants. They, not knowing the hour of his return, are rewarded for patiently waiting and watching for him. As soon as he knocks, they are there to open the door at once. The reward is a dinner he himself serves to the servants. Imagine a master serving his servants a dinner at that late hour of the night! This is not realistic. Could there be a hidden meaning to the story? What is it saying to our people in the pews?

Context

Context of Luke 12

Today's parable needs to be seen in the context of Luke 12. Verses 32-34 of today's pericope are related to the previous Sunday (Pentecost 11), when we considered the Parable of the Rich Fool and the emphasis upon material possessions. In contrast, verses 32-34 tell us of God's giving us his Kingdom, which consists of spiritual riches. As a result we are relieved of worry over material needs.

Verses 35-40 give us the parables of the Watchful Servants and the Unexpected Thief. In verses 41-48 Jesus elaborates upon the servants of the foregoing parable, showing the results of faithful and unfaithful service. The explanation resulted from Peter's question, "Lord, does this parable [Watchful Servants] apply to us?" (v. 41)

Context of the Lectionary

The First Lesson. (Jeremiah 18:1-11) This is the first in a series of three lections from Jeremiah. It contains the Parable of the Potter. Yahweh sends Jeremiah to a potter to get a message for God's people. Yahweh is the potter and Israel is the pottery. God's people are in God's hands. If the pot is not pleasing to Yahweh, he will destroy it and make another one. But if the nation repents, God will change his mind and will not destroy it. If the nation rebels, God will destroy the vessel (Israel) and make another one. Jeremiah is instructed to tell the people that unless they change their ways, they will be punished.

The Second Lesson. (Hebrews 11:1-3, 8-19) Today's Second Lesson is the first in a series of four from Hebrews 11-13. This lection consists of a definition of faith and the personification of faith in the persons of Abraham and Sarah. Their faith was expressed in their obedience to God's call and in their trust in his promises.

Gospel. (Luke 12:32-40) Last Sunday the Gospel taught us that life does not consist of things possessed. Today's Gospel urges us to accumulate spiritual values. Then follows the Parable of the Waiting and Watching Servants, who open the door for their master as he unexpectedly returns from a wedding feast. Similarly, the Son of Man will return unexpectedly like a thief in the night.

Psalm. (Psalm 14) Fools say there is no God and live wickedly.

Prayer of the Day. A prayer for forgiveness and for good things for which we are unworthy.

Hymn of the Day. "Rise, my Soul, to Watch and Pray." The hymn speaks of our need to keep a "Watch against the world" and a "Watch against yourself," for pride and sin lurk within.

Context of the Gospel Lesson

Today's Gospel consists of two paragraphs and two parables. The first (vv. 32-34) deals with the foregoing in chapter 12: trust in God to provide the physical necessities of life. Now Jesus teaches that God will gladly give us the Kingdom of spiritual riches. Therefore, Jesus' followers can sell their property and give the money to the poor, for they now have spiritual wealth which will neither decrease in value nor be stolen.

The second paragraph (vv. 35-40) does not appear to be related to the first. Probably verse 32 is meant as the transition: "It is your Father's good pleasure to give you the kingdom." When the Kingdom, in the person of the Son of Man (v. 40) comes, will God's servants be waiting and watching to receive it? The Parable of the Watching Servants tells of a master's servants who faithfully watch for and open the door at the unexpected return of the master from the wedding feast. For their faithfulness they are rewarded by the master, who serves them dinner.

The second parable is found in verses 39-40. If you knew when a thief would break into your house, you would be present to protect it. Since the Christ will return unexpectedly like a thief in the night, servants must be forever vigilant. This second parable emphasizes the unknown hour of the Parousia.

Context of Related Scriptures

Matthew 25:1-13 — The ten girls and their lamps.
(See v. 35: "Your lamps burning.")

Mark 13:33-37 — The doorkeeper is to keep watch.
(See v. 36: "Like men who are waiting for their master to come home.")
Matthew 24:43-44 — The unexpected thief. (See v. 39: "What hour the thief was coming.")
Luke 19:12-13 — Servants are given responsibilities.
(See v. 38: "Blessed are those servants!")
Luke 14:15-24 — The great feast. (See v. 37: "He will come and serve them.")

Precis of the Parable

Be as ready for whatever comes as were the servants whose master left to attend a wedding feast. They are to keep the lights burning and be dressed for action so that, when the master returns, they will be able to open the door for him immediately. If they stay awake and are ready to open the door, they will be glad. The master will reward them by having them sit down at table and serving them the meal himself. They will be happy if they are ready whether he comes early or very late.

Thesis: Christ will return unexpectedly.

Theme: Be ready for Christ's return.

Key Words

1. **"Burning."** (v. 35) Jesus urged the Disciples to keep their lamps "burning." It is night time when the servants wait for the master's return. Night is for sleeping. We turn out the lights and go to bed. However, when waiting for the master's return, it is not time for sleeping in the dark, but for staying alert in the light. We sleep in the night and awake in the day. It is not a matter of having lamps, but of having them "burning." Years ago there was an accident at a railroad crossing and the railroad was sued. The watchman was asked if he had been on duty when the accident had occurred. He assured them that he had been on duty. The railroad won its case and the president commended the watchman, for the case depended on his being on duty. The watchman explained. "I was there with my lamp, but I was scared they were going to ask me if my lamp was burning."

2. **"Knocks."** (v. 36) Why would a master knock on his own door to be admitted to his own home? Apparently he was a wealthy man able to afford servants. A stranger would be expected to knock, but who of us knocks on our own front door to be allowed to enter our home? Obviously,

the master is Christ who returns to his people. He does not come into our hearts uninvited. He does not break down the door and force us to believe. God respects our free will and he would have only those who want him in their lives. "O Jesus, Thou art standing outside the fast-closed door . . ."

3. **"Blessed."** (vv. 37, 38) The parable tells of a happy occasion. In v. 32 Jesus tells us that the Father is happy to give us the Kingdom with all its treasures. The master in the parable goes to a wedding feast, which is usually a happy event. When the faithful servants stay awake and open the door for the master, they are described as "blessed" or "happy." Jesus' great sermon on the mount describes God's people as happy (the Beatitudes). The servants are happy to have their master back at home. They are happy that their reward is a dinner served by none other than the master himself. True Christians are happy people. They have the pleasure of Jesus' company. They are happy to participate in the meal which Christ had prepared.

4. **"Serve."** (v. 37) Servants are to serve. Here in the parable is a surprise! The master serves the servants. The master rewards the servants for their faithful watching and for being always prepared to receive him when he returns. In the master we see Christ who said he came "not to be served but to serve." (Matthew 20:28) Again, we see Jesus as the servant who washes his Disciples' feet. To be great is to serve. That is contrary to the world's claim that to be great is to be served.

5. **"Watch."** (v. 38) The time of the master's return is measured by "watches." The first watch is at sunset, usually six o'clock. The second watch is three hours later at nine o'clock. The third watch comes three hours after midnight at three a.m. The later the master comes, the harder it will be for the servants to stay awake and watch. A Christian does not observe the watches, for he or she is constantly on the "watch" for Jesus to come into his or her life. To watch is to be alert and sensitive to Christ's unexpected coming, both in the here and now, and at the Parousia.

Contemplation

Insights

1. **What is the parable saying to us?** At the Ascension, Jesus, the Master, left his earthly home for a feast in heaven. At an unknown time he will return. We, the servants of Christ, are to be faithful in waiting and watching for his return. The longer he delays his coming, the more difficult it is for us to continue to be awake and to be ready for his return. If we servants are

alert and open the door for him, we will be rewarded with a messianic dinner when the Master himself will have us as his guests and will serve the meal to us. As a homeowner does not know when a burglar will break into a house, Christians will not know when Christ is coming. In that case, we need to maintain constant vigilance and be perpetually prepared.

2. Always on Duty. In the parable the servants are never to go to sleep. They are to watch and be ready to open the door at any time during the night. Christians are always servants of Christ. We do not have a thirty or forty hour work week. We, like Satan, never take or want a vacation from Christ. To be a servant of Christ is to be on duty all of the time. We are always on call for service. Therefore, we are not called to be successful or great, but to be faithful, tireless workers by day and night for always.

3. The Night Visitor. The master in the parable is attending a wedding feast. After the dinner he comes home that night. He does not stay and come home the next day. The hour of his night return is unknown, but before daybreak he will come. Christ, our Master, comes to us at night, too. It is night in our souls, and he comes in our night to bring us light. When we are in the night of doubt, sorrow, despair, or depression, Christ comes to us. He comes to us in the hour of our need. "The people who walked in darkness have seen a great light." (Isaiah 9:2)

4. The Knock of Opportunity. When the master returns, he knocks on the door of his house for his servants to open it that he might enter. Christ ever stands at the door for us to invite him in. He does not force himself upon us. We have the free will to shut him out of our lives. His knock is our opportunity to receive him. Must we wait a thousand or two years before he returns? We are living in an interim period, between his first and second comings. But does he not come to us also in this interim time? He does not necessarily come within the context of cataclysmic events such as Armageddon, but in the daily, ordinary, and common realm of human experience. He comes to us in the face of a needy person, in the eyes of an innocent child, in the bread of Communion, or in the water of Baptism. To hear the knock we must be attentive, awake, and sensitive. This calls for readiness and preparation on our part to seize the opportunity. The manager of a Ford assembly plant once told me, "Success is when opportunity and preparation intersect."

5. Happiness Is. Christians can be the happiest people in the world. Happiness is a life in Christ. The biblical word for happiness is "blessed." In this parable the word is used twice to describe the faithful servants. Christians have every reason to be happy. God is happy to give them the Kingdom of love, peace, and truth. (v. 32) The servants are happy because they are rewarded with a dinner served by the Master. In addition, Christians have the joy of salvation. They are happy because their prayers are answered. Why then do some Christians go about as though they have lost their last friend?

Homily Hints

1. It's Not So Bad to be a Servant! (12:35-38) To be a servant is not a popular ambition for many. We do not object to self-service, but we do not want to serve others. The servant concept is demeaning for many people. Most of us want to *be* masters who *have* servants. But in this parable we find that it is not so bad to be a servant of Christ because —
> A. Servants are alert — "Your lamps burning."
> B. Servants are ready for action — "Your loins be girded."
> C. Servants are happy — "Blessed."
> D. Servants are rewarded — "He will . . . serve them."

2. The Night of His Coming. (12:38-40) Usually we speak of the Parousia as "the day of his coming." But in the parable the Son comes at night, whether at the second or third watch. His coming at night may surprise us and catch us unprepared. He comes to us personally in the dark night of our souls when we are discouraged and doubtful. He comes to bring us light for our darkness.
> A. The night may be long — v. 38.
> B. In the night Christ comes unexpectedly — v. 39.
> C. Night time calls for readiness — v. 40.

3. If Christ is to Come to You. (12:35-38) We may know Christ only by hearsay and desire a personal experience with him. We may have lost faith and want Christ to re-enter our lives. Indeed, he is ever willing to enter our lives. He waits for us to open the door to his presence. But how do we open the door?
> A. Be sensitive to Christ's presence — "Your lamps burning" — v. 35.
> B. Be ready to serve him — "Let your loins be girded" — v. 35.
> C. Be awake to the possibilities of your life — "Open to him" — v. 36.

4. Look for Christ Today. (12:35-39) We believe Christ will return to earth some day to judge the nations and to establish a new earth and heaven. Christians have been waiting for almost 2000 years, and may have to wait 2000 years more for him to return. Can we stay awake and be girded for

118

action throughout this long night of waiting? According to many New Testament scholars, it was not Jesus but the early church that expected an imminent Parousia. Indeed, Christ may come in our generation. What can we do in the meantime? How can we experience Christ today? While we may be concerned about his return tomorrow, for some that tomorrow may never come. We need to look for Christ today.

    A. Where may Christ come? He knocks on your door — v. 36.
    B. When may Christ come? He comes unexpectedly — v. 40.
    C. What will Christ do? He comes to serve us — v. 37.

Contact

Points of Contact

1. Preacher Problems. One of our preacher problems is the timing of the subject matter of the parable. In the middle of the Pentecost season, we are presented with the subject of the Parousia. According to the church year, and the lectionary, we consider the Second Coming to fall either at the beginning or end of the church year, or both. In the people's minds, the Parousia is connected with Advent. It may be difficult to preach on this subject when the mood of the Parousia does not prevail.

Another problem is the frequency with which the subject occurs. The lectionary gives two parables concerning the end times for two Sundays in a row: this and next Sunday. This will challenge the preacher who is committed to preaching on all of the parables as they appear in the lectionary. To avoid repetition, sermons for both Sundays should be kept in mind during preparation.

2. To Whom does the Parable Apply? When Jesus finished giving the Parable of the Watchful Servants, Peter asked, "Lord, does this parable apply to us or do you mean it for everyone?" (12:41)

Does this parable dealing with Jesus' return and the messianic banquet apply to us, or only to those in Jesus' lifetime? Except for some fundamentalists, most mainline churches give only lip service to Christ's second coming. Norman Perrin claimed that the "coming of the Son of Man" passages did not come from Jesus but from the early church. C. H. Dodd wrote that this parable was not given to prepare the Disciples for a long and indefinite period of waiting for the Parousia, but to show the need of alertness in a crisis then upon them. In 1986 sixty-one percent of a group of New Testament scholars took the position that they did not think Jesus expected the end of the world in his generation.

Indeed, we believe that Christ will come again to wind up history, gather his faithful, and judge the nations. Although the time of his coming is unknown, we need to think of allowing Christ to come now into our lives and society. It is doubtful that Jesus intended for us to literally keep our lamps burning and our clothing ready for immediate action during the next 2000 years or longer.

It seems appropriate for us to contemporize this parable. Christ can come to us here and now. He comes not only in the extraordinary, but also in the ordinary events of life. He comes in time as well as in eternity. His presence can be seen in the ordinary, common, and secular experiences of life. The parable teaches us to be aware of the sacred in the secular. As with Jacob's experience, the Lord may be here without our knowing it. He comes to us in simple forms like bread in Communion and water in Baptism. With the disciples on the Emmaus road, Christ can be known in the breaking of bread. For Christ to become a reality to us, we need to become sensitive, aware, awake, and alert to the spiritual presence in a material world. In this sense, then, this parable applies to us and to every generation.

Illustrative Materials

1. Asleep. In 1987 a nuclear power plant in Pennsylvania was shut down by the Federal agency because it found men in the control room asleep.

The night the Titanic crashed into an iceberg and sank in the north Atlantic, the ship, *California,* was only nine miles away; but it did not come to the rescue. Why? Because the *California's* radio operator, fresh from a training school, was fast asleep in his cabin. Thus, the Titanic's distress calls were unheard.

2. Ready. The people at the time of the Passover (Exodus 12:11) were to be ready to march out of Egypt: "You are to eat it quickly, for you are to be dressed for travel, with your sandals on your feet and your walking stick in your hand."

One day in a cathedral, the cardinal was approached by an excited young curate. "Your Eminence," he cried, "a woman claims to have just seen a vision of the Savior in the chapel behind the main altar. What should we do?" "Look busy," the cardinal told him. "Look busy!"

3. The Door. In a certain church there was a stained glass window depicting Jesus in royal robes, a crown on his head, and with a lamp in his hand.

It was Holman Hunt's "Light of the World." One day a mother was explaining the scene to her little daughter. She explained that Jesus was standing at the door of our lives waiting for us to open it that he might come in. She called attention to the fact that the door had to be opened from within. At the conclusion of the explanation, the little one looked into her mother's face and asked, "Did he ever get in?"

4. Faithful Servants. Senator Mark Hatfield once visited Mother Theresa and asked her, "How can you face each day the sight of Calcutta's starving, sick, and dying people, knowing that you can never meet all of their needs?" Mother Theresa answered, "God does not ask me to be successful. He only asks that I be faithful."

5. Opportunity and Preparation. Several years ago at West Virginia University a piano teacher was popular with the students, who called him "Herman." One night at a university concert, a distinguished piano player suddenly became ill while performing an extremely difficult piece. No sooner had the artist retired from the stage when Herman left his seat in the audience and came to the stage, sat down at the piano, and with great mastery completed the performance. Later that evening at a party, one of the students asked Herman how he was able to perform such a demanding piece so beautifully without notice. He explained, "In 1939, when I was a budding young concert pianist, I was arrested and placed in a Nazi concentration camp. Putting it mildly, the future looked bleak. But I needed to practice every day. I began by fingering a piece from my repertoire on my bare-board bed. The next night I added a second piece and soon I was running through my entire repertoire, and I did this every night for five years. It so happens the piece I played tonight was part of that repertoire."

Proper 15 • Pentecost 13 • Ordinary Time 20
Common   Lutheran   Roman Catholic

---

10. Weather Signs

Luke 12:49-56

---

⁴⁹"I came to cast fire upon the earth; and would that it were already kindled! ⁵⁰I have a baptism to be baptized with; and how I am constrained until it is accomplished! ⁵¹Do you think that I have come to give peace on earth? No, I tell you, but rather division; ⁵²for henceforth in one house there will be five divided, three against two and two against three; ⁵³they will be divided, father against son and son against father, mother against daughter and daughter against her mother, mother-in-law against her daughter-in-law and daughter-in-law against her mother-in-law."

⁵⁴He also said to the multitudes, "When you see a cloud rising in the west, you say at once, 'A shower is coming'; and so it happens. ⁵⁵And when you see the south wind blowing, you say, 'There will be scorching heat'; and it happens. ⁵⁶You hypocrites! You know how to interpret the appearance of earth and sky; but why do you not know how to interpret the present time?"

As a weather reporter and forecaster, would you get the seal of approval of the American Meteorological Society? Some radio and television stations assure their listeners that their weather reporter carries this seal of approval.

Indeed, the people of Jesus' day would certainly have qualified. They knew that rain would come with a west wind and heat with a south wind. They were so good at understanding weather signs that Jesus was upset that they could not interpret the signs of their present time. In their time they had Jesus — his teaching, his life, and his miracles. Yet, they could not see that his ministry was the coming Kingdom of God on earth.

We are a weather-conscious people. Many radio stations give a weather report every half hour or more. We live by these weather reports. They tell us what clothing to wear, whether we need to take an umbrella, if we need to start early to the office because of fog or snow or ice. We depend upon the meteorologists to warn us of coming hurricanes, tornadoes, and floods.

We would not take a boat ride or plan a ski trip without first checking the weather. There are television channels which program nothing but weather reports, twenty-four hours a day.

The weather affects our lives. Our rockets can fail if they chance to be hit with lightning. The space shuttle, *Challenger* blew up after only seventy seconds of flight; one of the causes for the disaster was the freezing temperatures at the launch site. The weather can affect a person's attitude: a bright day cheers us up; a dark, rainy day may cause depression.

The weather is very much with us. We may know even more about it than the people of Jesus' day. But though we may have more accurate instruments with which to predict the weather, are we any better than Jesus' generation in our ability to interpret the present time? That is what this parable is all about: the ability to understand the present situation.

Context

Context of the Lectionary

The First Lesson. (Jeremiah 20:7-13) Jeremiah feels Yahweh has deceived him. He faithfully proclaimed Yahweh's judgment upon Judah. For this the people threatened his life. When he decided to stop preaching, he felt an inner compulsion to preach. In the end, faith returns to him and he praises Yahweh to whom he again commits his cause.

The Second Lesson. (Hebrews 12:1-2, 12-17) Surrounded and encouraged by a multitude of faithful people, we are to run our race of faith by looking to Jesus. This race involves a pursuit of peace and holiness. The time to repent is now, before the time comes when repentance will be impossible.

Gospel (Luke 12:49-56) A decision for Jesus means division. Jesus came not to bring peace but to cast fire on earth. His truth and principles will cause divisions among people, even within families. Then Jesus turns to the people and observes that, though they can read the coming weather from the source of the wind, they cannot interpret the times.

Psalm. (Psalm 10:12-18) The Lord knows the ways of the wicked but the righteous will be heard and strengthened.

Prayer of the Day. A petition for perfect faith that overcomes all doubts.

Hymn of the Day. "Lord, Keep us Steadfast in Your word" — a prayer by Luther that God will be victorious over Satan and will lead us out of death to life.

Context of the Gospel Lesson

The Gospel Lesson consists of two paragraphs which do not appear to be related. The first paragraph, verses 49-53, deals with Jesus' declaration that his coming will cause division among people even within families.

The second paragraph, verses 54-56, is addressed to "the multitudes," whereas the former paragraph was given to the Disciples. In this paragraph, Jesus has changed the subject from the division resulting from his teachings to the people's inability to read the signs of the times. Since verse 54 says he spoke to the crowd, it is difficult to understand why he would call them "hypocrites." (v. 56) The charge would suggest that he was speaking to the religious leaders of his day. The Parable of the Weather Signs is found in this second paragraph.

Context of Related Scriptures

Matthew 16:1-3 — In this passage the Pharisees and Sadducees asked Jesus to give them a sign from heaven. Jesus refers to the redness of the sky in the morning and evening, but in Luke he refers to the wind. In both cases Jesus says they are able to understand the signs in nature but cannot interpret the meaning of what is happening in the world.

1 Kings 18:41-46 — Elijah notifies King Ahab that the drought is about to end, because he sees a cloud of rain coming up from the sea.

Matthew 11:2-6 — When John the Baptizer sent his disciples to ask Jesus if he were the promised messiah, Jesus told them to go back to John and tell them what they heard and saw. These were signs of his identity.

Luke 19:41-44 — Heart-broken, Jesus weeps over Jerusalem and predicts her destruction due to the people's failure to recognize their savior in Jesus.

John 2:11; 4:54 — The miracles of Jesus are considered signs of his Sonship.

Jeremiah 8:1-7 — Birds, but not humans, know "the time of their coming."

Content

Content of the Pericope

vv. 49-50 — Jesus explains his purpose in coming: to cast fire on earth and to undergo a baptism of sacrifice.

vv. 51-53 — Jesus brings not peace but division, even within a family.

vv. 54-56 — The parable of the weather signs.

Precis of the Parable

In speaking to the people, Jesus points out that they know that a west wind brings rain and a south wind brings a heat wave. When the west wind comes, they say, "It is going to rain," and it does. When a south wind is felt, they say, "It's going to get hot," and it does. "You hypocrites!" Jesus exclaims, "Why are you able to read correctly the forces of nature but not the present time?"

Thesis: Interpret correctly the present time.

Theme: Know what is happening.

Key Words

1. **"Hypocrites."** (v. 56) Why would people listening to Jesus' teachings be called "hypocrites"? Usually we hear the word applied to Pharisees, scribes, and Sadducees. According to the popular meaning of the word, a hypocrite is an insincere actor trying to appear to be someone whom he or she is not. However, Jesus does not use the term to mean one who acts a false part, or one who pretends to be pious when he or she is not. Rather, Jesus uses the term "hypocrites" to mean those guilty of disbelief, wickedness, craftiness, or unprincipled actions. Jesus is referring to the people who are outwardly religious but inwardly ungodly. While they honor God with their lips, their hearts are far from him. (Isaiah 29:13)

2. **"Time."** (v. 56) The Greeks had two words for "time": *chairos* and *chronos*. *Chronos* was clock time: hours and minutes, as in "What time is it?" *Chairos* is the word used here. It stands for a critical or opportune time. It is the time when opportunity knocks. Jesus saw his ministry as the nation's time to be saved from disaster. Thus, he wept over Jerusalem because the people did not know or realize the time to accept salvation by receiving Jesus as their king.

3. **"Sky."** (v. 56) Jesus says here that the people could predict the weather by the signs of the earth and sky. But, in the parable, he refers only to the wind as a key to understanding weather. In Matthew's version of the parable (Matthew 16:1-3) Jesus does mention the sky. He states that whether the sky is red in the morning or evening indicates what kind of day it will be. Could Luke have been familiar with Matthew's account and therefore included the sky in this verse?

4. **"Present."** (v. 56) We are to interpret the "present" time. It is a matter

of what is happening today, in our generation. It is not past time. We cannot do anything to change past time except to learn from it. It is not future time. We cannot do anything about future time, for only God has the future in his hands. Today is the day. What is happening today that will affect our future? Things are happening every day, but what are they saying to us?

Contemplation

Insights

1. Forecast of the Future. In the parable the winds tell us of the coming weather conditions. A western wind means rain; a southern wind will bring heat. Likewise, the present times with their conditions tell us what to expect in the future. The signs of the times tell us what we can expect. They are warnings of things to come — maybe a hurricane or a tornado, maybe a calm and cool day. The forecast enables us to prepare accordingly.

2. Redeem the Times. *Chairos* is the Greek word used here for "time." It is not chronological time, *chronos,* but time in terms of crisis or opportunity. It may be an opportunity to escape disaster or to take advantage of an opportunity for peace, security, and well-being. To fail to take advantage of the opportunity spells judgment. In Jesus' day, the people did not recognize the "time" of their salvation, the visitation of the Christ. As a result, Jerusalem and the nation were destroyed. Now is the time — strike while the iron is hot! Make hay while the sun shines!

3. Know the Score. Because the people whom Jesus was addressing did not interpret the times, Jesus called them "hypocrites." As hypocrites they were insensitive to what was happening in their day. They did not see Jesus' ministry among them as the advent of the new age. Here was their messiah and they did not know it. What does it take to ascertain the spiritual significance of current conditions? It takes a spiritual disposition to recognize and understand spiritual realities. The people were outwardly, formally, routinely religious but they lacked the inner spirituality which would enable them to properly interpret conditions. Do we know what is going on with the weather of the world? Do we realize what present conditions are? Are we numb and callous to the point that we are totally oblivious to what is happening?

4. Your World Today. When Willard Scott gives the national weather report on the *Today* show, he concludes, "Now here is what is happening in your world today." Then, a local forecaster tells what the weather conditions are in your town or county. The national report comes down to the local situation. We may see the signs of national conditions, but what do they mean to your local town, congregation, or life? How does the world-wide or national situation affect your life? What will the wind of the parable bring to your locality — rain or heat?

5. Believe in Signs? When one ignores a sign we jokingly ask, "Don't you believe in signs?" When a sign says, "Bridge out," do we proceed as though there were no sign? Jesus refers to the winds as signs of coming weather. He refers to other signs of what is happening in his day, and upbraids the people for not interpreting their signs of the times. Signs are meant to speak to us. They give us information about speed limits, sharp curves, narrow bridges, or where to find food or fuel. Signs give us directions and show us how to get where we want to go. They speak to us for our own good. Jesus wants us to see the signs of the times and to be guided through or warned of what lies ahead.

Homily Hints

1. The Times are in Our Hands. (12:56) The times, past, present, and future, are in our hands in terms of our knowledge, understanding, and interpretation of them. The times affect our lives for good or ill. In this verse Jesus speaks of the "present time," but the "present" cannot be isolated from the past or future.

    A. The present time if affected by past time.
        1. The lessons of history for present day living.
    B. The future is affected by present time.
        1. Future shock or salvation?

2. What's Going on Here? (12:54-56) There are times when we do not know what is happening to us. An infant does not know what God did at baptism. Does anyone know what one is getting into at a wedding? Can anyone realize the implications and obligations of committing oneself? Things are happening all around us all the time, but do we understand what is going on? In which category do you belong?

    A. People who wonder what happened.
    B. People who watch things happen.
    C. People who make things happen.

3. What are Today's Times Telling Us? (12:54-56) We live in a sick society, a world of worldliness. Crime and wickedness abound. Most people are unhappy. We face a world plagued with a nuclear arms race, drug addiction, poverty, hunger, and over-population. The weather forecast is one of severe weather: earthquakes, hurricanes, and tornadoes. Do these say anything to us of the future?

A. Signs of spiritual hunger: drugs, alcoholism, suicides, crime.
B. Internal collapse of civilization: treason, fraud, bribery, moral corruption.
C. Need for repentance: "Repent or perish."

4. What any Fool Should See. (12:54-56) Conditions in contemporary society are so blatant and evident that anyone with a minimum of sense could see disaster ahead. The foreseeing of coming disaster should drive us to Christ and his way of life and spirit.
A. Nuclear arms will lead to world destruction.
B. The growing national debt of two and one-half trillion dollars will bring depression.
C. The population explosion with accompanying poverty, hunger, and illiteracy will result in a world revolution.

5. Signs to Live By. (12:54-56) We cannot live satisfactorily without signs on the highways of life. We need the information and guidance they give. We ignore the signs at the risk of our lives. There are signs other than those of the weather in today's parable.
A. The sign of good news — Luke 2:12.
B. The sign of faithlessness — Matthew 26:48.
C. The sign of power — John 4:54.
D. The sign of future — Luke 12:54-56.

Contact

Points of Contact

1. The World. How can we not be in contact with the meaning of today's parable with the world all around us? As Christians, especially as preachers, we need to know the world as well as the Word. We live in the world. We are subject to its conditions. We have a responsibility and message to the world. We cannot be ascetics and live apart from the world. The Christian's constant problem is how to be in the world and not of it. Can we be spiritual in a secular world?

We must know our world and be able to interpret what is happening and what the trends are, in order that we can present a message relevant to the world. Without relevance we have no message.

The signs of the present time may not forecast a safe future: moral corruption, poverty, nuclear weapons, hunger, over-population, and national hatreds. These conditions warn us of future disaster and at the same time give us urgent opportunities to turn the world right side up.

Indeed, our church people are probably better informed through the public media than any previous generation. What happens in Lebanon or South Africa is known as well, if not better, than what happens in our home towns. We have become world citizens and the whole world comes into our homes through the television screen. What happens in Moscow has implications for Washington and, through Washington, for your personal life. What happens to the rain forest in the Amazon affects the world's climate.

2. The Church. The "present time" also involves the church. In the parable Jesus was probably referring to his own coming and what it meant to his nation. The people could forecast the weather by signs in the sky, but they could not see that in Jesus and his ministry the Kingdom of God was present.

Can the people of the world today see and rightly interpret the existence and work of the church? Does the world hear what God is saying to it through the words and work of the church? In recent times the church has made solemn pronouncements on human rights, the economy, the sexual revolution, and nuclear arms. Does the world rightly interpret the church's message and work?

There is also a personal application of this truth. The local church makes her persistent witness to love and to mercy. She proclaims God's love for the sinful. She offers hope in the name of Christ to the disconsolate and depressed. The church sends out witnesses to visit in the homes, inviting people to become committed to the Christ and to join the movement. Does the non-Christian world interpret these overtures in terms of acceptance and response?

Illustrative Materials

1. Lessons of History. Dr. Charles A. Beard, dean of American historians, summed up the lessons of history which he had put in thirty volumes:
    A. "Whom the gods would destroy, they first make mad with power."
    B. "The mills of God grind slowly, yet they grind exceeding small."
    C. "The bee fertilizes the flower it robs."
    D. "When it is dark enough you can see the stars."

2. Today's Paradoxes.
    A. Omar Bradley: "We have grasped the mystery of the atom and rejected the Sermon on the Mount."
    B. We have more living but less life. In less than a century we have gained twenty-six years in the average life span. This is nearly equal to what was attained in the preceding 5000 years. In 1776 life expectancy was thirty-five. Today it is seventy-four.
    C. We have a sextant but no fixed star.

D. We have technique but no destiny.
E. We have material but no blueprint.
F. We have means but no ends.
G. We have speed without direction.
H. We have rights without duties.

3. The World's Seven Sins. "There are seven sins in the world: wealth without work, pleasure without conscience, knowledge without character, commerce without morality, science without humanity, worship without sacrifice, and politics without principle."

— Mahatma Ghandi

4. An Imperiled Planet. The World Commission on Environment and Development of the United Nations issued a report in April, 1987, stating that present conditions threaten the future of humanity. Among the threatening trends are the alteration of earth's atmosphere by the burning of fossil fuels, the destruction of the protective ozone layer by synthetic chemicals, the destruction of tropical forests, the accelerating extinction of plant and animal species, the spread of deserts, the acid poisoning of lakes and forests, and the toxification of air, soil, and water. Related to these trends are the problems of poverty, hunger, rapid population growth, the excessive outlays for arms, and the inequitable distribution of wealth.

5. The Best in Worst Times. In the chapel at Staton Hall, England there is a plaque remembering a man who in 1653 did something lasting: "When all things sacred throughout the nation were either demolished or profane Sir Robert Baronet founded this church whose singular praise is to have done the best things in the worst times."

6. Out of this World. A few years ago the news media told of a twelve-year-old boy who all his life had had to live in a prophylactic sterile bubble, because of his lack of immunity to all kinds of bacteria. Then he underwent an operation to implant healthy bone marrow in his own body, giving him immunity to the germs. When he was finally taken out of his antiseptic bubble, it was the very first time in his entire life that he was kissed by his mother.

Proper 16 • Pentecost 14 • Ordinary Time 21
Common Lutheran Roman Catholic

11. The Narrow Door

Luke 13:22-30

²²He went on his way through towns and villages, teaching, and journeying toward Jerusalem. ²³And some one said to him, "Lord, will those who are saved be few?" And he said to them, ²⁴"Strive to enter by the narrow door; for many, I tell you, will seek to enter and will not be able. ²⁵When once the householder has risen up and shut the door, you will begin to stand outside and to knock at the door, saying, 'Lord, open to us.' He will answer you, 'I do not know where you come from.' ²⁶Then you will begin to say, 'We ate and drank in your presence, and you taught in our streets.' ²⁷But he will say, 'I tell you, I do not know where you come from; depart from me, all you workers of iniquity!' ²⁸There you will weep and gnash your teeth, when you see Abraham and Isaac and Jacob and all the prophets in the kingdom of God and you yourselves thrust out. ²⁹And men will come from east and west, and from north and south, and sit at table in the kingdom of God. ³⁰And behold, some are last who will be first, and some are first who will be last."

Life is a series of doors. We cannot live without them. Day by day we are going through doors, locking doors, or are locked outside doors. We have all kinds of doors: bathroom, bedroom, kitchen, basement, office, laboratory, etc. Every room seems to have a door by which we enter or leave. A door can be an entrance or a barrier. Doors may have different colors. Traditionally church doors are painted red to symbolize the blood of Christ who is the door to the Kingdom. There are doors of various materials: bronze, wood, and glass. Some doors open outward and others inward. There are automatic, revolving, and ordinary doors. There can be single, double, or triple doors, high and low doors, wide and narrow doors.

In today's parable we have several doors: narrow, open, shut, and visible.

Jesus teaches a lesson on the necessity of living the faith as a means of entering the Kingdom of God. The day is coming when he, as master of the house will shut the door. Many will try to enter but will find the door closed. He will refuse to open the door for them, because they are evil-doers and have no part in him. Their agony of being excluded will be intensified when they see both Jews and Gentiles in God's Kingdom. This parable answers the question of a listener, "Lord, will those who are saved be few?" It is Jesus' answer to Universalists who claim that all will be saved.

Context

Context of Luke 13

In Luke 13 there are four parables of the Kingdom. The Parable of the Barren Fig Tree was considered on Lent 3. After the parables of the Mustard Seed and the Yeast, we have the Parable of the Narrow Door.

Context of the Lectionary

The First Lesson. (Jeremiah 28:1-9) In the temple the prophet Hananiah addresses Jeremiah in the presence of the priests and people. He forecasts the downfall of Babylon and the return of the exiles and temple treasures. When he is finished, Jeremiah prays that Hananiah's forecast will come true. However, he points out that former prophets had foretold doom for a wicked people like Judah. Whether Hananiah is a true spokesman of Yahweh will be shown if and when his forecast of redemption comes true.

The Second Lesson. (Hebrews 12:18-29) This is the third in a series of four passages from Hebrews 11-13. The experience on Mount Sinai was terrifying, but Christians experience a greater event: the heavenly Jerusalem consisting of angels, the redeemed, God, and Jesus. On Mount Sinai the voice of God shook the earth; but now his voice shakes heaven and earth. But the Kingdom of God cannot be shaken. For this we should worship God with reverence and awe.

Gospel (Luke 13:22-30) Not all people will be saved. Only those who enter through the narrow door of righteous living will enter the Kingdom.

Psalm. (Psalm 84) My soul longs for Yahweh's lovely dwelling place. The Psalm harmonizes with the scene in the temple in Lesson 1.

Prayer of the Day. God calls all nations to his Kingdom and gathers disciples near and far. We pray that we may be among those who confess

Jesus as Lord. The prayer is related to the parable in the Gospel.

Hymn of the Day. "A Multitude Comes from East and West" for the feast of salvation. The hymn corresponds to the parable in the Gospel.

Context of the Gospel Lesson

On his way to Jerusalem, Jesus taught the people as he passed through their villages. Luke does not tell us what prompted the person to ask, "Lord, will those who are saved be few?" Prior to this account Luke records the parables of the mustard seed and the leaven. These are not related to the above question. In answer to the question, Jesus gave the Parable of the Narrow and Closed Doors. He taught that the saved will be few because they must enter through the narrow door of righteous living.

Context of Related Scriptures

> Matthew 7:13-14 — Hell is a wide door, but heaven is a narrow door which few find because it is hard.
> Matthew 7:21-23 — At the judgment Christ will reject the wicked because, though they know him, they did not obey his commands to live righteously.
> Matthew 8:10-13 — Jesus commends the faith of a Roman officer for his faith.
> Matthew 22:11-13 — A man without a proper wedding garment is cast out.
> Matthew 25:1-12 — The shut door for five girls.
> Mark 10:24 — It is hard to enter the Kingdom of Heaven.
> John 10:1-10 — Jesus is the door of the sheep.
> Psalm 24:7-10 — Open the doors for the King to enter.

Content

vv. 22-23 — Jesus is asked if only a few will be saved.

v. 24 — Because the door is narrow, many will not be able to enter the Kingdom.

v. 28 — The terror of the rejected.

vv. 28-29 — The people inside the Kingdom.

v. 30 — The last and the first.

Precis of the Parable

On his way to Jerusalem Jesus stopped to teach in villages. In one of these towns a man asked, "Lord, will just a few be saved?" In answer Jesus urged his hearers to try to enter the Kingdom through the narrow door. Many will try but will be unable to do so. When the master of the house closes the door, some will knock and want to enter. But, the master will say "I have nothing to do with you. I don't know where you come from." Then they will say, "Of course, you know us. Don't you remember we once had a meal with you and we heard you teach in our village?" Again the master will reply, "I do not know you. You are none of mine. You are wicked people." Then the outsiders will become hysterical with grief when they look inside the house and see both the Jewish faithful and the Gentile converts from all over the world. The people who are last in this world will be first in the Kingdom and the first will be last.

Thesis: The narrow door to salvation will be closed to the wicked.

Theme: Life through a narrow door!

Key Words

1. **"Few."** (v. 23) Here is a question still being asked, "Will only a few be saved?" Universalists claim that since God is love, every person ultimately will be saved. He will empty out hell so that all will be in the Kingdom of Heaven. What made the man ask this question? What was there in Jesus' teaching that prompted the question? Did Jesus say, "Sell all and give to the poor" or "You must be perfect" or "You must deny yourself and take up your cross?" One sect limits the number of saved to 144,000. Others say, "Only if you belong to my religion, church, or race can you be saved." Jesus did not really answer the question, but he did say that many would not make it. This could lead to the conclusion that many not a few, would be saved.

2. **"Saved."** (v. 23) "Are you saved?" Some resent this question and approach to evangelism. It is the same as asking, "Are you going to heaven?" To be saved is to be in a right relationship with God, a relationship of peace, harmony, and well-being. To be saved is to be in God's Kingdom, to be one of God's people. The parable suggests that salvation is attained by entering the narrow door of the Kingdom.

3. **"Strive."** (v. 24) Jesus says we are to "strive" to enter the narrow door. To strive is to struggle. Our word, "agony," is derived from the word, "strive." The narrow door calls for agony of mind and spirit. Who ever said it was easy to be a Christian? Is it easy to repent? Is it easy to overcome doubt in order to believe? Is it easy to deny oneself? Is the cross an

easy burden? To enter the narrow door demands obedience to God's laws and living within the will of God. Have we given people the impression that becoming a Christian is just coming forward, shaking hands with the preacher, and answering a few questions to which the pastor even supplies the answers? On many doors is a sign, "Pull" or "Push." It takes effort ("strive") on our part to enter a door. The effort is righteous living.

4. **"Narrow."** (v. 24) The door to salvation is narrow. What does it mean to be "narrow?" It can mean righteousness in contrast to "iniquity." (v. 27) Sometimes we call people narrow because of their moral strictness. We would say, for example, that it is narrow to prohibit both sexes from bathing in the same swimming pool. Or, we may think of narrowness in terms of an individual rather than a corporate passage through a door. We cannot enter the Kingdom as a race, country, or class of people. We can only enter the door one at a time. Or, the door is narrow because there is only one way to salvation — faith in Christ by whose name alone we can be saved. Non-religions are not alternate ways to God.

5. **"Shut."** (v. 25) The door is shut and will not be opened again. There is a finality about it. At present the narrow door to the Kingdom is open universally, but the day is coming when it will be shut. Then the opportunity to be saved will be gone. When Saint Paul offered the open door to Felix, the governor said, "When I have an opportunity, I will summon you." (Acts 24:25) But the opportunity never again came, and the door was shut to Felix. The time of shutting the door is death, or it is the day of judgment at the Parousia.

6. **"Come from."** (vv. 25, 27) The master of the house says to those waiting to enter, "I do not know where you come from." Why did he not say, "I do not know you?" It has the same meaning, for who we are is where we come from. Where we come from tells who we are and what we are like. The master is saying that he has no relationship with them, for they are not of his kind. He refers to them as workers of wickedness. Goodness and evil have no connection. Truth and falsehood have no relationship. Christ and Satan do not come from the same place.

7. **"Householder."** (v. 25) Other terms for "householder" are master of the house, or head of the house, or man of the house. It refers to the one in authority, the one with the responsibility for the family. Undoubtedly, the parable refers to the judgment day and the householder is the Master, the King-judge in charge of his house, the Kingdom of God. This reminds us that Christ is both Alpha and Omega. He not only opens doors but closes the door of salvation. He is the one in charge and in his hands is our ultimate destiny.

8. "Gnash." (v. 28) Does it really matter whether one gets shut out of the Kingdom? In the parable the people of iniquity were most distressed at their plight. They wept and gnashed their teeth. The gnashing of teeth is an expression of extreme woe. Their condition was intensified when they saw the people of God in the house where they enjoyed life and peace. The parable does not suggest any punishment. God does not punish. Our sins punish us. We exclude ourselves from the Kingdom. We therefore reap the harvest of our wickedness — sorrow, regret, darkness, and death. This ought to be enough to motivate us to strive to enter by the narrow door into God's Kingdom of life.

Contemplation

Insights

1. Limited salvation. "Many will seek to enter and will not be able." (v. 24) The Parable of the Narrow Door teaches us that not everyone will be saved. Jesus does not teach universalism, the view that ultimately all people of all religions, or no religion, will be saved because God is merciful. God gives a universal invitation to enter his Kingdom — "whoever." But the "whoever" is limited by repentance and belief. (John 3:16) God wishes all to be saved, but not all are willing to believe in him or come to him for salvation. This truth gives function and urgency to the faithful to be or support evangelists and missionaries.

2. Limited opportunity. The door to the Kingdom is open for the present. In the parable Jesus teaches that it will not always be open. The opportunity to enter the Kingdom can be lost forever. Now is the time; today is the day of salvation. Tomorrow may be the day of the closed door. Death closes the door. Jesus' return also will close the door. Since we do not know the day of closing, we need to take advantage of the open door today.

3. The narrow door. Because the door to the Kingdom is narrow, the number entering is limited. It is not wide enough for a multitude, but so narrow that people must enter one by one. The road to the Kingdom is not a six-lane freeway but one lane leading to a narrow entrance. Because the door is narrow, a person needs to be slender, for a person burdened with the corpulence of dissipation cannot squeeze through. It is narrow because the Kingdom demands righteous living. This calls for striving and struggling. It is hard to deny oneself and to exercise self-control. It calls for being a moral person in an immoral society.

4. More than knowledge. The parable stresses that knowledge about

Jesus is not sufficient to enter the Kingdom. When some found the door shut, they begged to come in. But, Jesus denied knowing them, for he called them "workers of iniquity." Like some church members, they even ate with him and listened to his teaching. Nevertheless, they did not practice their religion. Some church members may have a false security of salvation because they are members of the church: they are called the "people of God," and belong to the society of the saved. They may have faith but not the works of faith. The problem boils down to whether we know Jesus or just know about him.

5. Dangers of narrow living. The "narrow door" places emphasis upon the need for righteous behavior. We can be too liberal and too tolerant. The Ten Commandments are not suggestions but moral absolutes. They demand strict obedience. However, we must be on guard against the dangers of this emphasis. It can lead to faith in works righteousness as the way to reconciliation with God. It can lead to Pelagianism or Semi-pelagianism. This emphasis on ethical living can be carried to the extreme of Puritanism. It can make legalists of us, and we can become Pharisees. To live righteously we may even enter into asceticism, a denial of and a separation from the world. There is no sinless place in the world. There is no hiding place from Satan. We must be in the world but not of it. A true Christian is one who participates in the world but refrains from participation in the sins of the world.

6. Tough religion. Jesus calls upon us to "strive" to enter God's Kingdom. This necessitates struggle. The church is often guilty of making it seem easy to be a Christian. Does the church have any requirements for membership? To live a godly life in a godless world is difficult. The cross is not a pillow but an instrument of torture and death. In contrast, we may take the easy way in life — the way of going with the crowd, the way of compromise. The narrow door calls for self-discipline and self-sacrifice. It is not the style of life for everyone because it is too difficult.

7. Servants. Today the emphasis is upon Christians as children of God, the people of God, the saved, and the redeemed. Indeed, this is true, for we have been adopted as children by God in Baptism and are therefore members of the Kingdom. By grace we are saved, and grace was received through the Word and the Sacraments. However, this is only one side of the truth. We are also servants of the King. "Servant" in the New Testament is a slave (*doulos*). A servant or slave exists to obey and serve the master whose will is to be done, and whose commands must be carried out. This calls for righteous and holy living. This is the narrow door of the parable. If we see ourselves only as children of God, we may neglect the pursuit of holiness with a false sense of security, believing that as children of God we are automatically saved. In other words, we as members of the church can be lost children of God, because we have not striven to enter the narrow door of righteous living.

Homily Hints

1. Doors of Life. (13:22-30) According to the parable we confront various doors in life. We have a choice of doors.
    A. Open door of opportunity — v. 25.
    B. Narrow door of righteousness — v. 24.
    C. Closed door of judgment — v. 25b.
    D. Glass door of vision — v. 28.

2. The Door of Salvation. (13:22-30) Salvation is being a member of God's Kingdom. To enter the Kingdom is to go through a door, from the world to God's realm. What is this door? Is it open or closed, narrow or wide, for everyone or a few? The door answers the man's question, "Lord, will those who are saved be few?"
    A. The door is now open — v. 24.
    B. The door is narrow — v. 24.
    C. The door will be closed — v. 25.

3. Proof of the Pudding. (13:22-30) The point of the parable is that followers of Jesus are expected to live godly lives if they expect to be saved as members of God's Kingdom. The source of godly living is faith in Jesus. It is not only knowing about him while going about our own ways of life. To know Jesus is to be related to him and to possess his spirit. The proof of faith is obedience in terms of moral quality and service rendered in the name of Christ. The proof of the pudding is in the eating. The proof of faith is the living of it.
    A. Proof of a true prophet — when it comes true — First Lesson.
    B. Proof of salvation — when God's voice is heeded — Second Lesson.
    C. Proof of faith — when faith works through love — Gospel.

4. An Evangelical Interpretation. The parable may lead to a glorification of good works as the means for entering the Kingdom. Like all other texts, this parable needs to be understood in the light of total Scripture. The parable emphasizes the need of holy living, but it needs to be seen in the light of the Gospel.
    A. Christ is the narrow door — only means of salvation — John 10:9.
    B. Faith in Christ opens the door to salvation — John 3:16.
    C. True faith is revealed in godly living — Luke 13:22-30.

5. Push or Pull. (13:24; Matthew 16:24) "Strive" is a key word. To live a godly life calls for effort. Anything worthwhile costs. In art, business, and the professions, excellence demands effort. On some public doors there is a sign saying "Pull" or "Push." The door calls for effort.

    A. Strive to deny yourself.

    B. Strive to carry your cross.

    C. Strive to follow Jesus in obedience.

6. The Glory of Being Narrow. In our time we frown on narrowness of thinking or living. We exalt tolerance and compromise. Universalism is an expression of this latitudinarian attitude. But, Christianity is a narrow religion. Truth is narrow — there is no room for falsehood. Goodness is narrow — a thing is either right or wrong. Christianity is narrow because —

    A. One God only — Isaiah 43:11.

    B. One Savior only — Acts 4:12.

    C. One way of life — righteousness — Luke 13:24.

7. What the World Wants. (13:22-30) The world wants and needs Christians to be examples of godliness. The world's respect and acceptance of the Gospel depend largely on Christians living holy lives.

    A. Thesis: Church is more concerned with the proclamation of a message rather than a demonstration of it.

    B. Antithesis: World gets the message primarily through demonstration.

    C. Synthesis: Proclamation with demonstration.

8. The Shut Door: On Which Side Are You? (13:25-29) A shut door may be good or bad, depending on which side of the shut door you happen to be. Are you in or out, lost or saved, warm or cold, accepted or rejected?

    A. Do you shut the door?

        1. Shut it for safety, protection, privacy?

    B. Is the door shut on you?

        1. Reason: "Workers of iniquity" — v. 27.

        2. Exclusion from heaven — vv. 28-29.

Contact

Questions

The Parable of the Narrow Door raises a number of questions which a preacher must answer before preparing a sermon on the pericope. They are disturbing questions which challenge the Gospel and strike at the heart of the Christian faith.

1. Are all people saved? Universalism is involved in this parable, because of the question which prompted its telling: "Lord, will those who are saved be few?" Universalists would say that not a few but all will be saved. To be "saved" means to be reconciled with God and welcomed in heaven. The Universalists base their position on the love and forgiving mercy of God. To them it is unthinkable and non-Christian to exclude anyone from paradise for eternity. It seems hard and cruel to claim that some will be lost, forever shut out of God's presence which means life and love and peace. What is the answer? In this parable Jesus teaches against Universalism. Contrary to God's will, some people will reject God and choose hell. According to the parable, many will go to hell because they are workers of iniquity.

2. Are we saved by our own righteousness? The parable seems to teach that only those whose lives are holy can enter the Kingdom of God. This is symbolized by the narrow door. The wicked find the door of the Kingdom shut. Morever, in the parable, Jesus urges his listeners to "strive" or struggle or work to get into the narrow door. It is not easy to live a Christian life in a non-Christian world. It calls for effort, denial, and sacrifice. If we are able to enter the Kingdom by our characters, where does the Gospel of grace come in? Are we saved by our good works?

What is the answer? In the parable, Jesus is emphasizing that religion, and not religiosity, saves a person. We are content to know about Jesus, to respect, admire, and listen — but not to accept him. The answer is that, in the light of the teaching of the whole New Testament, Jesus is the door to the Kingdom, and by faith in him we enter the Kingdom. But, faith in Jesus requires ethical expression. The book of the Bible which the church needs to remember is James, with its thesis that faith without works is dead.

3. Is Christ essential for salvation? Another possible disturbing question arises when, in the parable, Jesus tells of the anguish which the rejected will face when they see that the Jewish leaders and Gentiles from all parts of the world are in heaven. If we take this literally, it would seem to say that the godly before the time of Christ are in heaven and the Gentiles who have lived righteously are also in the Kingdom. Where then is Christ and the cross and redemption? Do we need Christ as Savior if people are in heaven without the gift of his atoning work?

Is there an answer? Again, we must keep the total context of the Bible in mind. Jesus says this to the rejected ones to make them realize what their wickedness costs them. It is another way to press the point that faith requires action. The truth remains: Christ died for our sins and through him we have access to God and to heaven.

Point of Contact

Does the congregation need to hear the message of this parable? The preaching of this parable is desperately needed because church people show a decline in living the Christian faith. We are prone to be content with sinful living. In 1987 the country was shocked by the sexual deviance of PTL leader, Jim Bakker; Oral Roberts, with his attempt to blackmail God for eight million dollars, was the laughing stock in the secular world, and an embarrassment to the church. The Roman Catholic Church reported that forty percent of its priests are not faithful to their vows of chastity. Church leaders are known to have committed adultery, embezzlement of funds, and excessive drinking of alcohol. If leaders fail to live Christlike lives, what can be expected of the laity? The imperative for our day is a fearless preaching on the need for holiness in life as an expression of faith.

It needs to be pointed out that the parable is directed to religious or church people, not to the world. The people in the parable claimed that they had had fellowship with Jesus and had heard him preach. Of course, the world needs to be called to repentance and faith, but church people need to be challenged to live their faith. People of the world need to turn to God; church people need to *re*turn to God. People of the world are expected to be worldly; people of God are expected to be godly.

Illustrative Materials

1. Cheap Grace.

"Cheap grace is the preaching of forgiveness without requiring repentance, baptism without church discipline, Communion without confession, absolution without personal confession. Cheap grace is grace without discipleship, grace without the cross, grace without Jesus Christ, living and incarnate."
— Dietrich Bonhoeffer in *The Cost of Discipleship*.

2. Unacceptable narrowness. When Pope John Paul II visited the South in the Fall of 1987, various leaders of Protestant churches were invited to meet with him for fellowship. While thirty-one heads of churches accepted, the president of the largest Protestant church in America declined the invitation.

A news item tells of a revival held in a Baptist church in Madisonville, Tennessee. The evangelist asked the people to bring their bright-colored bathing suits, decks of cards, and novels. While the worshipers sang, "I'll Never Turn Back," the preacher set fire to their suits, cards, and novels.

3. Faith without works. A Hindu was meditating while a child tottered near an oncoming train. When the Hindu was implored to rescue the child, he replied, "I'm not interested in people; I'm a holy man."

At a revival in north Georgia a man stood up and gave his testimony: "Brothers and sisters, you know I haven't been what I ought to have been. I stole hogs. I got drunk, told lies. I've played poker, cussed and abused women. But through all of this, there is one thing I haven't done. I ain't never lost my religion!"

4. Pluralism. A new chapel costing 4.8 million dollars was built for the Candler School of Theology, Emory University, Atlanta, Georgia. At the opening, the Dean of the school indicated that though the school had been founded by the Methodist church, "The chapel does not signify that a single religion is advocated by the administration."

Episcopal Bishop John T. Walker of Washington, D. C. discouraged people from supporting "Jews for Jesus." He explained, "If we truly believe that Jews are the people of God, we should not lend support to groups that seek to convert Jews to Christianity."

5. Charm of Character. An old eastern fable tells of a man who possessed a ring with a beautiful opal. Whoever wore the ring became so sweet and true in character that all people loved him. The ring was passed from father to son until it happened that a man had three sons. Before his death he had two other rings made exactly like the one. After his death the three sons learned that each had the magic ring, but which one was the original? They took the matter to court and the judge said, "Because the ring will make the man who wears it sweet and good, we will know the genuine ring by the goodness of his life." The one who was kind, truthful, brave, and just would know that he had the true ring.

Proper 17   •   Pentecost 15   •   Ordinary Time 22

Common   Lutheran   Roman Catholic

---

12. Places of Honor

Luke 14:1, 7-14

---

¹One sabbath when he went to dine at the house of a ruler who belonged to the Pharisees, they were watching him . . .

⁷Now he told a parable to those who were invited, when he marked how they chose the places of honor, saying to them, ⁸"When you are invited by any one to a marriage feast, do not sit down in a place of honor, lest a more eminent man than you be invited by him; ⁹and he who invited you both will come and say to you, 'Give place to this man,' and then you will begin with shame to take the lowest place. ¹⁰But when you are invited, go and sit in the lowest place, so that when your host comes he may say to you, 'Friend, go up higher'; then you will be honored in the presence of all who sit at table with you. ¹¹For every one who exalts himself will be humbled, and he who humbles himself will be exalted."

¹²He said also to the man who had invited him, "When you give a dinner or a banquet, do not invite your friends or your brothers or your kinsmen or rich neighbors, lest they also invite you in return, and you be repaid. ¹³But when you give a feast, invite the poor, the maimed, the lame, the blind, ¹⁴and you will be blessed, because they cannot repay you. You will be repaid at the resurrection of the just."

You read a parable like the one dealing with places of honor and you think, "That could never happen to me." But, it can happen, and it did happen to me. As a result, I can identify with the experience of the man in the parable who was told, "Give place to this man."

For a number of years I taught and served as chaplain for the summer session at the Candler School of Theology, Emory University. At the close of the term each year students and faculty had a banquet. Because I was the chaplain, each year there was a place for me at the head table. This one year I went to the head table to look for my name card. I went from place to place, but there was no card for me. By this time the banquet hall was filled and I had to find a seat at the other end of the dining room. Why I was deleted from the head table I never found out, but I will always remember the embarrassment I felt when, in front of all the students, I had to find a place at the back. The experience was good for my humility.

Today's parable tells of a similar situation. Jesus is invited to the home of a prominent Pharisee for dinner. He notices how some, out of pride, choose the honorable places near the host. To teach a lesson on humility to the assembled guests, Jesus tells about men at a wedding feast. He urged them to choose the lower seats so that they will not be asked to give up their places to a more honorable guest, and face the humiliation of taking a lower seat. The principle of the parable: the exalted will be humiliated while the humble will be honored. In this parable humanity's worst sin, pride, and the most difficult virtue to possess, humility, are considered.

Context

Context of Luke 14

Luke 14 gives us a series of discourses, a series of table talk. They are not necessarily related to each other and not chronological. In this chapter we have three parables and one miracle.

v. 1 — Jesus attends a dinner in the home of a Pharisee who was a "ruler."
vv. 2-6 — Jesus heals a man with dropsy.
vv. 7-11 — Parable of Places of Honor, recorded only by Luke.
vv. 12-14 — Jesus has a word of advice for his host.
vv. 15-24 — Parable of the Great Banquet.
vv. 25-33 — Parable of Counting the Cost.
vv. 34-35 — Saltless salt.

Context of the Lectionary

The First Lesson. (Ezekiel 18:1-9, 25-29) The individual is responsible for his or her sin. Children are not responsible for the sins of their parents. A sinner will die. A righteous person will live. Lesson 1 is the first of two selections from Ezekiel and is not intentionally related to the other two lessons.

The Second Lesson. (Hebrews 13:1-8) The author of Hebrews, in this last in a series of four lessons from Hebrews, urges the faithful to apply love in various areas of life: hospitality, concern for the imprisoned, marriage, and stewardship.

Gospel (Luke 14:1, 7-14) While attending a dinner, Jesus tells the guests the Parable of the Places of Honor, and urges his host to invite to dinner only those who would be unable to return the favor.

Psalm. (Psalm 15) Related to the First Lesson's message concerning a righteous person, the Psalm describes the characteristics of a godly person who dwells with Yahweh.

Prayer of the Day. The prayer picks up the humility theme of the parable: "Humble us by his example . . ."

Hymn of the Day. "O God of Earth and Altar" evidently was chosen to harmonize with today's parable, for the first stanza ends "But take away our pride."

Context of the Gospel Lesson

Verse one gives the setting for the parable. Jesus is the guest in the home of a ruler who happens to be a Pharisee. Apparently he arrives early, for he watches how some choose places of honor at the tables. At the same time the other guests are watching Jesus. The guests consist primarily of scribes and Pharisees. Among the guests is a man with dropsy. They watch to see if Jesus will break the Sabbath by healing the man. After putting his critics to silence, he tells the guests the parable about the choice of seats at a wedding feast. Then he addresses the host and urges him to invite the dispossessed and handicapped to future dinners.

Context of Related Scriptures

> Proverbs 25:6-7 — Seek not the top place in the king's presence.
> Matthew 23:1-12 — Pharisees love the best seats.
> Mark 10:35-45 — James and John ask for the chief seats in the Kingdom.
> Mark 12:38-40 — Scribes like to have the chief seats.
> Philippians 2:1-11 — Jesus is the example of humility.
> 3 John 9 — Diotrephes causes trouble by putting himself first.

Content

Content of the Pericope:

> v. 1 — The setting of the parable: Jesus attends a dinner at the home of a Pharisee-ruler.

vv. 7-11 — Jesus speaks a parable to the guests concerning pride and humility as seen in their choice of seats at a dinner.

vv. 12-14 — Jesus has a word for the host concerning future invitations to dinner: invite only those who are too poor to return the favor.

Precis of the Parable

When Jesus was a dinner guest in the home of a leading Pharisee, he observed how some chose the chief places of honor to be as close as possible to the host. He used the occasion to teach a lesson on humility by telling a parable. When you are invited to a wedding feast, or any dinner or banquet for that matter, do not take the best place. If you do, someone more important may come and the host will ask you to move. This will be embarrassing because in the presence of the other guests, you will have to take the lowest seat. Rather, when you arrive, take the lowest place so that when the host comes and sees you, he will say, "Come up to a better place." Then all at the dinner will witness your being honored. Jesus then explained that anyone who puts himself forward will be humbled, but that the humble person will be considered great.

Thesis: The proud will be humbled but the humble will become great.

Theme: Going down to go up!

Key Words

1. **"Ruler."** (v. 1) The host of the dinner to which Jesus was invited was a "ruler." He was not a ruler in terms of a local authority, governor, or king. It was a way of saying that he was a leading citizen of some importance and influence. Perhaps he was a member of the Sanhedrin, Israel's supreme court at the time. He may have been the leader of a local synagogue. Since he was a Pharisee, his other guests were for the most part fellow-Pharisees. This would explain why some chose the top seats at the dinner, for Pharisees were known as lovers of the best places. (Matthew 23:6) That Jesus was invited to the home of a religious leader reminds us that Jesus was not always associating with publicans and sinners.

2. **"Watching."** (v. 1) The dinner at the Pharisee's home turned out to be a watching match. The guests were watching to see if Jesus would break the Sabbath law by healing a sick man. They were watching to find fault with him. On the other hand, Jesus watched them — "He marked how . . ." (v. 7) He observed how proud they were in grabbing seats of honor. As they found fault with him, he found fault with their attitudes.

3. "Invited." (v. 7) Jesus tells this parable to the assembled guests. Was this the right time and place to criticize those who demonstrated pride taking chief seats? Was it an act of discourtesy? It shows that Jesus was an opportunist. He struck while the iron was hot. It was an opportunity to teach an important lesson. At the same time it shows us how fearless Jesus was in proclaiming truth even if it hurt. It is easy to understand why Jesus had bitter enemies.

4. "Places." (v. 7) Jesus noticed how the men who came tried to get the seats of honor at the head table, where the host would be seated. Often we do not get to choose where we sit. Some hosts use name cards, or the hostess asks us to sit at certain places around the dinner table. When we enter a restaurant, usually a hostess takes us to a table. In this case, the guests could find their own seats. This revealed what they thought of themselves, and how important they thought they were. The proud revealed their self-importance by going to the top places.

5. "Shame." (v. 9) The shame comes when the host asks you to move so that a more important person can have your seat. The shame is that in the sight of all present you must take the lowest seat, for by that time all the intermediate seats are occupied. You are embarrassed and humiliated. It is a shame when you go from first to last place in the respect others have for you. It is a shame when the president of a nation, because of a Watergate scandal, falls from the presidency to disgrace. It is a shame when a front-runner for the Democratic nomination for the presidency must drop out of the race because of adultery. What a shame for a couple that entertained millions on television, and received annually over a hundred million dollars from listeners, to be deposed because of sexual sins. How the mighty have fallen — from exaltation to humiliation!

6. "Exalts." (v. 11) A person who "exalts" herself is one who thinks more highly of herself than she ought to think. This results in pride or hubris. It is the central failing of humanity. It all began with Adam and Eve, who wanted to be more than human; they wanted to be like God. (Genesis 3:5) It is a case of blowing your own horn. It is expressed in the slogan, "I am worth it," or "I deserve it." It leads to arrogance and conceit. The person who exalts himself is self-centered and thinks of himself as "number one." The penalty for this sin is humiliation.

7. "Humbles." (v. 11) We either humble ourselves or we will be humbled in terms of humiliation. Probably humility is the most difficult virtue because it cannot be acquired. Like happiness, it is a by-product of other qualities. It is an unconscious virtue, and as soon as we are aware of it, we lose it. We can be proud of our humility. To be humble is to be your real and true self as God has made you. The real person may be hidden by superficial and unnatural accretions which must be scraped off like a woman's makeup before she retires. The reward of humility, according to Jesus, is exaltation.

Contemplation

Insights

1. Humility for the wrong reason. The parable may suggest that one can be humble for selfish reasons. We are advised to take the lowest place at a feast so that the host will come and ask us to take a more honorable seat. When this happens, we will be honored in the sight of all. Obviously, Jesus certainly was not teaching this as a motive for humility, but was giving an account of what could happen. If we had a selfish motive, it would be false humility. Yet, some people express humility in order to gain praise. One may say, "I am nothing. I am worthless." The person then expects the hearer to respond, "Of course, you are something and you are worth millions to many people."

2. False humility. Some think of humility as self-negation. One can have self-esteem and a sense of worth, and still be humble. Humility does not demand that we deny our worth or accomplishments. I do not have to disparage myself or my talents to be humble. With Saint Paul I can say, "I am what I am." God has made me what I am and any talent I have God gave me. I do not boast about myself, but I can feel good about myself.

3. Let others praise you. A humble person will not boast or praise him or herself. If there is any good thing about you, let others say it. In the parable the host comes to the humble person seated in the rear and says, "Friend, go up higher." In Philippians 2 Paul describes the humility of Jesus in becoming a servant who was obedient unto death. "But God has highly exalted him . . . ." Jesus did not claim any honor or glory for himself. The Father praised and glorified him. Self-praise is odious, a sign of pride. We should so live that others have reason to praise us.

4. An unconscious virtue. Humility is the scarcest human commodity. Anyone who thinks or says she is humble is not. It is a contradiction in terms when a person, in accepting an honor, says, "I am humbly proud." What the person means to say is, "I do not feel worthy to receive this award." That is far different from humility. Like happiness, humility is a by-product of other conditions. No one can consciously decide to be humble or acquire humility. It comes when a person is her real self without any pretensions or superficial poses.

5. A personal evaluation. At the wedding feast in the parable there were no name cards on the table nor, a host or hostess to take guests to their seats. It was a self-seating arrangement. It is assumed that the host was one of the last to arrive because his guests were already seated. When a guest arrived, he had to ask himself, "Where shall I sit?" The place he chose indicated what he thought of himself and his importance. In pride he could say, "I belong at the head table at the right hand of the host." A humble person would be comfortable in a less honorable seat.

6. The price of pride. The price is that "Every one who exalts himself will be humbled." (v. 11) In the parable the host says to a proud person, "Give place to this man." (v. 9) The proud one then with shame takes one of the lowest seats. "Pride goes before a fall," a proverb says. In May of 1987 this truth was illustrated by scandals that shocked both church and state: the PTL scandal, Iranscam, and the dropping out of the race for the Democratic presidential nomination by Gary Hart for his adultery. *Time* magazine commented, "Character becomes fate as hubris is defined anew. Behind all the revelations lurked arrogance, a modern hubris." Power produces pride and pride produces peril.

Homily Hints

1. From Top to Bottom. (14:7-11) In the parable the proud took top seats, but were sent to the back of the room. It is possible for one to go from pride to humility.

    A. Hubris — "How they chose the places of honor" — v. 7.

    B. Humiliation — "Give place to his man." — v. 9.

    C. Humility — "Go and sit in the lowest place" — v. 10.

2. The ABCs of Humility. (14:11) Our talk of the need to be humble may not be helpful. Our basic human nature makes us proud, for we are inherently self-centered. Since humility cannot be acquired by our effort, how do we become humble without falsely minimizing ourselves? Humility is a by-product of the following:

    A. Acknowledging your limitations and imperfections.

    B. Being aware of your indebtedness to others.

    C. Considering what God has done in and for you.

3. Who do You Think You Are? (14:7-11) At life's dinner table there are no name cards or host to tell you where to be seated, at the head or foot of the table. Where you choose to sit follows who you think you are. Are you worthy and deserving of the place of honor or not? Pride or humility depends upon your evaluation of yourself. Who do you think you are?

A. Do you think too highly of yourself? If so, pride.

B. Do you think too lowly of yourself? If so, depression.

C. Do you think honestly of yourself? If so, humility.

4. You're on Candid Camera! (14:1) When we are on candid camera, we do not know we are being watched. At the dinner in the Pharisee's house, there was a mutual watching by Jesus and the other guests. When we do not know we are being watched, we are off guard and our true selves are seen. This watching game between Jesus and us is still going on.

A. What did the guests see in Jesus — a helping, healing person — vv. 2-6.

B. What did Jesus see in the guests — pride or humility? vv. 7-11.

5. Who Shall Blow Your Horn? (14:11) An old adage says, "If you don't blow your horn, nobody else will." This gives one license to boast of one's self and accomplishments. Out of it come pride, arrogance, and conceit. A humble person will let others blow his or her horn. Because of your character and your attainments, others will be moved to honor and praise you. This is in keeping with humility.

A. To blow your own horn is to be proud — v. 7.

B. Why you would not blow your horn — v. 10.

1. God and you know who you are and what you have accomplished.

C. Your good works will cause others to blow your horn — v. 10.

Contact

Points of Contact

Today's parable deals with a universal problem, as old as the human race: pride as expressed in the parable of "how they chose the places of honor." At the same time, in this parable we deal with the most difficult of virtues to possess — humility. In preaching on this subject, we are dealing with a problem and need applicable to every person in attendance. Even the very best of us have pride peeping through the holes in our garments of piety.

1. Reasons for pride in the world:

Graduated from college *magna cum laude.*

Had dinner with a Senator.

Ran with the ball that made the winning touchdown.

Received a medal of honor for valor.
Was given the keys of the city.
Had the top grade on the exam.
Just came back from a trip abroad.
Our child was named a "whiz kid" by the media.

2. Expressions of pride in the church:

Members offended if recognition of gifts or services is not given.
Names of donors in windows, on chancel furnishings or pews.
Offended when not nominated or elected to a church office.
Angry with pastor for not visiting when one is sick, though he or
  she was not informed.
Defensive and hurt when constructive criticism is given.
Refuses to accept help or to learn.
Offended if the pastor cannot remember one's name.

Problems

1. Today's parable dealing with humility has a twin — the Parable of the Pharisee and Publican at prayer in the temple. If one continues with the Gospel lesson and brings to a conclusion this series on parables, one will face the same theme eight weeks from today — on Pentecost 23, Proper 25. In today's parable we see pride expressed in the choosing of places at a feast. Later, pride will be shown within the context of prayer. With this twin-parable on pride in mind, a preacher may want to deal with only a segment of the subject rather than try to handle the whole subject at this time.

2. Another problem deals with Jesus' relating the parable to the guests whom he saw express their pride in themselves by seeking places of honor. Was it courteous of Jesus to criticize and attack the proud guests at a dinner occasion where the atmosphere should be one of table fellowship and good spirit? Would it have been better if Jesus had dealt with the problem at another place and time? In defense of Jesus we might say that Jesus seized the most opportune time to teach a lesson on humility. As a result of his criticism, he probably was considered a *persona non grata*.

3. A third problem deals with the motivation for humility. It is possible to see a selfish motive resulting in false humility within this parable, when Jesus says that one should take the lowest seat in order for the host to request he move up higher. If one chooses the lowest place in order to be elevated to honor, it is an unworthy motivation. In defense of Jesus, we need to understand that Jesus is not teaching this kind of motivation. He is simply telling a story in which a host asks a humble person to take a place of more prominence.

Illustrative Materials

1. Pride.

Benjamin Franklin: "A man wrapped up in himself is the smallest package in the world."

A sign in a barbershop: "For the greatest such as I, it is difficult to be humble."

Bruce Barton: "Conceit is God's gift to little men."

An ad in *Psychology Today*: "I love me. I am not conceited. I'm just a good friend to myself. And I like to do whatever makes me feel good."

2. Egotism.

A woman was seen with a T-shirt saying: "I am his because he deserves the best."

Richard Burton: "I rather like my reputation . . . a spoiled genius from the Welsh gutter, a drunk, a womanizer. It's rather an attractive image."

Truman Capote: "I'm an alcoholic. I'm a drug addict. I'm a homosexual. I'm a genius."

Marvin Gaye: "I am good-looking, intelligent, articulate, arrogant, and an artist."

There is a story about a little boy who was going to show his father how he could hit a baseball. He asked his father to go with him to the park across the street from their home. He explained, "Dad, I want you to see how I can hit the ball!" He threw the ball up in the air, aimed carefully, swung as hard as he could, and missed it! The ball dropped in the dust. The boy yelled, "Strike one!" He turned to his father and said, "Don't worry about it, Dad. The bases are loaded, the fans are cheering — it takes only one to win the game." He threw the ball a second time and missed it. The boy yelled, "Strike two!" He explained, "That's all right, Dad. There is one left. It's going to go over the fence. You won't believe it." Again he swung with all his might and the ball again fell in the dust. Just then his mother called the two of them for dinner. As the two headed to the house, the boy said to his father, "Gee, Dad, I guess that really proves it — I really am a fantastic pitcher!"

3. Humility.

Author unknown: "Pray to God for humility, but forget to thank him when you think you've got it."

———

Alex Haley, author of Roots tells of the lesson taught him by his friend, John Gaines: "If you see a turtle on the top of a fence post, you know he had some help."

———

In 1979 Red Sox star, Carl Yastrzemski had his 3000th hit. When he was asked whether all the attention he was getting would go to his head, he explained, "Well, in my career I've been up to bat over ten thousand times. That fact alone keeps me from getting a swelled head."

———

"No man's really any good 'til he knows how bad he is or might be; 'til he's realized exactly how much right he has to all this snobbery, and sneering, and talking about 'criminals' as if they were apes in a forest ten thousand miles away; till he's got rid of all the dirty self-deception of talking about low types and deficient skulls; 'til he's squeezed out of his soul the last drop of the oil of the Pharisees; 'til his only hope is somehow or other to have captured one criminal, and kept him safe and sane under his own hat." — G. K. Chesterton.

4. Chief Seats. An elderly, well-dressed man walked into a crowded coffee shop and crossed the dining area to where a busy waitress was clearing dishes from a table. "Where's a nice place for a retired executive to sit?" the man asked pompously. Without looking up, she answered, "Florida."

Proper 18 • Pentecost 16 • Ordinary Time 23
Common Lutheran Roman Catholic

13. Counting the Cost

Luke 14:25-33

²⁵*Now great multitudes accompanied him; and he turned and said to them,* ²⁶*"If any one comes to me and does not hate his own father and mother and wife and children and brothers and sisters, yes, and even his own life, he cannot be my disciple.* ²⁷*Whoever does not bear his own cross and come after me, cannot be my disciple.* ²⁸*For which of you, desiring to build a tower, does not first sit down and count the cost, whether he has enough to complete it?* ²⁹*Otherwise, when he has laid a foundation, and is not able to finish, all who see it begin to mock him* ³⁰*saying, 'This man began to build, and was not able to finish.'* ³¹*Or what king, going to encounter another king in war, will not sit down first and take counsel whether he is able with ten thousand to meet him who comes against him with twenty thousand?* ³²*And if not, while the other is yet a great way off, he sends an embassy and asks terms of peace.* ³³*So therefore, whoever of you does not renounce all that he has cannot be my disciple."*

A nationwide network of banks placed a full-page ad in a recent magazine with the headline: "Before you start looking, better find out how much house you can afford."

Once they had the reader's attention, the ad continued:

"When most of us look for a home of our dreams, we lead with our hearts. We see the wood in the den and the tile in the bathroom and the morning sun in the kitchen. But we don't see the need to talk about money just yet. That can wait. So, starry-eyed, we fall in love with a house; before we know how much house we can afford. How human, how worrisome and how unnecessary. Because the last thing on your mind should be the first place you start."

Not looking ahead and counting the cost is a universal problem. We express the problem in phrases like "Look before you leap," or "Don't bite off more than you can chew." We ask, "Do you know what you are getting into?" For instance, I asked myself this question when I got into scraping a three-year layer of paint which was peeling off the floor of the deck in front of our mountain cottage. The deck was a horrible eye-sore, and so I decided to scrape off the paint down to the natural wood, and then apply a wood preservative. After several hours of hard work in the blazing summer sun, and covering only a few square feet, I began to question my decision to indulge in the project. Had I counted the cost of the physical energy, the discomfort of the sun, and the sweat of hard work?

This principle applies to every area of life: marriage, parenthood, education, vocation, and religion. In today's parables Jesus applies it to discipleship. He urges his many followers to Jerusalem to count the cost of becoming one of his disciples. When they know that his invitation to follow is at the same time an invitation to die, they may change their minds.

The advantage of knowing what price you have to pay is knowing whether you are capable of paying the price. It prevents you from starting and not finishing, as when building a house or tower. This saves you from the disgrace of not being able to complete what you started. There is something tragic about not completing a worthy project. The world has an "Unfinished Symphony," and because it is so good, we wish it had been finished. In Europe a certain town planned to build the highest cathedral in the world, but only the chancel was built. It is an unfinished cathedral. In the parables Jesus warns us against an unfinished life, for a finished life is a life of discipleship. No life is complete until it is a life in Christ.

Context

Context of the Lectionary

The First Lesson. (Ezekiel 33:1-11) This is the second of two lections from Ezekiel. Last Sunday we learned that each person is responsible for his own sin and not that of others. Today we hear that a preacher as a watchman is responsible for the sins of her people if a warning is not given. But if the warning is sounded and the people reject it, the preacher is not held responsible for their sins. The warning may be related to the parables of the tower and the opposing army, for in these parables Jesus urges us to be aware of what lies ahead.

The Second Lesson. (Philemon 1-20) Paul writes a personal letter to Philemon asking him to take back his run-away slave, Onesimus, as a Christian brother, because under Paul's influence, he had become a Christian.

This lesson, also, makes a connection with the parables of the Gospel lesson. Paul gives advance notice to Philemon of Onesimus' return and asks him to receive him in a manner appropriate to a Christian.

Gospel. (Luke 14:25-33) Jesus urges the multitude through two parables to count the cost of discipleship. The price is putting Christ first in all things and in all ways.

Psalm. (Psalm 94:11-22) The Lord defends and protects us from the wicked.

Prayer of the Day. We pray that, in his love and power, God, in spite of our weaknesses, will make us firm in the faith.

Hymn of the Day. "Take my Life, That I may be." In harmony with the Gospel's parables, the hymn provides us with a prayer of consecration of our total selves to Christ.

Context of the Gospel Lesson

Jesus is on his way to Jerusalem for the last time. Crowds went with him (v. 25) expecting a victory celebration when he would be accepted as king. The multitude expected him to establish an empire based on truth and justice. Seeing the great numbers following him for the wrong reasons, Jesus felt he had to banish their false hopes by telling them the cost of being one of his disciples. He was interested in recruits rather than spectators who came to see the show. The twin parables of the tower and the army come between two pronouncements about self-denial (vv. 25-27, 33) being the price of discipleship. Jesus is not as interested in the quantity of followers as he is in the quality of disciples.

Context of Related Scriptures

> Matthew 10:37-38 — Matthew puts Luke's account (14:26) in a positive form. One who loves family more than Jesus is unworthy of discipleship, whereas Luke's version uses "hate."
>
> Mark 10:35-40 — Jesus asks James and John if they are willing and able to pay the price of having the chief seats in the coming Kingdom.
>
> Luke 9:57-62 — Would-be disciples are rejected.
>
> John 6:60-69 — Surface disciples abandon Jesus when the truth about him is declared.
>
> Acts 9:15-16 — At his conversion Paul is told that suffering is the price of being a disciple.

Content

Content of the Pericope

v. 25 — The setting for the parables.
vv. 26-27 — The cost of discipleship.
vv. 28-30 — The parable of the tower: count the cost.
vv. 31-32 — The parable of kings going to war: ability to pay the cost.
v. 33 — The total cost of discipleship: renunciation.

Precis of the Parables

As Jesus was on his way to Jerusalem, large crowds went with him. When he saw the multitude following him, he turned to them and explained, "No one can be my disciple unless he loves me more than he loves his father, mother, wife, children, brothers, sisters, and even himself. Unless one carries his cross and follows me, he cannot be one of my disciples. If any of you wants to build a farmhouse, he first figures what it would cost to build it. If he has only enough money to lay the foundation, people will laugh at him. They will say, 'He began but was not able to finish the job.' Or, if a king with 10,000 men goes out to fight a king with 20,000, he will determine whether he is able to face the larger force. If not, he will ask the other king for terms of peace." Jesus concluded, "No one can be my disciple unless he gives up everything he has."

Thesis: A disciple is one who puts Christ first.

Theme: Look before you leap!

Key Words

1. "Hate." (v. 26) "Hate" the members of your family? Does Jesus really mean that? Did he not say, "Love your enemies . . . ?" (Matthew 5:44) If your family were your enemies, Jesus would still have you love them. "Hate" is not meant here in the popular sense of the word. In Scripture love and hate are matters of the will rather than of the emotions. To love is to accept and submit; to hate is to reject and refuse to submit to. In this verse "hate" means to place family and self in second place to Jesus as the price of discipleship. The *Good News Bible* interprets "hate" in this fashion: "Whoever comes to me cannot be my disciple unless he loves me more . . ." As Christians it is not that we do not love family and self, but that we love Christ more than these.

2. "Cross." (v. 27) One cost of discipleship for each of us is carrying "his own cross." It is not Jesus' cross, for no one can die for him. His cross was one of redemption, and only God in Christ could pay the price of sin. What is a Christian's cross? It is not the hardship or suffering that come from a wicked world. All people, Christian or non-Christian, are subject to the world's tragedies. A cross is something voluntarily endured for another's good in terms of suffering and sacrifice. Jesus suffered and died for our redemption, not for his sins because he had none. Christians walk in Jesus by sacrificing for the world's welfare.

3. "Tower." (v. 28) A "tower" refers to a major building which would be costly. Probably it was a farmhouse. It was a project that would be a major event and would require much expenditure of substance and work. The questions a builder faces are, do I have sufficient resources to complete the structure? Have financial arrangements been made? Are the materials available? The inability to finish the job is a reflection on the intelligence and wisdom of the builder. He becomes a laughing stock to the community if he cannot finish.

4. "Count." (v. 28) "Count" or figure or estimate the cost of what you want or want to be. Look ahead. Investigate. Inquire. How much is this going to cost? Get an estimate on car repairs — can you afford them? You want to build a house — what will it cost? Going to war — is there an even chance to win? Going to college — need a scholarship, willing to put in hours of study daily, able to hear disturbing ideas? You want to be a Christian? What will be expected of you?

5. "Renounce." (v. 33) A Christian at baptism is asked, "Do you renounce the devil . . . ?" Here Jesus is calling upon each prospective disciple to "renounce all that he has." What then is left for a Christian? He has left only Christ, for as Saint Paul wrote, "For me to live is Christ." (Philippians 1:21) To renounce is to say "Goodbye" or "Farewell." A Christian says goodbye to everything that is considered more important than Jesus. For instance, the rich young ruler was unable to renounce his wealth and therefore rejected discipleship. To renounce does not mean to get rid of everything or anybody, but to subordinate them to second place to Jesus. Therefore, a rich person can be a true Christian by placing wealth in the service of the Kingdom.

6. "Cannot." (vv. 26, 27, 33) "Cannot" is a very definite word. It is not "maybe" or "possibly" or "should." Very clearly and absolutely Jesus says certain people "cannot" be his disciples. There is no room for discussion, argument, or compromise on this issue. You can or you cannot be a disciple depending upon your paying the price of discipleship. Since some are unwilling to pay the price, it means exclusion from the Kingdom of God. There is no universalism here. Pay the price or else!

Contemplation

Insights

1. **Life's Most Important Decision.** To be or not to be a disciple of Jesus is life's most important decision. At infant baptisms sponsors make the decision for the baby. At confirmation the child, who has come of age, either confirms or rejects the decision. Since no greater decision can be made, the decision should not be based on an emotional feeling or impulse only. The feeling and enthusiasm may soon disappear and the person may later regret the decision. The decision for Christ should be based upon reasoned consideration and reflection of what it means to be a Christian and what it will cost. To provide this, many churches invite prospective members to a six-week or longer course in order for them to learn what it means to be a Christian, and what will be expected of them. As a result, they will enter the Christian faith with open eyes.

2. **Complete Commitment.** According to Jesus, no half-hearted or lukewarm person can be a disciple. It is a matter of all for Jesus or none for Jesus. Three times Jesus uses the word, "cannot," to express the call to total commitment to him. Jesus will not take second place in a disciple's life. The disciple must love Jesus more than family or self, must take up his cross, and must renounce everything. In the parables Jesus is saying that prospective disciples need to know this before making a decision to follow him. Is Jesus asking too much of us? Is it possible for a person to pay this high price?

3. **Less is better?** When Jesus sees a multitude following him to Jerusalem, he explains to them what it will cost to follow him. He is more interested in quality than quantity of followers. Gideon could defeat an army with 300 rather than with 20,000 troops. Jesus turned the world upside down with only twelve men who were fully dedicated and committed to him. Mainline protestant churches have become concerned about the loss of members and are engaged in a church growth emphasis. Should today's church be more concerned about spiritual rather than numerical growth?

4. **Look before you leap!** A wise person will learn what lies ahead in order to be prepared for what might come, and to have adequate resources for future demands. Sometimes a swimmer will dive into a strange body

of water without knowing its depth. The water turns out to be shallow and he suffers a broken neck and total paralysis. It is a part of wisdom to know what is coming and what is expected of us. When we foolishly obligate ourselves, we ask, "Why did I get myself into this?" or "If I had only known." Jesus applies this wisdom to discipleship: know what you are getting into and what will be required of you. Then you are in a position to know whether you want to follow him.

5. First things first. What or who comes first in our lives? Who or what is "number one"? In the twin parables Jesus teaches us that we should know in advance that he must come first in our lives. God the Father expects the same, for the First Commandment says, "You shall have no other gods before me." Jesus said, "Seek first the kingdom of God . . ." In today's Gospel lesson, Jesus also says, "Whoever of you does not renounce all . . ." Of faith, hope, and love, love is the greatest. Jesus must come first as Son of God, King of the Kingdom, and Shepherd of love. If Jesus comes first, then I will pattern my life after him, obey his commands, and follow his example of service and sacrifice.

Homily Hints

1. Is it too Hard to be a Christian? (14:25-33) This text is probably the most demanding of any passage in the Bible. In contrast the emphasis in many churches is upon how easy it is to be a Christian — "only believe," "just come forward," "you will be blessed." We have forgotten that Christianity is a tough religion. How hard is it to be a true Christian?
  A. One must love Jesus more than family — v. 26.
  B. One must love Jesus more than self — v. 26.
  C. One must love Jesus more than comfort — v. 27.
  D. One must love Jesus more than possessions — v. 33.

2. The Question of Discipleship. (14:25-33) Is there a difference between being a Christian and being a disciple? Are all Christians disciples? In this passage we learn the truths of discipleship.
  A. The call to discipleship — "If anyone comes to me" v. 26.
  B. The cost of discipleship — vv. 26, 27, 33.
  C. The crisis of discipleship — vv. 28-31.

3. Go for it! (14:25-33) We look at the terrific cost of discipleship. Shall we or shall we not pay it? Are we afraid we may fail? Is it asking too much of us? Shall we slip back to our old way of life or go for it by launching out into deep waters?
  Let's go for it —

A. Take the risk of an unfinished life — vv. 28-30.
B. Have courage to face possible failure — vv. 31-32.
C. Hope for the best — v. 32.

4. Twin Truths of Twin Parables. (14:28-32) In today's Gospel lesson we have two parables. Both are related to each other concerning the cost of discipleship. In these parables Jesus asks us to look ahead and see what is required of a Christian. Consider the twin truths —
    A. Have sufficient resources to attain your objective — vv. 28-30.
       1. Do I have what it takes to be a disciple?
    B. If you have insufficient resources, lower your objective — vv. 31-32.
       1. If I can't be chief, I can be a brave.

5. Can You Take what it Takes? (14:28-32) Before we can decide whether to pay the price, we need to know what the price is. One parable deals with building a house or tower, and the other deals with going to war. A Christian is involved in both and the Christian asks, "What does it take?"
    A. What does it take to build a life? — vv. 28-30.
       1. Faithfulness — the danger of not finishing.
    B. What does it take to fight a war? — vv. 31-32.
       1. Who are the enemies of a Christian?
       2. What are the prospects of winning the war?

Contact

Points of Contact

1. Quantity or Quality? Today's parables and Gospel context bring up the question of the church's present emphasis on numbers. In the last decade the mainline protestant churches have lost millions of members. To regain the loss the church is emphasizing "church growth" in terms of numbers. Critics have called it the "Numbers Game." This issue confronts the preacher: shall the emphasis be on numerical or spiritual growth? On his way to Jerusalem, Jesus saw the crowds following him. They thought they were on a victory march rather than on a death march. Accordingly, Jesus tells two parables to persuade them to consider what it will cost to be one of his followers: self-denial, a cross, and renunciation. On the one hand, numbers are important because numbers are souls. On the other hand, Jesus does not want nominal disciples, but fully dedicated and surrendered followers — quality more than quantity. Can we have quality as well as quantity? To have both is the challenge of a preacher.

2. Is Jesus asking too much? In these parables Jesus is asking the most from us who choose to be his disciples, and wants us to be aware of what he expects of us. Are we able? Do we have the necessary resources?

In order to attract new members, some preachers have been emphasizing how easy it is to be a Christian in contrast to Jesus' hard way to discipleship. Television evangelists especially promise listeners that faith in Jesus will bring them health, success, and material prosperity. All you have to do to be a Christian is to believe. Come to the front during the singing of the final hymn and shake the pastor's hand as a symbol of accepting Jesus. Is the church making it too easy to be a Christian? In some churches, to be an active member is to take Holy Communion at least once a year, or to make a contribution, no matter how small, to the church's budget. To get new members we say, "Join our church and have a place for your wedding, a preacher for your funeral, a free hall for your wedding reception, a club for youth, trips for senior citizens, and camps for your children. Compare our church with others: we offer better programs for all ages, better church school teachers, a choir for every age group, a lovelier sanctuary, and a dynamic preacher. Our church is worth passing many other churches on the way to ours. You will find a friendly and happy people."

With this approach, how many people would be attracted to today's parables, with their cost of discipleship in terms of denial, sacrifice, and renunciation? If people are not attracted to a tough religion, shall we preachers change the subject of the parables to something more comfortable?

3. Christian or Disciple? In a recent sermon, a preacher urged his people, who he said were ninety-nine percent Christians, to become disciples of Christ. Is there a difference? Can one be a Christian and not a disciple? Who is a disciple? Is he or she not one who accepts and follows Jesus as Lord and Savior? Who then is a Christian? Is the person not one who also believes in Jesus as Lord and Savior? To be a Christian is to be in Christ, and to be in Christ is to be in the church, for the church is the body of Christ. A person is accepted as a disciple at the time of baptism, and at the same time is engrafted into the church. Can one then ask Christians to be disciples? One is a Christian or is not a Christian. To be a Christian is to be a disciple. One denomination calls itself "The Church." In parentheses is an explanation: "The Disciples of Christ." This is true of every church: Christians are disciples of Christ.

4. Christ or Family? In today's pericope Jesus opens up a problem every married minister faces: Who comes first — family or Christ? In the passage, Jesus stresses that a disciple must "hate" the family in terms of placing the members of the family in second place. In a pastor's life, which of the two comes first? For a pastor to put Christ first is to put the church first. This can cause problems in the pastor's family. He or she is criticized for neglecting the family. Shall a pastor refuse to perform a wedding, conduct a funeral, teach a Confirmation class, go to the bedside of a dying member, neglect sermon preparation, or attend a church meeting because it interferes with the family's plans? Every married minister faces this problem: how to put Jesus first without neglecting wife and children. But, as to who should come first, Jesus is very clear about it. Unless you love Jesus more than any member of the family, you cannot be a disciple of his.

Illustrative Materials

1. Gospel of Thomas. In the Gospel of Thomas there is the Parable of the Assassin. Jesus said, "The Kingdom of the Father is like a man who wished to kill a powerful man. He drew the sword in his house and stuck it into the wall, in order to know whether his hand would carry through: then he slew the powerful man."

2. Counting the Cost. As a joke, friends locked a prospective groom into an iron cage. In front of it they placed a large sign, "Getting Married."

In a wedding service the couple is cautioned about possible trouble ahead: "And although by reason of sin, many a cross hath been laid thereon, nevertheless our gracious Father in heaven doth not forsake his children in an estate so holy and acceptable to him, but is ever present with his abundant blessing."

If Luther had only known! In a sermon he said, "I would rather be stretched upon a wheel or carry stones than preach one sermon. For anyone who is in this office will always be plagued; and therefore I have often said that the damned devil and not a good man should be a preacher. If I had known, I would not have let myself be drawn into it with twenty-four horses."

3. Death. In May 1987 an American warship, *Starke,* was attacked by an Iraqi plane in the Persian Gulf. Thirty-seven Americans were killed. When one enlists in the Navy, the price one may have to pay is death.

4. Martyrdom. Religious News Service reports that some 330,000 Christians each year are martyred for their faith around the world. One in every 200 Christian workers is being killed on the mission field. Archbishop Laud, a Puritan hero of England, was sentenced to die for his faith. As he stood on the scaffold, his last words were, "Lord, I am coming as fast as I can."

5. Jesus First. Once a farmer found a great swarm of bees in a near-by woods. He thought it would be good to have bees on his farm so that he could have honey. So he bought a hive and then caught a dozen bees and put them in the hive. The next day he caught twelve more. But fast as he caught them, they flew back to the woods. In desperation he asked a bee-keeper why his bees did not stay in his hive. He was told "the only way to move a swarm of bees to your place is to catch the queen bee. Catch her and all the bees will follow."

6. Able to pay the price? A few years ago a little band of handicapped climbers roped themselves together, ice axes in their hands, to climb to the top of Mount Ranier. Nine of them were blind, two were deaf, one an epileptic, and another an amputee. Nine of them reached the top and planted the flag on the summit. Later they met with President Reagan in the Rose Garden outside the White House.

7. Renunciation.

"I am no longer my own, but Thine. Put me to what Thou wilt, rank me with whom Thou wilt; put me to doing, put me to suffering; let me be employed for Thee or laid aside for Thee, let me be empty; let me have all things, let me have nothing; I freely and heartily yield all things to Thy pleasure and disposal."

— John Wesley.

8. Price of sin. Surgeon General C. Everett Koop estimates that by the year 2000, 100 million lives will have been lost through AIDS acquired through sexual intercourse and contaminated needles.

It costs American society $20,000 a year to keep an inmate in prison.

Unwed American mothers are costing the United States $17.8 billion to support 3.7 million families.

Proper 19   •   Pentecost 17   •   Ordinary Time 24
Common   Lutheran   Roman Catholic

---

14. Lost and Found

Luke 15:1-10

---

¹*Now the tax collectors and sinners were all drawing near to him.*
²*And the Pharisees and the scribes murmured, saying, "This man receives sinners and eats with them."*

³*So he told them this parable:* ⁴*"What man of you, having a hundred sheep, if he has lost one of them, does not leave the ninety-nine in the wilderness, and go after the one which is lost, until he finds it?* ⁵*And when he has found it, he lays it on his shoulders, rejoicing.* ⁶*And when he comes home, he calls together his friends and his neighbors, saying to them, 'Rejoice with me, for I have found my sheep which was lost.'* ⁷*Even so, I tell you, there will be more joy in heaven over one sinner who repents than over ninety-nine righteous persons who need no repentance.*

⁸*"Or what woman, having ten silver coins, if she loses one coin, does not light a lamp and sweep the house and seek diligently until she finds it?* ⁹*And when she has found it, she calls together her friends and neighbors, saying, 'Rejoice with me, for I have found the coin which I had lost.'* ¹⁰*Even so, I tell you, there is joy before the angels of God over one sinner who repents."*

At a convention of 420 parachutists held in Arizona in 1987, a group of four jumped from a plane at 9000 feet. Gregory Robertson noticed as they were falling that Debbie Williams was in trouble. She was tumbling like a rag doll, because she had slammed into the backpack of another chutist and been knocked unconscious. Robertson went to her rescue. He straightened into a vertical dart, arms pinned to his body, ankles crossed, head aimed at the ground, and dove toward Debbie at a speed of 200 miles per hour. Ten seconds before impact, at 3500 feet, Robertson caught up with Debbie, and with six seconds left, yanked the rip cord of her emergency chute and then pulled his own rip cord. Both drifted to earth. Debbie landed on her back with a skull fracture, nine broken ribs, and an injured kidney —

but alive! Never before in history had there been such a daring rescue of a life at 2000 feet.

In contrast, it may seem rather prosaic and uneventful when we hear today's parables of the lost sheep and coin. If we could save people from spiritual death, as Robertson so spectacularly and courageously saved a physical life, we would be doing what Jesus was teaching in the parables: seeking souls who are in danger of destruction. Would that we had the same determination and courage to save souls as Robertson had in saving Debbie from death! He risked his life to save her. Are we risking our lives to save souls from eternal death?

Context of the Lectionary

The First Lesson. (Hosea 4:1-3, 5:15 — 6:6) Yahweh calls his wicked people to return to him. Through Hosea Yahweh addresses Israel, the northern kingdom, in the eighth century. Because of their wickedness Yahweh has a controversy with Israel. He withdraws from his people. Sensing the absence of God, the people return to Yahweh, but it is a superficial religiosity rather than true religion. The call to return to God harmonizes with the parables of the lost sheep and coin which were sought, found, and returned to the owners.

The Second Lesson. (1 Timothy 1:12-17) Christ came to save sinners. This lesson is the first of seven selections from 1 and 2 Timothy. Paul thanks God for his mercy in Christ for forgiving, accepting, and calling him as an apostle after he had been a blasphemer and persecutor of God's people in the church. This lesson also harmonizes with the parables of the lost in the Gospel lesson, for Paul was lost and was found.

Gospel. (Luke 15:1-10) The lost are found. The lectionary returns us to Luke 15, a chapter of three parables dealing with the lost. On Lent 4 we considered the Parable of the Prodigal. Now we deal with a sheep and a coin. A man lost a sheep and a woman lost a coin. Both found what they had lost, and heaven joined them in rejoicing when the lost were recovered.

Psalm. (Psalm 77:11-20) In reviewing Yahweh's dealings with Israel, we see that he led his people like a flock of sheep. This concept of Yahweh as a good shepherd is in keeping with Lesson 1.

Prayer of the Day. In keeping with the theme of seeking and saving, we say in the prayer that God's mighty power is expressed chiefly in showing mercy.

Hymn of the Day. "Jesus Sinners will Receive." The hymn focuses upon the parable of the lost sheep with the refrain: "Jesus, sinners, will receive."

Note: It is significant that all three lessons are given in semi-in-course fashion. On this Sunday there is perfect unanimity on the theme of the Gospel's two parables: Lesson 1 — an appeal to return to the Lord; Lesson 2 — Christ died to save the lost; Gospel — the found sheep and coin; Psalm — The Lord leads his people like a shepherd; Prayer — God's power is in his mercy; Hymn — Jesus receives sinners.

Context

Context of Luke 15

Luke 15 begins a section (chapters 15-19) that deals with outcasts. The section contains a number of parables which demonstrate God's love for the despised and the condemned. The parables of God's love for the unfortunate are in contrast to the condemnatory attitude of the "righteous" people. These chapters illustrate Paul's statement that "God shows his love for us, in that, while we were yet sinners, Christ died for us." (Romans 5:8) The parables in Luke 15 indicate that God wills "sinners" to be gathered in the Kingdom. Jesus' attitude toward sinners is not motivated by humanitarianism, but is the evidence of the purpose of God. The love of God goes out to seek and save the lost.

Context of the Gospel

The setting for the parables: Jesus is criticized for fellow-shipping, talking, and even eating with "sinners." To justify and defend his practice, he tells the twin-parables of the lost sheep and coin. They can be considered as one because the principles are the same: lostness, recovery of the lost, and joy over the recovery. One deals with a man's loss and the other with a woman's loss. In both cases there was distress over the loss. Both searched and found the lost. One of the lost items was inanimate and the other was an animate creature. Both were the property of the owners. Both were of value to the owners. Jesus is justified in associating with the sinners because they were lost and are now found. He was rejoicing in their return to God.

Context of Related Scriptures

Isaiah 40:11 — God is a shepherd who gathers his sheep in his arms.
Ezekiel 34:11-16 — As Israel's shepherd Yahweh will seek the lost and bring back the strayed sheep.
Matthew 18:12-14 — Matthew tells the parable of the lost sheep in

relation to Jesus' teaching against despising little children. It is given in an ecclesiastical setting, reflecting a church problem at the time.

Mark 2:15-17 — Scribes object to Jesus' eating with sinners and tax collectors.

Luke 19:1-10 — Jesus seeks and saves Zaccheus.

John 10:1-18 — Jesus is the good shepherd who gives his life for the sheep.

James 5:20 — Bringing back a sinner saves a soul from death.

Content

Content of the Pericope

vv. 1-2 — Pharisees and scribes criticize Jesus for associating with sinners.

vv. 3-7 — Jesus' defense — Part I: the parable of the lost sheep.

vv. 8-10 — Jesus' defense — Part II: the parable of the lost coin.

Precis of the Parables

One day a large number of "sinners" including tax collectors came to hear Jesus teach. Among them were Pharisees and teachers of the law who criticized Jesus for associating with outcasts to the point of even eating with them. In his own defense Jesus tells them the following parables.

Suppose, he said, that one of you owns one-hundred sheep and one gets lost. What would he do? He leaves ninety-nine in the pasture and goes in search of the missing one until he finds it. Then with great joy he puts the sheep on his shoulders and carries it home. He calls his friends and neighbors to rejoice with him because he says, "I have found my sheep which was lost." In the same way heaven will rejoice over a sinner who repents over ninety-nine so-called "righteous" people who think they do not need to repent.

In like manner, suppose a woman who had ten silver coins should lose one. What does she do? She turns on the lights, sweeps the house, and searches diligently until she finds it. Then, like the shepherd, she calls in her friends and neighbors and says, "Rejoice with me, for I have found the coin I lost." In the same way, Jesus concluded, God's angels celebrate when one sinner repents.

Thesis: God rejoices when sinners repent.

Theme: When angels sing!

Key Words

1. "Sinners." (vv. 1, 2) "Sinners" came to hear Jesus. Does that mean everybody? Are not all people sinners? Jesus is criticized by religious leaders for associating with sinners to the point of eating with them. But who are the sinners? In Jesus' day, sinners were either those who were unethical or who were in certain occupations, such as tax collectors and prostitutes. That the "sinners" came to hear Jesus, indicates that these people had repented and sought the truth of God as Jesus proclaimed it.

2. "Lost." (vv. 4, 8) Jesus does not use the word "sinner" for those who disobey God's will. He refers to the sinners as "lost." What does it mean to be lost? Who is the lost person? According to the parable of the sheep, a person who is lost is one who strays from the fold. It is one who no longer is in the fellowship of God's people, the church, which is the society of the saved. To be lost is to be apart, estranged from God. According to the coin parable, a lost person is out of circulation. He is not in his appropriate place; he is misplaced. He is somewhere where he has no business being. One can ask a lost person, "What are you doing here? This is no place for a child of God." A lost person, then, is a sinner, for in the parable Jesus refers to the lost as a sinner: "There will be more joy in heaven over one sinner who repents . . ."

3. "One." (vv. 4, 7) What is "one" among so many? What is one compared with ninety-nine sheep, or one to ten coins? It depends on the evaluation we give to one. According to the parable, God rejoices over one repentant person more than over ninety-nine who do not need to repent. The one sheep and the one coin were worth the time and effort to search for them. The sheep was valuable to the shepherd, not only because it was his property, but because he loved his sheep. Love puts the highest price on a person. The one coin was precious to the woman who was probably a poor widow. The ten coins were her life's savings and she could not afford the loss of one-tenth of her assets. Need gives a person or article importance and value. The good news is that God loves us, one by one, enough to seek our return to him.

4. "Until." (vv. 4, 8) As the shepherd searched until he found the sheep, and the woman until she found the coin, God never gives up on us until he finds us lost souls. Here we see the persistent love of God for sinners. It was no easy task for the shepherd to find the lost sheep. Where should he look? In what direction should he go across the vast open terrain? Moreover, a lost sheep when scared lies down and refuses to stand up. The shepherd's call would be useless. Finding the sheep would mean literally stumbling on it, for it would be lying in the grass, probably unseen.

Likewise, it took persistence for the woman to find the coin. The house was dark; she had to light a lamp. The floor was a dirt floor covered with straw. The coin would be unseen under the straw or dust. She had to work to find it, gather up the straw and sweep. Years ago before mechanical refrigeration, ice was cut off frozen lakes and stored in ice houses, where sawdust was used on the floors. One day a worker lost his watch which fell into the sawdust and could not be seen. He waited for the noonday whistle to blow and the workers to leave for lunch. The place became silent. He put his ear to the floor and heard the tick-tick of his watch. At once he went to the place, brushed off the sawdust, and he found his watch. The woman in the parable had similar difficulty finding her coin in the straw and dirt of her floor.

5. "Shoulders." (v. 5) The shepherd finds his sheep scared, lonely, bewildered, helpless, and hopeless. The sheep is too tired and weak to follow the shepherd back home. In tenderness he lifts the sheep to his shoulders and carries it home. He places the sheep around his neck as though he were hugging it in an expression of affection. The shepherd not only hunts and hunts until he finds the lost one, but in love carries it back to the fold. Here we see a demonstration of God's love for the lost sinner.

6. "Together." (vv. 6, 9) Both the shepherd and the woman called together their friends and neighbors to rejoice with them because they had recovered the lost. Why did they not simply feel good inside themselves and be happy that the sheep and the coin were found? Good news and joy need to be enjoyed with others. One cannot have a party by oneself or celebrate in solitude. Joy is a cup that runs over. You want others to share in the joy. The happiness is so great that you cannot keep it confined within yourself.

7. "Repentance." (vv. 7, 10) Jesus teaches in these parables that God rejoices when one person repents. He rejoices because repentance means that the person has returned to God and to the fold. The person is back home with God. Repentance, therefore, is not a condition of salvation, but the result of salvation. God has searched and found the lost sinner and brought her back. Because of the return, God is happy. Is the happiest day of the church the day when people join the church by renouncing the devil and confessing Christ as Lord?

Contemplation

1. **Lost until found.** The lost are lost until they are found. The sheep did not find its way home. The coin did not cry out, "Here I am!" The lost cannot find their way home to God. They can think, wish, hope, weep,

170

and even pray, but they are helpless. Someone needs to find them. It is a terrible thing to be lost. Eventually it means desolation, destruction, and death. In view of the plight of the lost, there is an urgency about our seeking the lost as ambassadors of God.

2. Are you worth it? Is a sinner worth the time, trouble, and effort to seek him or her? The parables answer, "Yes." The sheep was of value to the shepherd as the coin was to the woman. One sheep was worth leaving ninety-nine to go in search of it. One coin was worth the cleaning and searching of the entire house by the woman. At another time, Jesus taught that one person is so important that God knows us each by name and even the number of hairs on our heads. We are God's property. He purchased us with the blood of Christ. We belong to him. This is what makes us precious, worth his searching for us. The parables say to us, "God wants you."

3. A seeking God. Biblical scholars claim that most of what Jesus taught can be found in the Old Testament, but one unique teaching was that God seeks, yearns, and searches for humanity. In the parables, the sheep does not seek the shepherd and the coin does not find the woman. The sheep and the coin do nothing and say nothing. All is done by God — "saved by grace alone." There is no confession of straying or of doing anything wrong. It is God who goes after the sinner, searches until he finds, carries the sheep home, and has a party to celebrate success. How does God do this today? If God does it all, why are not all people saved from their lostness? In the parables God worked through the shepherd and the woman. Today God continues to use people as his instruments to find the lost and to bring them into the fold, the church. It is through the witnessing and visiting of Christians that sinners are brought back to God. As Jesus said, "The harvest is plentiful but the laborers are few." (Matthew 9:37) Therefore, we need to pray that the Lord will send laborers to harvest souls.

4. Where are the lost? When anyone or anything is lost, we usually ask where the person, animal, or object could possibly be. We say, "Now where did I put my glasses?" or "What was the last thing I did?" or "Where was he the last time I saw him?" The twin parables tell us the two places where the lost can be found. The sheep was found in the "wilderness," in the wide open spaces of grazing land — out in the world. The lost are in the world. Millions of them are not connected with a church. They do not pray, read the Bible, or got to church — signs of being at home with God. The coin on the other hand, was lost in the woman's home. The strayed can be in the church. We call them our "inactive members." In the average congregation they comprise forty percent of the total membership. The lost are in our homes, in our families, and in our churches. The lost are both out and in the church. For this reason evangelism is at the center of the church's work and mission: if we care about the lost, we will be constantly about the business of finding and re-finding lost people.

5. God never gives up. In each case, neither the shepherd nor the woman stopped looking for the lost until he or she had found it. They represent God's continual and persistent efforts to call sinners to repent. God never gives up on us no matter who we are, what we have done, how many times we have failed him, or how often we have broken our promises. Through the centuries he has appealed through prophets and priests, kings and peasants to call us home to him. His last and greatest effort to find us was the sending and sacrificing of his Son for us. Through Jesus, God is ever saying to humanity, "Come and I will give you abundant life."

Homily Hints

1. Our Seeking God. (15:3-10) It is not we who seek God but God who seeks us. This insight is the unique contribution Jesus made to our understanding of God. In the parables the shepherd and the woman are active seekers; the lost are entirely passive. They teach us that we do not find God, but that God finds us. God is the Hound of Heaven who pursues us through the ages and through our lives until we surrender and are found by him. Why does he seek us?
A. Because he knows we are lost — "lost" — vv. 4, 6, 8.
B. Because he wants us — "goes after" — v. 4.
C. Because he thinks we are worth saving — "go after the one" — v. 4.
D. Because he loves us — "lays it on his shoulders" — v. 5.

2. What Must You do to be Lost? (15:3-10) The question we usually ask is "What must we do to be saved?" But the saved are always prospects for being or becoming lost. The lost sheep was one of one-hundred; the coin was one of ten. Reports tell us that within five years of joining, fifty percent of the new members leave the church or become inactive. They come in by the front door and slip out the back door. Mainline protestant churches are concerned about the wholesale loss of members. Why do the "found" get lost again?
A. Because like the sheep they stray from the flock — v. 4.
1. They stop coming to church.
B. Because like the coin they are misplaced by carlessness — v. 8.
1. Lost because of the sins of others.

3. You Can't Win Them All? (15:4-10) When we fail, a friend tries to console us by saying, "You can't win them all." In the world that is often the case. In the Christian sense, we can win them all. In a worldly sense, why bother to find one sheep when you have ninety-nine, or why fret about one lost coin when you have nine others? In the parables, the one is important enough to leave the ninety-nine to go for the one-hundredth sheep. Each person is so valuable and important that each one must be found for God.

Yes, you can win them all —

A. If you search for the missing one — vv. 4, 8.
B. If you care enough to search — the shoulders of love — v. 5.
C. If you persist in your search — "until" — vv. 4, 8.

4. Our Wonderful God. (15:4-10) The parables tell us how wonderful God is to all, especially to sinners. The hero in the parables is not the sheep or the coin but God in the person of the shepherd and the woman. As sinners who have grieved and offended God, as sheep that have gone astray, we deserve nothing but exclusion and death. Here is a story of amazing grace.

A. God thinks sinners are worth saving — "one" — vv. 4, 8.
B. God never gives up on sinners — "until" — vv. 4, 8.
C. God carries sinners back with love — "shoulders" — v. 5.
D. God rejoices that sinners are re-united with himself — "Rejoice" — vv. 6, 9.

5. How to Make God Happy! (15:4-10) During Passion Weeks we think of the sorrow of God because of the cross — his Son was a man of sorrows. When we disobey God, we think of his wrath — he is angry with us. By our rejection of the Spirit, we grieve and offend God. When do we make God happy? In the parables Jesus tells us that God and the angels sing for joy when sinners repent. How then can we make God happy?

A. When we ourselves repent by confessing sin and asking pardon.
B. When we bring others to repentance through evangelism and missions.

Contact

Points of Contact

1. To whom are we preaching? Visualize your Sunday morning congregation. Who are they? The lost or the saved, the hunters or the hunted? Do you identify them with the ninety-nine faithful sheep, with the ninety-nine who need no repentance? Or, are they represented by the lost sheep and coin? Are they the ones that need to be found? Or, maybe you think of them as the shepherd and the woman who do the searching. Could the congregation be a mixture of all three? Who you think they are will determine the objective of your sermon. Do they need saving? Are they lost souls?

Are they smug in their self-righteousness needing no repentance? Do they need to be motivated to seek new members for the church?

2. Outsiders or insiders? It appears as though these twin parables of the lost sheep and coin deal only with people inside the fold, the church. The sheep was one of the one-hundred; the coin was one of the ten. They belonged to their owners, the shepherd and the woman. When the sheep and coin were found, the membership did not increase — it remained one-hundred or ten. There is a question, then, in fairness to the text, whether these parables should be used for evangelism and missions to win non-Christians to faith in Christ. The parables deal with the straying of the sheep, the leaving of the fold. Today we call them our inactive members or "dead wood" of the church. They no longer come to church or contribute toward her work. The church then becomes a field for evangelism.

But, shall we limit these parables to the inactive members? There are millions of people outside the church in need of being brought under the leadership and protection of the Great Shepherd. We have every reason to seek the lost outside the church rolls. As Christians we follow the example of Jesus who said he came to seek and to save the lost. (Luke 19:10) Jesus did this because his Father sent him to save the world. In like manner this is the Christian's mission, for Jesus said, "As the Father has sent me, even so send I you." (John 20:21) In this case, members of the congregation are under-shepherds who go out to the wilderness to search for lost souls.

3. One or two? In today's Gospel lesson, we again have two parables. Shall a preacher deal with the one or the other or both? A study of the two shows that the truths and principles they teach are the same: lostness, searching, finding, joy. The differences are non-essential: man or woman, animate or inanimate losses. The repetition of the parable emphasizes the importance of the truths portrayed. Thus, it seems practical and wise to consider both parables as the text for the sermon.

Points to Ponder

1. Can we fall from grace? These two parables bring up this controversial subject. Can a Christian fall from grace? In the parables the sheep and coin belong to the shepherd and woman. Through searching they are recovered to their original situation. It would seem that the answer would be: "Yes, you can fall from grace and be lost."

On the other hand, the sheep and coin, though lost, still belonged to the shepherd and the woman. The sheep and coin were never disowned. Therefore, they did not fall from *grace* but from *faith*. The sheep was a lost sheep of the shepherd. The coin, though lost, was still the property of the woman. One, then, can be a lost child of God when faith is lost. But we can never fall from grace because God is forever faithful. He never casts out or disowns any of his children regardless of their disobedience.

2. Leave the Ninety-nine? A disturbing question arises from the parable of the lost sheep. It says that the shepherd "leaves" the ninety-nine to go in search of the lost one. Does this imply that the shepherd neglected the ninety-nine and left them unprotected for the sake of one? If so, it does not make sense. Some have suggested that he left the ninety-nine in the care of fellow-shepherds until he returned.

This question arises sometimes within a congregation. The regular members feel neglected because their pastor calls upon prospective members. He or she spends time calling, instructing, and preparing prospects for membership. Of course, this problem exists only in those churches where the pastor places evangelism at the head of the priority list.

3. Are they lost? Fundamental to doing something about these parables is whether we, clergy or laity, are really convinced that people not in Christ and not in the church are lost souls. If people live respectable and responsible lives, are they not as well off as church members? What if we decide they are lost? What does it mean to be lost? According to Scripture, lost souls are separated from God. To be apart from Christ is the same as being a branch cut off from the vine. Its destiny is misery, suffering, and death. The end of death is eternal hell. Do we believe this? If so, do we care whether the lost are found for Christ? If we care enough, we will search until we find the lost soul.

Illustrative Materials

1. Lost Without Knowing It. Daniel Boone was wandering in the wilderness. While trying to find his way, he was asked, "Are you lost?" "No," replied Boone, "but I've been mighty bewildered for three days!"

2. Value of the Lost. How much is a coin worth? In the market of 1987, an ounce of gold cost between $400 and $450; an ounce of platinum, $350 to $700; an ounce of silver, $5 to $10.

3. Lost Soul Wanted? One day a rabbi's son came in from a game of hide-and-seek with tears streaming down his face. His father asked him what was wrong. The son explained that he had hidden himself but that no one had come to find him. The rabbi embraced his son tenderly and said that perhaps now the boy could understand how God felt.

4. Who Wants Garbage? The town of Islip, Long Island, had a barge of 3200 tons of garbage and shipped it south. Six states and three countries refused to take it. Finally the garbage was returned.

5. Who Wants a Sinner? Larry Singleton raped a teenager and then cut off her forearms, and threw her in a ditch to die. He served eight years of a fourteen-year sentence. In April, 1987, he was paroled, but no town in California would have him. One town after the other forced the Corrections Department to move him.

6. Prone to Lose. Americans are prone to lose things as well as souls. Norman Cousins tells us that the cash lost each year in America amounts to about seventy-five dollars per capita. For most people in the world, the total average income is sixty-nine dollars per person. Americans lose more money each year than almost anyone else earns.

7. Keeping Saved. How can we keep from getting lost? A teacher took her fifth grade class to see the sights of Manhattan. Since she was not taking any assistant leaders with her to handle this group of youngsters in the crowded streets, some parents were not sure they wanted their children to go. When they returned, one mother asked her son how their one teacher was able to handle all the children and not lose one in the traffic and crowded sidewalks. She wanted to know how they were able to get across busy streets without anyone getting hurt. At that age he was not very talkative, but he explained, "All she told us was 'Keep hold of the rope.' " The teacher had had a long rope and asked each pupil to hold it as they went from place to place. The church is the rope, and as long as we hold on to the rope in fellowship with fellow-Christians, we will keep from getting lost.

8. Counting the sheep. Dr. William Hinson, pastor of First Methodist Church, Houston, Texas, took sixty-four teenagers to Europe. He was concerned that all of them return home safe. As he stood at the London airport boarding gate, he counted the kids. There were sixty-three — one was missing. He began to run here and there, calling in restrooms, running, calling, looking, calling. Suddenly he saw the sixty-fourth — a sixteen-year-old girl casually buying candy and a movie magazine. He grabbed her hand and they raced to the gate. The attendant was closing the plane's door as they squeezed in. The girl was saved by the count. In the parable, the shepherd counted his sheep up to ninety-nine and then he realized his one-hundredth sheep was missing.

Proper 20 • Pentecost 18 • Ordinary Time 25

Common   Lutheran   Roman Catholic

---

15. The Clever Crook

Luke 16:1-13

---

¹*He also said to the disciples, "There was a rich man who had a steward, and charges were brought to him that this man was wasting his goods.* ²*And he called him and said to him, 'What is this that I hear about you? Turn in the account of your stewardship, for you no longer can be steward.'* ³*And the steward said to himself, 'What shall I do, since my master is taking the stewardship away from me? I am not strong enough to dig, and I am ashamed to beg.* ⁴*I have decided what to do, so that people may receive me into their houses when I am put out of the stewardship.'* ⁵*So, summoning his master's debtors one by one, he said to the first, 'How much do you owe my master?'* ⁶*He said, 'A hundred measures of oil.' And he said to him, 'Take your bill, and sit down quickly and write fifty.'* ⁷*Then he said to another, 'And how much do you owe?' He said, 'A hundred measures of wheat.' He said to him, 'Take your bill, and write eighty.'* ⁸*The master commended the dishonest steward for his prudence; for the sons of this world are wiser in their own generation than the sons of light.* ⁹*And I tell you, make friends for yourselves by means of unrighteous mammon, so that when it fails they may receive you into the eternal habitations.*

¹⁰*"He who is faithful in a very little is faithful also in much; and he who is dishonest in a very little is dishonest also in much.* ¹¹*If then you have not been faithful in the unrighteous mammon, who will entrust to you the true riches?* ¹²*And if you have not been faithful in that which is another's, who will give you that which is your own?* ¹³*No servant can serve two masters; for either he will hate the one and love the other, or he will be devoted to the one and despise the other. You cannot serve God and mammon."*

It was not only sex (allegations of adultery, wife-swapping, prostitution, homosexuality, and bisexuality) that brought down Jim and Tammy Bakker's PTL Television evangelism program in the spring of 1987, but also money and greed. Between 1984 and 87 the Bakkers received $4.8 million. In addition to living in a million dollar mansion on Lake Wylie, South Carolina, the Bakkers had two homes each costing $600,000, a mountain chalet in Gatlinburg, and two cars — a Mercedes and a Rolls Royce. As separation pay the Bakkers requested $300,000 per year for life for Jim and $100,000 for Tammy, the lakeside mansion in South Carolina, two cars, and a security staff. As leaders of PTL, they had begged their 13,000,000 listening families on a network of 161 TV stations for money, supposedly for charitable causes, but for what actually turned out to be their own financial well-being. So great was their greed that the PTL went into bankruptcy with debts totalling $70 million. As a result of this, his church said, "You can no longer be steward."

This greed on the part of religious leaders is nothing new. The very next verse following today's parable (16:14) tells us that the overhearing Pharisees "were lovers of money." In the sixteenth century the Roman Church was so greedy for money that salvation was sold through the indulgence traffic. Is there an explanation for this greed then and now? It is based upon the false gospel of prosperity. In Deuteronomy 28, Yahweh promises prosperity to those who keep the Law. Wealth is an indication of God's favor. The Bakkers preached and practiced that God wants his people to have the best and the most of this world's goods — mammon. It is a part of today's popular heresy: the gospel of success, health, and prosperity.

It is natural and normal for Christians to be concerned about the material side of life. We are physical creatures living in a materialistic world. We must have bread to live. We do have to pay the rent or the mortgage. Food costs money. Clothes are expensive. We need money to raise and educate our children. We must put aside funds for retirement. The material concerns are a very vital and essential part of our lives. The Bible recognizes this fact. The New Testament says more about money than about any other subject. One-third of Jesus' parables deal with money. As Luke 15 is known as the "lost" chapter, Luke 16 is the "money" chapter. In this chapter we have two parables, this and next Sunday's, concerned about material possessions. Thus, for two Sundays we will be considering the use and sharing of our money. Today's parable tells us about a clever crook who used money to provide for his future. He was commended not for being a crook but for being a clever one.

Context

Context of the Lectionary

The First Lesson. (Hosea 11:1-11) In spite of Israel's wickedness, Yahweh cannot give up his people. Yahweh has loved his people, Israel, since Israel was a child. He, like a dear mother, taught the child to walk, and took him in his arms of tender compassion. In spite of this, Israel turned to other gods. For this the judgment of conquest by Assyria came to Israel. However, Yahweh cannot give up his people, and promises to restore the captives to their homes.

The Second Lesson. (1 Timothy 2:1-7) Christians are to pray for all people. Paul urges the church to pray for all people, including the government, so that people may live in peace. God would have us do this because he, the only God, wants all to be saved by faith in Christ. To this end Paul was appointed as a preacher and an apostle.

Gospel. (Luke 16:1-13) The parable of the dishonest steward. Jesus uses a scoundrel to teach a lesson on the proper use of material possessions.

Psalm. (Psalm 107:1-9) In harmony with Lesson 1, the Psalmist calls upon us to thank God for his steadfast love shown in his deliverance from distress.

Prayer of the Day. We ask God to set us to our tasks in Kingdom work.

Hymn of the Day. "Father Eternal, Ruler of Creation." The message of the hymn is in the refrain: "Your kingdom come, O Lord; your will be done."

Context of Luke 16

As Luke 15 is known as the "lost" chapter, Luke 16 may be called the "money" chapter, because Jesus deals with the use and sharing of material possessions. In the first thirteen verses Jesus tells a parable about a shrewd manager who used material arrangements to protect his future well-being. This is followed by Jesus' saying that no one can serve God and money. The Pharisees who loved money laughed at Jesus' teaching on wordly possessions. After a brief statement on the law and divorce (vv. 16-18), Jesus tells another parable about a rich man and a beggar. (vv. 19-31) This latter parable is assigned to next Sunday — Lazarus and Dives. For two Sundays then, we will have the material side of life on our minds: the use and misuse of wealth.

Context of the Gospel Lesson

After telling the story of the prodigal son, Jesus turns to his Disciples and tells them, within the hearing of the Pharisees, a parable about a dishonest steward. After the parable Jesus urges faithfulness in the use of finances, and warns his men that they cannot serve two masters, God and money. God and mammon are rival gods and no one can serve both at the same time.

Context of Related Scriptures

> Matthew 6:24-34 — Do not worry about material needs.
> Luke 12:16-21 — Gaining the world to lose a soul.
> Luke 12:57-59 — Use of practical wisdom to settle a dispute outside court.
> Luke 18:18-23 — A rich ruler prefers money to discipleship.
> Romans 14:12 — We are accountable to God.
> 1 Timothy 6:6-10 — The root of all evils.

Content

Content of the Pericope

There is a division of opinion concerning the length of the parable. Some scholars think the parable ends with verse 7 others with verse 8a, and another group would take it through verse 9. It makes a difference where the parable ends because it affects the interpretation. If it ends with verse 7, Jesus and not the owner of the estate commends the rascal. If it ends with verse 8a, the owner does the commending. If it ends with verse 9, Jesus explains the point of the parable. This diversity of opinion lends to two possible outlines:

Outline A —
> 16:1a — Jesus addresses the Disciples.
> 16:1b-8a — Parable of the dishonest manager.
> 16:8b-12 — Interpretation of the parable.
> 16:3 — Conclusion of the interpretation.

Outline B —
> 16:1a — The setting of the parable.
> 16:1b-7 — The parable.
> 16:8-10 — Jesus comments on the parable.
> 16:11-13 — Applications of the parable.

Precis of the Parable

Jesus told this parable to his Disciples. A wealthy man had a manager of his estate. It was reported to him that his manager was wasting his property. So he called on his manager and asked, "What is this I hear about your wasting my goods? You will please give an account of your dealings and submit your final report, for you can no longer be my manager." So the manager said to himself, "I am about to be fired. What in the world shall I do? Since I had a desk job for years, I am not physically able to do manual labor such as digging ditches. And I am too proud to beg. I know what I'll do. I will make friends who will feel obligated to take me into their homes." So he called in all who owed money to the owner. He asked one, "How much do you owe?" He replied, "One-hundred barrels of olive oil." "Well, quickly change the bill to fifty." He asked another how much he owed. He answered, "A thousand bushels of wheat." "Then change that to 800." The manager was commended for his shrewdness because people of the world are more clever than the people of light.

Jesus went on to say that we should make friends with our money so that when the money no longer counts, we may be welcomed into an eternal home. If we are faithful in small amounts, we will also be faithful with large sums. If we are faithful in worldly wealth, we will be faithful with spiritual wealth. If we are not faithful with the assets of other people, we will not be faithful with our own. Above all, be faithful to God, for no one can serve both God and money. To love one is to hate the other.

Thesis: The main point of the parable depends upon your choice of the purpose of the parable. According to Jesus' original purpose, the parable deals with the facing of a crisis, because Jesus was facing a crisis at the time. Another view is based upon Luke's application of the parable to the early church — the proper and wise use of wealth.

Since the chapter deals with "mammon" and Jesus' comments following the parable deal with the proper use of money, it seems that the thesis of the parable would deal with finances: the proper use of money.

Theme: Money — master of servant?

Key Words

1. "Steward." (v. 1) The word "steward" is not commonly used in conversational language. It may call for explanation. A steward is one who is employed to manage a household or an estate. The parable tells us that the owner was a rich man who apparently employed another man to run his farm. Today we probably understand a steward in terms of a manager, overseer, or superintendent. A steward is not the owner, only the one responsible for the welfare of the property and/or business. God made humankind the stewards of the earth, but we act as though we own it.

2. "Account." (v. 2) The rich corner owner called for an accounting of the manager's stewardship. "Bring in your account books, sales, and purchases, profit and loss. Let me see what you have done." This accounting is in order because, when anyone is given a responsibility to manage, the owner has the right to receive an accounting. The immediate call for the accounting was the report of mismanagement. Because we have been given responsibility, God is holding us accountable. He will ask, "What have you done with your life? What use did you make of your talents?" In Romans 14:12, Paul writes, "So each of us shall give account of himself to God."

3. "Master." (v. 8) The Greek word is *kyrios*, meaning "lord." There is a question as to whether "lord" or "master" applies here to the employer or to Jesus. On the one hand, "master" may refer to the owner of the estate. Accordingly, the rich man commends his manager for his shrewdness in getting his friends to take care of him during his unemployment. But, why would a man commend an employee who not only wasted his goods but by clever deception stole from him? Some conjecture that the steward did not steal from him, but reduced the debts by foregoing his own interest on the them. If this view is taken, the parable continues through verse 8a.

On the other hand, "master" or "lord" may refer to Jesus. This view is supported by the fact that in the same sentence Jesus states that the sons of the world are more shrewd than the sons of light. In addition, Jesus continues his remarks dealing with possessions and the right use of them. According to this position, the parable ends with verse 7. Since there is no certain answer, the preacher must make a choice.

4. "Shrewd." (v. 8) In the parable this is a super-key word. The manager is commended for his prudence, or shrewdness. Jesus calls upon his Disciples to match the shrewdness of non-Christians. What does it mean to be shrewd? Shrewdness is a practical, realistic, hardheaded cleverness and good sense. It calls for wisdom, and creative imagination in finding a solution to a problem. It is adequately illustrated in the parable: the manager is very clever by making the debtors obligated to care for him by reducing their debts, without the owner's or the debtors' knowing what his scheme was. In the end the owner admires his cleverness, the debtors are happy, and he is taken care of. It was a pretty good trick!

5. "Unrighteous mammon." (v. 9) "Mammon" is an Aramaic word for wealth. Mammon was an oriental deity synonymous with wealth. It is a word dealing with money and material possessions.

"Unrighteous mammon" does not refer to possessions or wealth as being inherently evil. As Paul said, it is the love of money that is the root of evil. Unrighteous mammon is dirty money. The main objection to mammon is that it is God's chief rival; money is a popular god. It is, some say, what makes the world go round, the answer to all human problems, the source of happiness. Money is unrighteous when it displaces God from first place in our lives.

6. "Eternal habitations." (v. 9) As the manager used money to be taken into the homes of debtors, Jesus is saying that by making friends with money, we will have a home in heaven some day. This may suggest that by giving we may earn a place in heaven. If so, we would fall into the trap of works righteousness. If we use our money to feed the hungry, clothe the naked, and endow institutions and movements that improve the human condition, we will make friends with God who will welcome us to our eternal home. This harmonizes with Jesus' statement, "Inasmuch as you have done it unto the least of these my brethren, you have done it unto me."

Contemplation

Insights

1. You are accountable. The rich owner in the parable called upon his manager to give an account of his stewardship. When the steward was employed, he was given the responsibility and authority to manage the estate in place of the owner. Whenever we are given a responsibility, we are obligated to give an account. God is the owner of all. He has made us what we are and all we have came from him. God is going to ask us for an accounting. What have we done with our lives, talents, and possessions? Because the manager wasted his goods, he was asked to submit a report. Because we may be wasting God's resources, he is going to ask us to give an account to him.

2. Face the facts. Though he was a despicable crook, the manager had some good points. One of them was his ability to face the facts of his situation. When he was told he had lost his position, he did not pity himself or blame his predicament on others. He did not try to flee from the problem, and he did not fight the decision. He faced the fact that he was fired. He knew he was too physically weak to do manual labor. He realized that he was too proud to beg. Then he put his mind to work and decided upon a solution to his problem.

3. A lesson from the world. The manager was shrewd — bright, intelligent, imaginative, crafty, and clever. It was this quality that earned him commendation. Jesus pointed out that people of the world were smarter than people of God. Business people are clever and expert in promoting their business, but often these same people on church boards forget to apply that expertise to church work. If church people would put the same study, intelligence, and energy into the church as they do into their sports, professions, and businesses, the Kingdom of God would soon cover the earth, resulting in peace and justice.

4. Money with a good purpose. Money can be a blessing. It can clothe the naked and feed the hungry. It can provide a home for the homeless sleeping on city streets. Money can be used to make friends. The manager in the parable used money for this purpose. The only fly in the ointment was that the money was not his. Nevertheless, the principle is still good and, used for constructive purposes, it can be a blessing. In the parable Jesus urges us to use money that we might make friends with God, who will receive us into his eternal home. God is pleased and glorified when we use money to help the needy, and to extend and support his church. We hope to hear him say some day, "Well done, thou good and faithful servant."

5. Where we part company. In this parable Jesus exhorts us to follow the example of the world in being wise, shrewd and clever in doing the work of the Kingdom. We are to be like the world and emulate the children of darkness. But only to a point! We can be crafty but not crooked. We cannot use dishonest means to gain a worthy goal. The end does not justify the means. In no way does Jesus approve of the manager's dishonesty, but he admires how clever he was in providing for his future.

Homily Hints

1. Making the Best of a Bad Situation. (16:1-7) Life has its crises and none can escape them. It may be the loss of a job, financial bankruptcy, divorce, or bereavement. The steward in the parable faced a crisis: "You can no longer be steward." What can one do in a crisis situation? The manager gives us a model —

    A. Face the reality of the situation — "You can no longer be steward" — v. 2.
    B. Be shrewd in working out a plan — "I have decided what to do" — v. 4.
    C. Put the plan into operation — "Sit down quickly and write" — v. 6.

2. What to do with Your Money. (16:1-13) Because many do not know what is the best thing to do with their money for protection and growth, they turn to financial advisors and planners. Let the parable be our financial guide in determining what to do with our money —

A. Provide for the future — v. 4.
B. Be honest — vv. 1, 5.
C. Make friends — vv. 4, 9.
D. Be faithful — vv. 10-13.

3. Personal Questions. (16:1-7) The dishonest steward had some hard questions to face and to ask. The questions led to serious consequences. When certain questions that may incriminate us are asked, we may take the Fifth Amendment and refuse to answer. In the parable there are questions we may have to face —
A. "What is this that I hear about you?" — v. 2.
1. An accusatory question for a guilty one.
B. "What shall I do?" — v. 3.
1. A desperate question for one in a jam.
C. "How much do you owe?" — v. 7.
1. A life-saving question involving a solution.

4. Some Good in the Worst of Us. (16:1-9) The clever crook in the parable was as unethical as one may be. He was guilty of wasting his owner's property. He was dishonest and a liar. He not only wasted his employer's resources but cheated him out of money owed him. He was deceptive and insincere in dealing with debtors, his base motivation for doing good to save his own hide. In spite of this and even more, Jesus commended him, or at least the owner did, for his shrewdness. In the worst of us, there can be found some good. One can say even the devil has a good point — he is not lazy!
The good we can see in bad people —
A. The steward faced the facts of life — v. 3.
B. The steward was smart to find a solution — v. 4.
C. The steward provided for his future — vv. 4, 9.

Contact

Point of Contact

In preaching on the subject of money or material possessions, we are dealing with a top subject or problem for most people. For many, money is not "a" but "the" top subject. It deals with earning a living, or an occupation, or a profession. For those with insufficient funds, money is of utmost concern for paying the bills or debts. For those with savings, money presents the problem of how best to invest it. For this and next Sunday the parables deal with "mammon" — the use and sharing of money. For many money is a sore subject and they do not want it mentioned in the pulpit.

For this reason, some preachers never bring up the subject in sermons. Nevertheless, money is a universal need and problem to the point that it can be our real god. Since Jesus did not avoid the subject, neither should the pulpit.

Points to Ponder

   1. **Shall I preach on this parable?** It is considered the most difficult of all Jesus' parables. There are conflicting interpretations. People may get the impression that we are approving unethical behavior. Why risk it? The easy way out is to choose a text from the other two lessons. Would that be a cop-out? If Jesus told it, there must be a worthwhile truth in it that merits a sermon.

   2. **Could we be preaching works-righteousness?** In his comments on the parable Jesus says we should make friends with our money that we may be received into "eternal habitations," or heaven. Who are "they" (v. 9) — people or God? If God, then it would seem that, by our funds, we gain God's favor to get into heaven. Therefore, we must be on guard that we do not give this impression. We preach the gospel of justification by grace alone through faith alone. Our charitable gifts, indeed, please God but they do not save us.

   3. **How can we avoid dishonesty?** We need to make clear and to emphasize that Jesus is not approving stealth nor deception but sagacity, shrewdness, and cleverness. He is calling upon us to be as smart as the world in the use of our money. The challenge we preachers have is to keep separate the virtue and the evil in this parable. It would have been better if Jesus had had the manager use an honorable method of gaining friends for his future care. At least, it would have made it easier for preachers!

Illustrative Materials

   1. **Making Provision for the Future.** Sigmund Freud told about a sailor who was ship-wrecked on a South Sea island. He was seized by the natives and treated as a king. That was very pleasing until he learned that it was their custom to make one man a king for a year and then banish him to a desert island where he would starve to death. The sailor determined that he would outwit the islanders. As king, he commanded the gardeners to transplant trees to the barren island and start crops growing so that, when his term of kingship was over, the island to which he was to be banished would not be barren but fruitful.

2. Good in the Bad. A few years ago a clergy person was on his way to Riverside Church in New York to worship. A man with a gun came up to him and demanded his wallet. The thief explained, "I do not do this for a living. I am out of work and desperate for money to live. You have a job and I don't." He took the money and handed back the wallet. The thief left but soon returned and asked, "Do you have any change?" The parson reached in his pocket for some quarters, but the robber gave him back two of his dollars so that he would have money to get home.

3. Making the Best of a Bad Situation. In a chapel at Staton Hall, England, there is an inscription telling about a man in 1653, a year of turmoil, who did his best:

> "When all things sacred throughout the nation either demolished or profane, Sir Robert Shirley Baronet founded this church whose singular praise it is to have done the best things in the worst times and hoped them in the most calamitous."

A man was wedged between two hungry tigers. Pursued by tiger A, he was chased over a cliff and hung precariously on a vine dangling from the side of a hill. Glancing below he saw tiger B. Above his hands two mice gnawed steadily on the vine. His eyes discovered a clump of strawberries. With one hand he picked the fruit, eating and exclaiming, "How delicious!"

4. Two Masters. In northern Ireland a man stood in the middle of a narrow piece of wood that spanned a small, rushing stream. Feeling his precarious bridge giving way beneath him, he exclaimed to the open skies, "God is good, but the Devil isn't bad either!"

5. Waste Not.

> Food: The United States Accounting Office estimates that annual food waste is valued at $31 billion. That is enough to feed 49 million people.
> Suicides: Each year in America almost 6000 teen-agers commit suicide and two million try it and fail.
> Smoking: Cigarette smoking is responsible for the deaths of 350,000 Americans each year.
> Alcohol: 98,186 people die annually from excessive alcohol consumption.

6. Materialism. In 1923 a group of the world's most successful men met at the Edgewater Beach Hotel in Chicago. Assembled were the president of the largest steel corporation, the greatest wheat speculator, a man who was to be president of the New York Stock Exchange, a member of the President's cabinet, the canniest investor on Wall Street, a future director of the World Bank for International Settlements, and the head of the world's largest monopoly. A few years later their experiences were: Charles Schwab died in debt. Richard Whitney became insolvent. Albert Fall was pardoned from prison in order that he might die at home. Jesse Livermore, Leon Fraser, and Ivan Krueger committed suicide. All learned how to make money. None of them learned how to live. All the bulls became lambs.

7. Dishonest Cleverness. At a certain corporation valuable things were missing. A security firm was hired to search every employee as he left at the end of the day. The workers did not seem to mind having their lunch boxes opened. But one man every day went through with a wheelbarrow full of trash. The guard checked the garbage, but found nothing worth stealing. Finally the guard asked, "I know you are up to something. I never find anything worthwhile. It is driving me crazy. What is the meaning of all this? I promise not to report you." The man shrugged and said, "It's simple. I'm stealing wheelbarrows."

Proper 21 • Pentecost 19 • Ordinary Time 26
Common   Lutheran   Roman Catholic

---

16. Rich Man, Poor Man

Luke 16:19-31

---

[19]*There was a rich man, who was clothed in purple and fine linen and who feasted sumptuously every day.* [20]*And at his gate lay a poor man named Lazarus, full of sores,* [21]*who desired to be fed with what fell from the rich man's table; moreover the dogs came and licked his sores.* [22]*The poor man died and was carried by the angels to Abraham's bosom. The rich man also died and was buried;* [23]*and in Hades, being in torment, he lifted up his eyes, and saw Abraham far off and Lazarus in his bosom.* [24]*And he called out, 'Father Abraham, have mercy upon me, and send Lazarus to dip the end of his finger in water and cool my tongue; for I am in anguish in this flame.'* [25]*But Abraham said, 'Son, remember that you in your lifetime received your good things, and Lazarus in like manner evil things; but now he is comforted here, and you are in anguish.* [26]*And besides all this, between us and you a great chasm has been fixed, in order that those who would pass from here to you may not be able, and none may cross from there to us.'* [27]*And he said, 'Then I beg you, father, to send him to my father's house,* [28]*for I have five brothers, so that he may warn them, lest they also come into this place of torment.'* [29]*But Abraham said, 'They have Moses and the prophets; let them hear them.'* [30]*And he said, 'No, father Abraham; but if some one goes to them from the dead, they will repent.'* [31]*He said to him, 'If they do not hear Moses and the prophets, neither will they be convinced if some one should rise from the dead.' "*

What parable would make a man with three doctoral degrees (medicine, philosophy, theology) leave civilization with its culture, education, and comforts for a primeval forest in Africa? Upon reflection on this parable, he gave up his Bach organ concerts, his writing on theological books, and his medical practice to go to darkest Africa, to minister physically and spiritually to the poor and illiterate black natives of its darkest depths. This man was Albert Schweitzer, named the greatest man of the Twentieth century. Upon pondering the Parable of Lazarus and Dives, he decided he should go to Africa to help the Lazaruses of that continent. Apparently he saw himself as Dives and felt a responsibility to help the most helpless. As we begin to prepare a sermon on this parable, we know what power it has to move people to care for and to share with the needy at home and abroad.

In this parable we have three worlds. One is the world of Dives, the world of the rich. Another is Lazarus' world — that of the poor, hungry, and dispossessed. Both worlds face a final world, the world after life on earth. Can these two worlds be brought together? Can they be reconciled? The parable tells us what happens to these two worlds in the coming final world.

Context

Context of Luke 16

Today we continue with the "money chapter," Luke 16. Last Sunday we considered the Parable of the Unjust Steward who used dishonest methods of providing for his future well-being. It was a case of the wrong use of money — a clever but wrong use. Now we consider the second parable in Luke 16, dealing with the need to share our physical resources with the less fortunate in our society, the poor. It is not a story of the rich becoming richer nor the poor becoming poorer, but a story of how a rich man became poor and a poor man became rich. In the former parable we had a case of the wrong use of money. Now we see a case of the non-use of money, a failure to relieve human need, and the eternal consequences thereof.

Context of the Lectionary

The First Lesson. (Joel 2:23-30) Yahweh promises to send material and spiritual blessings to his people. This lection is the second in a series of nine lessons from the Minor Prophets: Hosea to Malachi. In relation to today's Parable of Lazarus and Dives, we see that God provides sufficiently for all of our physical needs so that no one needs to go hungry as Lazarus did. God also provides his Spirit which will motivate us to share our affluence with the needy.

The Second Lesson. (1 Timothy 6:6-19) True riches are spiritual. Although this pericope is the third in a series of seven selections from 1 and 2 Timothy, it is appropriate for the Parable of Lazarus and Dives. In this lesson Paul warns Timothy that the love of money is the root of all evils and urges him to command the rich in his congregation to generously share their wealth with the poor.

Gospel. (Luke 16:19-31) Lazarus and Dives. A helplessly poor beggar and a "filthy" rich man have their conditions reversed in the next world, so that the beggar now receives the riches of heaven and the "rich" man faces the poverty of hell. The question then arises of how people can escape the fate of Dives.

Psalm. (Psalm 107:33-43) The Psalm reinforces the message of Lesson 1 — Yahweh blesses his people with an abundant harvest because of his constant love.

Prayer of the Day. We pray that God will give us grace to overcome our frailties and our failings. Among our failings is the refusal to share our wealth with the needy.

Hymn of the Day: "Oh, Praise the Lord, my soul." Praise the Lord, for "the hungry he supplies with bread."

A review of the Lessons and Propers shows a unanimity regarding the sharing of our resources with the poor:
1. Out of his love God abundantly provides us with physical and spiritual resources. (Lesson 1, Psalm, and Hymn)
2. They who have should share with those who have not. (Lesson 2, Prayer)
3. The eternal consequence of not sharing. (Gospel)

Context of Related Scriptures

Psalm 106:15 — Fatness of body but leanness of soul.
Deuteronomy 8:11-20 — Affluence tends to make people forget God.
Mark 8:11-12 — No sign nor miracle will be given to create faith.
Mark 12:18-27 — The Sadducees deny the resurrection of the dead.
John 11:1-44 — Lazarus returned from the dead.
2 Corinthians 8:8-15 — Jesus became poor to make us rich.
James 2:14-17 — The poor need more than words.
1 John 3:17-18 — To love God is to share.

Content

Content of the Pericope

16:19-21 — Lazarus and Dives on earth.
16:22-26 — Lazarus and Dives after death.
16:27-31 — Epilogue: Dives' concern for his brothers.

Some New Testament scholars are of the opinion that verses 27-31 were not included in the original parable. They claim this section was added by the early church as a response to the fact that Jesus' resurrection did not cause people to become Christians. Faith in Christ was not to be based on the miracle of the resurrection but on the Word, the Law, and the prophets. However, the epilogue can be considered an authentic part of the parable, because it is all of one piece. When Dives learns that there is no hope for his getting out of hell, it is a natural response for him to be concerned about his brothers and the possibility of their experiencing the same fate.

Precis of the Parable

There was once a rich man, Dives, who lived in a palace, wore expensive clothing, and daily ate gourmet meals. At the same time there lived a poor man, Lazarus. He was carried to the rich man's gates to beg. His body was covered with sores which stray dogs licked because he was too weak to chase them away. He was only too glad to eat the cast-off food from the rich man's table. In due time Lazarus died and angels carried him to heaven, where he was with Abraham and God's faithful people. The rich man also died but went to hell, where he was tormented. He looked up to heaven and saw Abraham and Lazarus. He begged Abraham to send Lazarus to cool his tongue with a drop of water, for he was burning up with the heat. But, Abraham reminded Dives that, on earth, Lazarus had suffered while Dives had lived in comfort. Now the situation was reversed. Furthermore, Abraham explained that he could not send Lazarus even if he wanted to because a great canyon, which no one could cross, separated heaven and hell. Then, Dives begged Abraham to send Lazarus to warn his five brothers lest they come to the same fate. But Abraham said, "They have Moses and the prophets; let them hear them." Dives protested that this was not enough. If someone from the dead would go, they would repent. Abraham assured him that, if they did not hear the Law and the prophets, they would not be convinced by one from the dead.

Thesis: Compassion through sharing.

The parable is not primarily intended to deal with the furniture in heaven or hell, nor proof of life after death, nor who goes to heaven and hell. Some, like Jeremiah, do not consider Lazarus to be the main character, but rather the five brothers of Lazarus. The thrust of the parable then would deal with the need for hearing Moses and the prophets rather than depending on a miracle as a stimulus to repentance. In the light of the context of this chapter's concern with "mammon," the parable deals with sharing one's wealth with the poor out of compassion. The concern for the brothers is a natural result of the knowledge that hell has no exit and of the experience of hell's misery.

Theme: The peril of plenty, or, the poverty of affluence.

Key Words

1. **"Rich man."** (v. 19) Jesus did not give his name but the church calls him "Dives." The *Latin Vulgate* translated "rich man" as "Dives," and he has been known as such ever since. According to the parable he was a wealthy person. This was evident in his expensive clothing, daily feasting, and his palatial home, for Lazarus had chosen the gates of his estate as a good place to beg for alms. Probably Dives was a Sadducee, because Sadducees were aristocrats, wealthy, and unbelievers in life after death. Dives was a "good" man who was a respected citizen. His only fault was his failure to share his wealth with the needy such as Lazarus.

2. **"Poor man."** (v. 20) In all of the parables this "poor man" is the only one given a name: "Lazarus." In Hebrew the name is "Eleazer" meaning "God is my help." He was properly named, because he received no help from any human, only from God. He was the poorest of the poor. He was so poor that he had to beg for food and was glad to get the garbage from the rich man's mansion. He was so physically weak that he could not stand to beg; he lay at the gates of the palace. He was sick, for his body was covered with sores which stray dogs licked because he did not have the strength to chase them off. Lazarus was a helpless, hungry, and dispossessed person living in poverty, illness, and deprivation.

3. **"What fell."** (v. 21) In the *King James Version*, the word is "crumbs;" in the *Good News Bible* it is "bits of food." The *New English Bible* calls it "scraps." In Jesus' day wealthy diners used pieces of bread to wipe their mouths and hands as we use napkins. Then the bread was discarded as garbage. Since Lazarus was lying outside at the gates, he could not have been inside to grasp the discarded pieces of bread. When the garbage was discarded, he probably was brought the scraps of bread which he was glad to eat. In today's world, it would be the same as our poor searching garbage cans and dumpsters for food.

4. **"Hades."** (v. 23) The Greek word for "Hades" is *aidns*. In Hebrew it is *Sheol*. The *King James Bible* translates it as "hell." In the Bible Hades is the abode, place, or world of the dead awaiting judgment. After judgment the dead go either to heaven (paradise) or hell *(Gehenna)*. In the parable, Hades includes both paradise and hell. Lazarus goes to heaven where

Abraham is, and Dives falls to hell where he is in torment of the fire associated with hell. Lazarus had hell on earth and now Dives has hell after death.

5. "Father Abraham." (v. 24) Abraham was considered the father of the Hebrews who made the original covenant with Yahweh. He is pictured in the parable as the leader of those in heaven. Dives prays to Abraham for mercy and begs him to send relief through Lazarus. Why, one may ask, did Dives pray to Abraham rather than to God? Does this indicate that, to Dives, Abraham was his god, or that Dives had no belief in God? This reminds us that the parable is not to be taken literally or allegorically. The parable is a story with a central message: give to the poor out of compassion, not out of fear of hell. Of course, we pray to God and not to Abraham.

6. "Chasm." (v. 26) Even if Abraham had wanted to relieve Dives' suffering, there was no way for one to go from heaven to hell. A great "chasm" or canyon divided the two, and no one could bridge the gap. Of course, today we might say we could fly over it. Did we not cross the chasm between earth and the moon? The significance of the chasm is that, after death, there is no repentance, no chance to get to heaven. Where we shall spend eternity is decided here and now on earth.

7. "Beg." (v. 27) We have here a change of beggars. Lazarus begged for food at Dives' palatial gates. Now Dives begs for water to cool his tongue, and for someone to go to his brothers to warn them of hell. To beg is to do more than make a simple request. To beg is to appeal and to beseech. It denotes intensity of desire and desperation. The need is critical. Life is at stake. Luther reminded us that all of us are beggars — beggars for the Bread of Life, for truth, for God's acceptance.

8. "Repent." (v. 30) The *Good News Bible* translates "repent" as "turn from their sins." Dives wants Lazarus to go to his brothers that they might not also come to hell. This corrects the impression one gets at first from the parable: that the rich go to hell and the poor automatically go to heaven. Entrance to heaven or hell depends upon faith and repentance. Dives is here confessing that he and his brothers did not have faith in a life after death, and accordingly had no concern for the poor. Since he now knows there is a hell for unbelievers and the wicked, he wants his brothers to "turn from the sins" of unconcern for the poor. Entrance to heaven depends upon a person's true repentance.

9. "Hear." (vv. 29, 31) Dives' request that Abraham send Lazarus to warn his brothers was refused. Abraham told him it was enough for them

194

to hear Moses and the prophets. But Dives insisted that only one coming from the dead would convince them to repent. Again Abraham assures Dives that not even one from the dead could cause them to repent. It depends upon their hearing Moses and the prophets. Of course, "Moses and the prophets" consisted of the Bible in Jesus' day. Today we would say, "Law and Gospel." The key to salvation is not in a spectacular miracle, such as a resurrection, but in the humble, ordinary proclamation of truth and grace as recorded in the Scriptures. Salvation is in the hearing of the Good News, and hearing involves accepting and obeying. This emphasizes the primacy of the Scriptures and the indispensability of proclaiming the truth of the Bible.

Contemplation

Insights

1. A missed opportunity. Wealth is no guarantee of righteousness; and poverty is no guarantee of wickedness. A rich person is not doomed to hell. A poor person does not automatically go to heaven. A poor person can be an unbeliever and can live immorally. A rich person can be a devout and faithful follower of God. Jesus had both rich and poor men as disciples. Salvation is more than the the lack of possession of worldly goods. Being rich is not a crime but an opportunity. In the parable Dives missed his opportunity.

2. The day of decision. The parable teaches us that where we will spend eternity is decided while we are on earth. We choose life or death here and now. There is no repentance after death. We cannot get a transfer from hell to heaven. A great gulf wider than the Grand Canyon separates the two and no one can cross over. To make a decision for Christ now becomes an urgent and serious matter.

3. Almost perfect. Dives was an almost perfect person. The parable leads us to believe he was a good man — a faithful spouse, a just father, a good citizen, a religious man devoted to the synagogue. His Achilles heel was his failure to share his money with a poor, hungry man. Apparently, this one thing caused him to land in hell. What price stinginess! Behind his stinginess was his lack of compassion for the poor. Behind his lack of compassion was his unbelief in a future life.

4. A symptom of spiritual deficiency. Dives did not share because he did not care that Lazarus was poor, hungry, and diseased. Why did he not care? As a Sadducee, he did not believe there was a life after death. If death ended all, there was no judgment and no hell. Death wiped out everything. He could say, "Eat, drink, and be merry, for tomorrow we die." Why then should he care about the impoverished and suffering? While it lasted, life was to be enjoyed. When Dives learned that hell was a reality and there was no escape, he became concerned for his five brothers, for they, like him, were without faith and concern. He was anxious to have Lazarus to go to them with the facts, so that they could repent and believe.

5. The saving Word. What can cause people to repent, to turn from their hard-hearted ways and become helpers of needy humanity? The epilogue of the parable reveals that hearing the Word, Moses, and the prophets, is the only way people will come to repentance, be persuaded to change their ways, and go from stinginess to generosity. No miracle or sign will convince sinners to change. In spite of Jesus' return from the dead, presently two-thirds of the world's population do not believe. The Word has the power to convince and to transform. Social action will not change people. A change of environment will not make people good. Goodness comes from the heart, and only the Word can change it. For this to happen, people need to hear the Word. Teaching and preaching the Word therefore is the primary task of the church.

Homily Hints

1. What it Takes to Help. (16:19-31) In this parable we are not given an example of one who alleviated the problem of hunger and poverty. What must we have or do to be a part of the solution?
   A. Care — Dives had no compassion for Lazarus.
   B. Share — Dives failed to share his food with Lazarus.
   C. Dare — Dare to give, to help.
   D. Compare — the condition of Dives and Lazarus in Hades.

2. The Solution to Poverty. (16:19-31) What a claim to make! A solution to poverty! The world is divided into the haves and have-nots. Some live in luxury. Millions are homeless, hungry, and helpless. What can be done about it?
   A. God has provided plenty for everybody.
   B. Millions are deprived of food and housing.
   C. The solution is distribution — sharing.

3. Which are You? (16:19-31) In the parable we have three characters. With which, if any, do you identify?
   A. Are you another Dives?
   B. Are you a poor Lazarus?
   C. Are you one of the brothers in need of repentance?

4. The Poverty of Affluence. (16:19-31) Dives was a poor rich man. He seemed to have everything, but in the end he had nothing. Affluence can make us poor. Consider the poor wealthy Dives.

    A. He, though rich, was poor in compassion — No compassion.

    B. He was bereft of life eternal — No paradise.

    C. He was anxious about his brothers — No peace of mind.

5. Facts of Life after Life. (16:19-31) Though the parable is not primarily concerned about the facts of existence when life on earth is ended, it does give us important facts.

    A. Heaven and hell are real.

    B. We shall know each other.

    C. There is no repentance after death.

    D. Selfishness leads to hell.

6. The Peril of Plenty. (16:19-31) To have too much is as bad as having too little. There is peril in plenty. This is demonstrated by Dives. Consider the peril of plenty —

    A. We have a false sense of security.

    B. We neglect the Lazaruses of life.

    C. We forget God.

    D. We end up in hell.

Contact

Points of Contact

1. Today's world of Lazarus: hunger, poverty, disease, illiteracy. In today's world many share the economic plight of Lazarus in the parable. Seven-hundred and thirty million people are hungry and long for the scraps from the rich people's tables. Forty thousand children die daily from malnutrition. One billion people (twenty percent of the world population) are destitute and lack the necessities of life. In America people are also poor and hungry. In 1984 33.7 million lived under the poverty line of $10,989 per year. Two million are homeless. It has been called "a national disgrace."

2. Today's world of Dives: affluence, wealth, luxury. Twenty percent of the world's population has seventy-one percent of the world's production. Another twenty percent has only two percent of the production. For instance, in Gautemala ninety percent of the land is owned by five percent of the population.

In America ten percent of the people own seventy-two percent of the stocks. One percent possess thirty-five percent of America's wealth. Twenty percent receive fourty-one percent of the national income. With six percent of the world's population the United States uses thirty-three percent of the world's energy.

A sample of wealth: When Imelda Marcos fled with her husband from the Philippines, she left behind 1060 pairs of shoes, fifteen mink coats, 507 gowns, sixty-five parasols. The Marcos wealth is estimated at $5 billion.

3. Today's lack of sharing. Like Dives, today's rich do not share adequately with the less fortunate. The rich get richer and the poor get poorer. The poor in America grew from twenty-five million in 1978 to thirty-four million in 1984, while those with an annual income of $35,000 or more increased from twenty-nine to thirty-four percent.

People have been allowed to starve while food was being sold for profit. In the 1800s Ireland had a famine because of a potato blight. Two million starved to death while enough corn and cattle to feed the whole of Ireland was shipped across the Irish Sea as rent due to English landlords. Likewise, under Stalin in 1932 and 1933 at least five million people in the Ukraine starved to death while Russia exported a half million tons of grain.

Productivity does not mean availability. America is presently overburdened with farm surpluses. In 1987 the United States had surplus milk. Outside Kansas City, huge caves contain enough cheese and milk to feed every person in the United States for two years. Likewise, excess grain is getting to be a burden on the nation. The blessing of the 1986 harvest has turned into a curse. The United States does not know where to store the grain or where to get the money to pay for the storage. Farm supports are costing the American taxpayers twenty-four billion dollars annually.

4. Life after death? As a Sadducee, Dives did not believe in immortality. This affected his concern for the beggar at his gates. Are there people today who share Dives' position?

In 1986 *The Reader's Digest* reported a Gallup poll involving 1500 American adults. The poll revealed:

70% believe in a life after death.

67% believe they are going to heaven.

53% believe in hell.

Points to Ponder

Before the preparation of a sermon on this parable begins, we need to ponder several dangers in preaching on the subject.

1. The danger of glorifying the poor. Lazarus is the hero of the parable. As a poor, suffering man, he goes directly to heaven. There is a tendency to say, "Blessed are the poor." We can feel sorry for the poor and be help-ful to the poor, but it would be a mistake to idolize or romanticize the poor. People in poverty are not necessarily saints. They need repentance and faith as much as do the rich.

2. There is danger of condemning the rich. Dives can rightfully be con-demned for his insensitivity to the needs of Lazarus, and for not sharing his affluence. As we tend to make saints out of the poor, we may make devils out of the rich. It is not sinful to have possessions. Rich people can be honorable, honest, and helpful. One bad case of Dives should not make us condemn all wealthy people.

3. The danger of proclaiming works-righteousness. Lazarus gets to heaven because he suffered physical privation. Dives went to hell for his lack of compassion. It is therefore easy for a preacher to leave the impres-sion that what we give or do not give determines where we will spend eter-nity. The whole plan of salvation is not given in one parable. This parable simply teaches that we who are able should help others in need. Not to do so has eternal consequences. Both rich and poor are saved by grace alone through faith. Dives did not share because he lacked faith in life after death.

4. There is danger of literalism. The parable tells a story with figurative language. It would be a mistake to take the passage literally in its descrip-tion of heaven and hell. Behind the figurative language certain truths stand out: the reality of heaven and hell, the impossibility of repentance after death, the nature of heaven as fellowship with God's people, and hell as the ab-sence of God.

Illustrative Materials

1. Dare to Give. At a certain revival a rich man was called upon to give his testimony. He said: "When I was a boy, I earned a fifty-cent piece for cutting a lawn. That night I went to the revival service. When the offering was taken, I questioned whether I should put the fifty-cent piece in the plate. I decided to give it. Since then God has blessed me with wealth and I be-lieve it was because, when I was a boy, I gave him all I had." When he returned to his seat, a little grey-haired lady touched him on the shoulder and whispered, "I dare you to do it again!"

2. Together in Death. In the mountains not far from Madrid, a huge mausoleum was built into one of the mountains. A half million tons of granite were removed for it. On top of the mountain a 500 foot high cross was erected. It was built as a memorial to those who fought in the Spanish

Civil War. Fifty thousand from both sides of the conflict are buried there. In war they were far apart as enemies. In death they are together. According to today's parable the dead in Hades are not together. Dives and Lazarus were separated by a great gulf. One was in heaven and the other was in hell. On earth the dead may lie side by side in the same mausoleum, but in the world after death people are divided into heaven and hell.

3. Christ the Giver.

"Jesus left his purse to Judas Iscariot, his body to Joseph of Arimathea, his mother to John, his clothes to the soldiers, his peace to the Disciples, his Supper to his followers, his self as an example and servant, his gospel to the world, his presence to God's people."

— Unknown author.

4. Abundance is Not Enough. Before taking his life, a youth wrote to Helmut Thielicke:

"You are the only one whom I am telling what I intend to do. You can tell my parents. They will be thunderstruck. They never knew me, despite all their care of me. They think I am a real sonnyboy when I fall with gusto into my favorite food which my mother prepares so lovingly. They think they have fed me, but I am starved. They made a home for me, but I was cold and homeless."

5. Lack of Concern. Lilly Tomlin, the commedienne, once surprised her audience by suddenly, in the middle of a routine, collapsing on stage. She literally fell over. After several moments of silence, still lying flat on her back, she whimsically accused her audience, "I noticed none of you got up to see if anything was wrong." Then with a cynical twist, she commented, "Remember, we're in this — alone!"

6. Selfish Giving. In a midwestern university there was an experiment on students' sharing and giving. Each student was to bring a dime. To what would they give it? One possibility was to give it for the famine in India where people were starving. Another possibility was to give it to the hungry in a ghetto where there was need for groceries. The third possibility was to give it to the University which was in need of a copier. Eighty percent of the money was given for the copier.

7. America as Dives. With six percent of the world's population, we consume forty percent of the resources of the world. At the present rate

of use, many metals, petroleum reserves, and gas will be exhausted within the next one-hundred years. We spend six times as much on tobacco as we give away in aid for hunger. The amount of grain needed to produce the whiskey consumed in the country would feed twenty million people. We produce three billion pounds of canned pet food to feed ninety million pets. We spend $400 million a year on chewing gum. The average American consumes 500 pounds of grain and one-hundred pounds of sugar each year.

8. Giving as Opportunity. When we were building a new church on Peachtree Street in Atlanta, we had barely enough funds to pay for the building itself. We depended upon memorials for the stained glass windows and chancel furnishings. There was not a dollar available for an organ. Hearing about our need, a non-member asked me to meet her in the safe deposit room of a large downtown bank. She took out of her deposit box securities worth $40,000 and gave them to me to purchase an organ as a memorial to her mother, who was a member of my denomination. As a young pastor I was flabbergasted. I had never seen so much money and I was overwhelmed with gratitude. With stammering feeble words I tried to tell her how grateful the congregation was for this very generous gift. I will never forget her reply: "Thank you for the opportunity."

Proper 22   •   Pentecost 20   •   Ordinary Time 27

Common   Lutheran   Roman Catholic

---

17. A Decent Obsession

Luke 17:5-10

---

⁵*The apostles said to the Lord, "Increase our faith!"* ⁶*And the Lord said, "If you had faith as a grain of mustard seed, you could say to this sycamine tree, 'Be rooted up, and be planted in the sea,' and it would obey you.*

⁷*"Will any one of you, who has a servant plowing or keeping sheep, say to him when he has come in from the field, 'Come at once and sit down at table'?* ⁸*Will he not rather say to him, 'Prepare supper for me, and gird yourself and serve me, till I eat and drink; and afterward you shall eat and drink'?* ⁹*Does he thank the servant because he did what was commanded?* ¹⁰*So you also, when you have done all that is commanded you, say, 'We are unworthy servants; we have only done what was our duty.' "*

A few years ago a best-selling novel by Colleen McCullough was entitled *Indecent Obsession*. It was the story of a nurse in Australia with a sense of duty to care for veterans of World War II. Even when she fell in love and had her one chance to fulfill her dream of being a wife, mother, and homemaker, she declined the invitation to marry because she felt that she had a duty to care for the afflicted. McCullough called it an "indecent obsession."

In the parable of the master and servant Jesus would call duty a "decent obsession." It is decent because of who we are, who God is, and what our relationship is to him. He is God, our Master, who owns us. We are his slaves because with the blood of Jesus he bought us. Because of this relationship, we are duty-bound to serve him for no other reason, such as thanks.

At a time when rights are demanded and duties are forgotten, today's parable cries out for attention and proclamation. It supplies a needed truth for our times.

Context

Context of Luke 17

Luke 17 consists of a number of assorted sayings by Jesus. Luke gathers a number of left-over sayings which are not integrally related to each other. The parable of the farmer and his slave does not come directly out of the context.

    17:1-4 — The sin of causing others to sin.
    17:5-6 — Faith the size of a mustard seed.
    17:7-10 — The parable.
    17:11-19 — The healing of ten lepers.
    17:20-37 — Signs of the Kingdom's coming.

Context of the Lectionary

The First Lesson. (Amos 5:6-7, 10-15) Do good and live; do evil and perish. Amos pleads with Israel to return to Yahweh that the people may live. If the people remain in their sinning, they are doomed. In relation to today's parable, Amos is saying that the people are not doing their duty by disobeying God's laws. If the nation would repent by doing their duty of obedience, they would be forgiven and given life.

The Second Lesson. (2 Timothy 1:1-14) Paul gives encouragement to his spiritual son, Timothy. With this lesson, we begin a series of four selections from 2 Timothy. As his spiritual father, Paul reminds Timothy of his "duties" as a minister: to keep alive the Spirit given to him at his ordination, to suffer for the Gospel, and to hold fast to the truth as Paul proclaimed it. In relation to today's parable in the Gospel, one might say that here we are reminded of the duties of a Gospel minister.

Gospel. (Luke 17:5-10) The Apostles ask Jesus to increase their faith, and Jesus teaches them that they have a duty to serve God. In the Gospel lesson is Jesus' parable concerning a master and his slave.

Psalm. (Psalm 101) Harmonizing with Amos' call for righteous living in Lesson 1, the king in the Psalm promises not to tolerate evil people, but to approve only the godly.

Prayer of the Day. Our prayer is for forgiveness because we have been trying to judge over God. In relation to the parable, we confess that we have been acting like the master rather than like the slave.

Hymn of the Day. "O Jesus, I have Promised" In this hymn we acknowledge Jesus as "my master and my friend" and promise to "serve you to the end." In relation to the parable, we admit that we are slaves of the Master and that our duty is to serve him.

Bringing it all together. When we look at the Lessons and Propers in relation to the Gospel's parable, we are given our duties to God in terms of right living. (First Lesson, Psalm). In the Second Lesson, we have the duties of a minister of the Gospel. In the Prayer and Hymn we acknowledge that we are slaves and are duty-bound to serve Christ.

Context of Related Scriptures.

> Job 1:6-9 — Does Job serve God for nothing?
> Matthew 25:26-30 — A worthless servant.
> Luke 12:35-37 — In this case servants are served.
> John 13:3-5 — As servant Jesus waits on his Disciples.
> John 15:15-16 — Friends and not servants.
> 1 Corinthians 9:15-18 — Paul had a duty to preach.

Content

Content of the Pericope

The pericope contains two unrelated subjects. Prior to the parable, Jesus hears the Disciples' request to increase their faith. Without a transition the parable follows.

> 17:5-6 — The Apostles request an increase in faith.
> 17:7-9 — The parable of a farmer and his slave. The parable consists of three questions. (An illustration of Jesus' indirect method of teaching.)
>   1. "Will any one of you . . . ?"
>   2. "Will he not rather say . . . ?"
>   3. "Does he thank . . . ?"
> 17:10 — Jesus applies the lesson of the parable to the Disciples.

Precis of the Parable

Would anyone of you with a slave working in your fields say to him when he comes from the field at the end of the day, "Come, sit down, and have your dinner?" Rather would he not say to the slave, "Prepare the evening meal, put on your apron, and serve dinner. After I have eaten and drunk, then you can have your supper." Does the master thank the servant for obeying his orders? It is the same with you. When you have done all that is commanded, say, "We are merely slaves; we have only done our duty."

Thesis: Our duty is to serve God.

In and through the parable Jesus teaches that we do not keep books on God. We do not keep account of our services that we can claim merit. God is not obligated to us because we serve him. We are his slaves obeying his commands. As slave, it is our duty to obey. Our very best deserves no credit, praise, or thanks, because we are only doing what we are supposed to do. Thanks for doing our duty is not in order. We are to thank God but God never thanks us for serving him.

Theme: A time to thank and a time not to thank!

Key words

1. **"Servant."** (v. 7) The Greek word used here is *doulos* meaning slave, or bondservant. The person is not a servant employed by the farmer but is a slave. He was bought by the farmer. The slave is his property and is obligated to obey his master's orders. Saint Paul refers to himself as a slave of Jesus Christ. We are bought with the price of Christ's blood.

2. **"Sit down."** (v. 7) Here is a touch of humor! Can you imagine a master preparing a meal for a slave and asking him at the end of a hard day's work in the field to sit down and eat the dinner he had prepared? It would be so ridiculous that the hearers of the parable would have had a good laugh. For doing our duty of obeying the Master's commands, God does not provide a festival dinner of appreciation!

3. **"Till."** (v. 8) The master appears to be a slave-driver. It seems cruel of the master. After all, the slave worked hard all day plowing or tending the sheep. He is dead tired. The farmer commands the exhausted slave to get busy, prepare and serve a meal for him. Then the slave may have his meal. So, who comes first? The answer is in the positions and roles of the persons involved. A master is the master. He is above his slave. He is first and must come first. A slave comes second, if not last, in line. Likewise, God is first, for we are his slaves. Thus, the first point of the Decalogue commands us to put God first.

4. **Thank."** (v. 9) Does or should the master thank the slave for obeying orders? The implied answer is "No." An army officer does not thank a private for obeying his orders. That is expected of him. That is his

responsibility. As slaves of God, we do not deserve thanks for serving and obeying him. Thanks are in order only when someone gives or does something for us without any obligation to do so. If something is done or given out of duty, there is no reason to give thanks.

5. "Commanded." (v. 9, 10) Who has the right to command? It is the one who is our superior and one who has the authority to command. A master has the right to command a slave. God has the authority to command his slaves. A command is to be obeyed. It is the duty of a subordinate to obey. The master does not thank the slave for obedience. He is not doing the master a favor for which he could expect thanks. What does our Master command us? Jesus ordered us to love one another, to help the needy, and to make disciples of all nations. Do we expect to be thanked for our obedience?

6. "Unworthy." (v. 10) Jesus teaches here that after we have done all we are commanded to do, we are not to expect thanks, but to say that as unworthy servants we did our duty. "Unworthy" does not mean worthless, as the servant in the Parable of the Talents was when he failed to make use of his one talent. "Unworthy" means that we are only servants, nothing more, and that as servants we simply did our duty when we obeyed. In humility we know who we are — slaves of Christ.

7. "Duty." (v. 10) Because of who and whose we are, we have certain duties. A citizen has the duty to serve his or her country. A spouse has the duty to be faithful. It is the duty of children to honor their parents. It is the duty of slaves to obey their masters. "Duty" in our time is an unpopular word. The "in" word is rights — civil, human, minority, and political rights. But, for every right there is a corresponding duty.

Contemplation

Insights

1. The rationale for duty. What constitutes "duty"? Why does one have duties? Duty is the result of a relationship. Because of a relationship with government, one has a duty to fellow citizens. Because of a relationship to a family, one has a duty to the other members of the family. If we have a relationship with God, we have a duty to worship, serve, and obey him. God is our Master; Christ is our Lord. He is that because we voluntarily accepted him as Lord. We surrendered all to him. We pledged our allegiance to him as Master. In turn, we have a duty to him, for we are his slaves.

He bought us. We are his and belong to him. Consequently, we are duty-bound to obey his commands.

2. Duty deserves no reward. When we have obeyed the commands, when we have done what is rightfully expected of us, when we have done our duty, do we deserve or expect a reward or thanks? Jesus urged his men to say, "We are only servants and we have done our duty by obeying your commands." For doing our duty, we have no right to expect God to thank us for it. God is not obligated to us for the service rendered. We dare not expect God to reward us with plenty, success, health, or good fortune. We are not to expect God to prepare a dinner of appreciation for our doing what we should do.

3. When giving thanks is out of order. Can we say thanks too often? If and when we express gratitude for someone's doing his or her duty, the giving of thanks is out of order. To express thanks is proper when a person is not obligated to give a gift or do a favor. Jesus says we are not to say "thank you" when a slave fulfills orders. Does a captain thank a private for obeying his orders? Is a father thanked for providing for the family? A mother for nursing, caring for, and training her child? Is a child thanked for minding his or her parents? No, because these are duties to be performed without thought of reward or gratitude. By doing our duty we are not doing anyone a favor, and therefore we deserve no thanks.

4. The fulfillment of duty. A duty is to be performed whether we wish to perform it or not, whether we like it or not. It is something we must or ought to do. It is a matter of conscience whether or not we fulfill our duties. We may have a duty to perform, which we do not like and would rather not do. A soldier may be given the duty to inform parents that their son was killed in action. A judge sometimes has a duty according to law to sentence a person to death. Because duties may be unpleasant and difficult, we may try to dodge the doing of our duties. We want privileges but not responsibilities. We march and cry for rights, but who says anything about our duties?

Homily Hints

1. Don't Thank Me! (17:7-10) If I have rendered service, if I have obeyed my superior's commands, don't thank me, because —
    A. Who is God? God is my Master.
    B. Who am I? I am a slave of my Master.
    C. What am I to do? Do my duty by obeying my Master.

2. Can One Thank Too Much? (17:9-10) Obedience to God does not obligate God to thank or bless the doer. ~~In human relations we do not~~ thank people who have done their duty. In this case, giving thanks is inappropriate. Duty flows from a relationship which obligates. Thanks is for acts or gifts that are done or given without any obligation. When we do good and obey God, we are simply doing our duty which is to obey God's commands.

    A. Service is not for the accumulation of merits for God's acceptance.

    B. Service does not obligate God to bless us.

    C. Service is our duty to obey God.

3. Answers through Questions. (17:7-10) Jesus used the method of questions to give answers. Jesus puts the questions to his Disciples, challenges them to think, and leads them to answers.

    A. What would you do — "Will any one of you . . . ?" — v. 7.

    B. What would you say — "Will he not rather say . . . ?" — v. 8.

    C. Would you say thanks — "Does he thank . . . ?" — v. 9.

4. If We are Going to do our Duty. (17:10) Knowing what our duty is and doing it are two different things. We clamor for rights but are silent when we consider our duties. When duty is mentioned, our faces fall. We consider the subject negative, a kill-joy. How can we reach the point when we will be glad to do our duty?

5. It's Not so Bad to be God's Slave. (17:7-10) The parable deals with a farmer-master owner and a servant-slave. Christians are also slaves of Christ, the Master. He bought us with his blood. We are not our own. We are the property of God, and are subject to his authority and will. No one wants to be a slave of another human, but to be a slave of God is not so bad, because —

    A. Slaves of God have the security of ownership.

    B. Slaves of God have no fear of being disowned.

    C. Slaves of God have all their needs met.

    D. Slaves of God have the joy of service.

Contact

Points of Contact

1. Demand for thanks. Today's parable has something to say to members of every congregation. Most of the members expect and demand recognition, appreciation, and thanks for what they give or do for the church. The average pastor is always frightened of having left out a name when it comes time to publicly thank those who had a part in church functions such as revivals, Vacation Bible Schools, fish fries, or retreats. Pity the pastor who omits the name of one who donated a poinsettia at Christmas or a lily at Easter! This demand is also expressed in the necessity to place brass plates on church furnishings such as altars, pulpits, fonts, and pews. Often the names of donors are permanently worked into stained glass windows. Why all this? Because people want to be recognized and thanked for service or gifts. But the parable tells us we should not want recognition or thanks, for as servants we are only doing our duty. The most effective worker or leader is one who gets the job done without caring who gets the credit.

2. Rights or Duties? Today's society is clamoring for rights: women's rights, civil rights, minority rights, political rights, labor rights, etc. It seems as though we have forgotten the other side of the coin — duties. No one demands that we perform our duties. We want privileges, but not responsibilities. We want to live together as man and wife without the duties and commitment of marriage. We want to be free without any discipline. Today's parable gives the preacher an opportunity to stress the need and importance of recognizing and performing our duties as citizens and as Christians. On the one hand, we have duties to the state and, on the other, we have duties to God.

Points to Ponder

1. Is God a slave-driver? The farmer-master in the parable appears to be a slave-driver. He makes his slave work hard in the fields all day long. The slave comes home tired, dirty, exhausted, and hungry. The master then demands that the slave get busy with the preparation and serving of the master's evening meal. After the master has eaten, then the slave is to find something for himself. Does the master here represent God? Is this an attractive or correct protrait of the Father? Rather, is Jesus not teaching us that God, who is over and above us, by virtue of being God demands first place in our lives?

2. No rewards for service? In the parable the servants do not expect thanks, because they know they were just doing their duty by obeying the commands of the master. Is Jesus saying that thanks are not in order when we obey him, since to obey is our duty? Jesus is saying that to serve for the sake of appreciation or thanks is not proper. We are to serve because it is our duty to obey his orders. Though we do not serve to get thanks, it is always encouraging to recieve thanks, know that our loyalty to the Master is appreciated. In other passages we are taught that the servants of Christ are rewarded for their services. Yet, the service is not rendered to get reward.

3. For duty only? The emphasis in this parable is upon our duty to obey God's commands. Is that all there is to Christian service — duty? For most people duty is a dirty word. We don't like it. We do not want anyone to tell us we "must" or "ought." It is a negative concept and we rebel against it. Wise preachers are careful not to use these two words. Duty is related to "must" or "ought." There is no joy or pleasure in it. Christian service certainly, is the preforming of our duty, as slaves have a duty to obey their master. Christians can rise above the level of duty because they *want* rather than *have* to do good. They want to serve because they love Christ and are grateful to him for saving them from the peril of sin.

Illustrative Materials

1. Do it for Thanks? Years ago Jane Addams ran a social service center in the Chicago loop. One of her social workers complained to her one day that, in spite of all she had done for a certain family, they had not even thanked her. Jane Addams asked, "Is that why you did it — for thanks?"

2. The only Reward. Ignatius Loyola prayed:

> "Teach us, good Lord,
> to serve you as you deserve;
> to give and not to count the cost;
> to fight and not to heed the wounds;
> to toil and not to seek for rest;
> to labor and not to ask for any reward,
> save that of knowing that we do your will."

3. A Scout's Oath. When I was a Boy Scout, I remember saying the Scout's Oath. Standing at attention and with the raised right hand making the Scout sign, we said, "I promise to do my *duty* to God and my country, to obey the Scout laws . . . "

4. Only Our Duty. Some years ago Ann Landers made a trip to China. Upon her return, she told of the fine service rendered by various Chinese servants. When they were complimented, they said, "We have only done what was our duty."

5. Duty to Obey. "A Christian society is not going to arrive until most of us really want it and we are not going to want it until we become fully Christians. I may repeat, 'Do as you would be done by' 'til I am black in the face, but I cannot really carry it out 'til I love my neighbor as my self; and I cannot love my neighbor as myself 'til I learn to love God, and I cannot learn to love God except by learning to obey Him."

C. S. Lewis

6. Reward of Service.

Wilhelm Loehe: "And what is my reward? I serve neither for reward, nor thanks, but out of gratitude and love; my reward is that I am permitted to serve."

7. Carry on with Duty.
A discouraged minister had a strange dream. He thought he was standing on the top of a great granite rock, trying to break it with a pickaxe. Hour after hour he worked with no result. At last he said, "It is useless. I will stop." Suddenly a man stood by him and asked, "Were you not given this task? If so, why are you going to abandon it?" My work is in vain. I can make no impression on the granite," said the minister. Then the stranger solemnly replied, "That is nothing to you. Your *duty* is to pick, whether the rock yield or no. The work is yours, and the results are in other hands. Work on."

8. Faithful to his Master.
Archibald Rutledge told the story of meeting a turpentine worker whose faithful dog had just died a few moments earlier in a great forest fire; the obedient servant would not desert his master's dinner pail, which he had been told to watch. With tears running down his face, the old man said, "I always had to be careful what I told him to do, 'cause I knowed he'd do it."

Proper 24　　•　　Pentecost 22　　•　　Ordinary Time 29

Common　　　　　　　Lutheran　　　　　　　　Roman Catholic

18. The Uncaring Judge

Luke 18:1-8

¹And he told them a parable, to the effect that they ought always to pray and not lose heart. ²He said, "In a certain city there was a judge who neither feared God nor regarded man; ³and there was a widow in that city who kept coming to him and saying, 'Vindicate me against my adversary.' ⁴For a while he refused; but afterward he said to himself, 'Though I neither fear God nor regard man, ⁵yet because this widow bothers me, I will vindicate her, or she will wear me out by her continual coming.' " ⁶And the Lord said, "Hear what the unrighteous judge says. ⁷And will not God vindicate his elect, who cry to him day and night? Will he delay long over them? ⁸I tell you, he will vindicate them speedily. Nevertheless, when the Son of man comes, will he find faith on earth?"

It's just not fair! Life in this world is not fair for many people. We live in a world of injustice, discrimination, prejudice, and tough luck. It is therefore easy to become discouraged. We throw up our hands and say, "What's the use?" In our hopelessness we may even cease to pray. We are discouraged — why pray? There may be no answer to prayer. God is silent. God may be in heaven, but can he do anything about my plight on earth? Prayer doesn't seem to change me or my lot. Prayer doesn't put bread on the table, protect me from vandalism, or get me a job.

Conditions in Jesus' day led the Disciples also to become discouraged with prayer. Jesus had just explained that the Kingdom of God would not come in visible form, that with his return there would be destruction and death. They would be victims of the world's tribulations and sorrows. So, Jesus urged them to keep on praying and not to become discouraged over these conditions.

In our day we have every reason to become discouraged to the point of giving up our prayers. We face a nuclear winter. In government we face scandal after scandal over which we have lost respect for the integrity of leaders. Crime increases each year. Moral absolutes have been dropped for permissive life-styles. The impact of modern values — secularism, materialism, violence, moral license — threatens Christian civilization. The Middle East is aflame with racial and religious hatred.

In the midst of these chaotic times, our only recourse is prayer. Like the widow in the parable, we are urged to keep on praying in the assurance that a good and loving God cares enough about us to answer our plea.

Context

Context of Luke 17

The Parable of the Uncaring Judge is to be seen in the context of the preceding material beginning with 17:20. In answer to a question raised by the Pharisees, Jesus tells of the coming of the Kingdom of God. Associated with the coming of the Kingdom is the Parousia and the destruction of those not prepared to receive Christ. This is not a bright picture of what is to come. Then, Jesus gives the parable to his Disciples (18:1-8) to encourage them to keep on praying. He concludes the discussion with the question, "When the Son of man comes, will he find faith on earth?" The parable, therefore, seems to be related to the Parousia, as Jesus encourages the Disciples not to lose faith in his return, but to keep on praying for the Kingdom of God to come, just as he taught them to say in the Lord's Prayer: "Thy kingdom come."

Context of the Twin Parables

Ten Sundays ago we dealt with the twin parable, a Midnight Friend (Luke 11:5-8). The theme of this parable is duplicated in today's parable. While the theme of perseverance in prayer is the same, the situations are entirely different. The Midnight Friend parable is one section of Jesus' teaching on prayer. The situation is humorous and light-hearted. At midnight a friend is aroused from sleep by one who requests bread to feed a visitor. We hear the banging on the door and the protests of the sleepy friend. In the Parable of the Uncaring Judge, the situation is far more serious. A poor, helpless widow clamors persistently for her rights. Because she nags him to death, the judge grants her request. Moreover, this parable is related to the Second Coming. The Disciples are facing a hostile world and the Parousia is slow in coming. There is reason for their becoming discouraged. To encourage them to keep praying and to keep their faith, Jesus tells them the story of the widow and the judge. If persistent appeals get an answer from a judge who neither fears God nor cares about people, how much more will a good God answer speedily the appeals of his people! Thus, while the principle is the same in both parables, the Parable of the Uncaring Judge is surrounded by the framework of the coming of God's Kingdom. In keeping with this subject, Jesus appropriately asks, "Will the Son of man find faith on earth when he comes?"

Context of the Lectionary

The First Lesson. (Habbakuk 1:1-3; 2:1-4) The righteous will live in spite of wicked people because they are faithful to God. Habbakuk is a prophet during the Babylonian exile. He sees how righteous Jews are oppressed by cruel Babylonians. He cries out to Yahweh to explain why he does nothing about it. He climbs up his watchtower for an answer to his complaint. God's answer: help, though slow, is coming, and good people will live because they are faithful to God.

This lesson harmonizes with today's parable. A helpless woman cries out for help to a godless judge. Help comes slowly as she keeps repeatedly crying out for justice. Because of her faithful appeal the judge yields. The lesson says, "Persist in your faithfulness to God."

The Second Lesson. (2 Timothy 3:14—4:5) Paul urges Timothy to fulfill his ministry. Paul is giving his spiritual son, Timothy, some instructions for his ministry. In keeping with today's parable and its theme of perseverance, Paul is urging Timothy to persist: "continue in what you have learned," "be urgent in season and out of season," "be unfailing in patience," and "always be steady." This pericope says, "Be persistent in fulfilling your ministry."

Gospel. (Luke 18:1-8) The Parable of the Uncaring Judge and the Widow. We learn from the parable that we should persevere in prayer and faith until Jesus comes again.

Psalm. (Psalm 119:137-144) In spite of trouble and anxiety, a believer finds joy in God's commands, for they are just.

Prayer of the Day. In keeping with the theme of perseverance we pray, "that your church throughout the world may persevere with steadfast faith in the confession of your name."

Hymn of the Day: "If You But Trust in God to Guide You" In a time of weeping, anger, and distress, keep believing in the promise of God that he will never leave nor forsake you. In keeping with today's parable, the hymn tells us, "Keep the faith."

Getting it all together. In an amazing way the lessons and propers deal with the theme of perseverance. In Lesson 1 they who persevere in faith during adverse times will live. Paul urges Timothy in Lesson 2 to persist so that his ministry will be fulfilled. The parable in the Gospel deals with perseverance in prayer and faith. The Psalmist in a time of trouble keeps believing in God's promises of deliverance. The prayer asks God to make us faithful in confessing Jesus' name to the world. The Hymn calls us to remain steadfast in faith when times get rough. The material for this Sunday drives home the message from every angle — keep the faith. Continue praying. Don't stop serving. Do not become weary in well-doing. When Jesus returns, then he will find faith on earth.

Context of Related Scriptures

Exodus 22:22-24 — Widows are not to be mistreated.
2 Chronicles 19:5-7 — What God expects of judges.
Isaiah 1:17 — Widows are to be defended.
Isaiah 62:1 — A prophet refuses to be silent until God saves.
Luke 11:5-13 — Parable of the Friend at Midnight.
Romans 15:30 — Prayer calls for striving.
Ephesians 6:18 — Paul appeals for perseverance in prayer.
1 Thessalonians 5:17 — Pray without ceasing.

Content

Content of the Pericope

What is the content of this passage? Does it relate only to persistence in prayer, or to the coming of the Kingdom of God? Is the entire passage from Jesus, or is some of it the work of the early church? Where does the parable end as Jesus gave it? Does it end with verse 5? If so, the parable deals only with persistence in prayer. In this case, the parable repeats the point of the Friend at Midnight. (Luke 11:5-8). Or, does the parable end with verse 8a? Is verse 8b an editorial addition reflecting the early church's concern for the failure of the early return of Jesus?

The position we take will determine how we preach the parable. If we separate the parable from the foregoing passage on the Second Coming and eliminate verses 6-8 as an editorial interpretation, the parable will deal with persistence in prayer only. If we accept the entire passage as coming from Jesus and consider it within the context of Luke 17, we will deal with the theme of persistence in general, including faith in Jesus' return, the coming of the Kingdom, and prayer. In the parable, we have the principle of perseverance applied generally, particularly with regard to the Parousia. Most New Testament scholars accept the pericope as coming from Jesus and dealing with the vindication of the elect awaiting the Parousia. The parable seems to be saying, "Keep on praying 'Thy kingdom come' and your faith will be vindicated."

Precis of the Parable

To teach the Disciples not to be discouraged and to pray always, Jesus told a story about a judge who neither feared God nor cared for people. In the same town was a widow who came repeatedly to him asking for her rights. She kept begging, "Help me get justice!" For a long time the judge ignored her appeals, but she kept on pleading time after time. Finally, the judge reasoned within himself: "Though I don't fear God nor care about people, I will give the widow her rights because her nagging is driving me crazy." Jesus then explained, "Do you hear what the judge said? If a corrupt judge will respond to persistent appeals, how much more will a good God speedily answer the cries of his people who pray to him day and night! Indeed, God will answer their prayers speedily. But, when the Son of man returns, will he find faith on earth?"

Thesis: Be persistent in praying for God's Kingdom to come.

Theme: Don't ever give up!

Key Words

1. "Always." (v. 1) Throughout the parable the emphasis is on praying "always." The widow got her request by her "continual coming" to the judge. God is sure to hear his people who pray "to him day and night." Paul taught, "Pray unceasingly." "Always" does not mean uttering a prayer twenty-four hours a day. We are not to pray *continuously* but *continually*. We can pray continually, for prayer is more than words. It can be attitude or thought. It is a living every hour of the day in the conscious presence of God.

2. "Lost heart." (v. 1) In the *King James Version* this is translated as "faint" and in the *Good News Bible* it is "never become discouraged." Why do we not "always" pray? We become discouraged and stop praying. God may be silent to our praying, and we become discouraged and ask, "Why pray?" Are we talking to ourselves? We pray "Thy kingdom come," and we have been doing it for 2000 years. Still the Kingdom has not come on earth. So, why pray on? We pray for world peace, but wars continue to flourish (Afghanistan, Nicaragua, Middle East.) We pray for Jesus to come, but it may be 2000 years more before he comes. So we give up praying. We are discouraged because our prayers are not answered.

3. "Pray." (v. 1) Pray for what? Persistence is no guarantee that a prayer will be answered. It depends on what we pray for. We can pray until dooms-day, but there will be no answer if we do not pray according to God's will. Pray for God's Kingdom to come? Yes! Pray for human justice and rights? Yes, the widow did. Pray for peace, for health, for spiritual strength? By all means. Though we pray night and day, God will not respond if the peti-tion is not according to his will or for our good.

4. "Judge." (v. 2) The parable is commonly called the Parable of the Unjust Judge. Although Jesus referred to him as "unrighteous" or "cor-rupt" (v. 6), he did nothing illegal nor immoral according to the parable. His main fault was his callousness to human need. He had no love, no con-cern for unfortunate people like the widow. The cause of his hard-heartedness was his lack of fear of God. He was a godless judge who had therefore no concern for the welfare of humans. He is a man who did the right thing for the wrong reason. Our inhumanity to "man" is rooted in our fearless-ness of God. Where there is no fear of God, there is no respect for "man."

5. "Widow." (vv. 3, 4) We do not know what it was, but an injustice was done to this woman. She was desperate and helpless. As a woman, in her day she had no rights. She was too poor to bribe the judge to grant her request. She could call on no influential friends to influence the judge in her favor. Her only weapon was her persistence. This was based on the rightness of her cause in which she believed with all her heart. Desperation makes us persevere in crying for help. When we are helpless in our desper-ate need, we will continually cry to God for mercy.

6. "God." (v. 7) To some it may be offensive to compare God with the judge of the parable. It is not a comparison but a contrast! Here we see what good a "bad" man can do for selfish reasons. God is not like that. If a callous judge is moved by persistent appeals, how much more will a good and gracious God give to his people when they persevere in their pray-ers. The parable is telling us we have a good God who hears and answers the prayers of the oppressed. And he does it "speedily." There is no need to beg and beg endlessly. Persistence does not persuade God to help.

7. "Faith." (v. 8) Will there be faith on earth when Jesus returns? Will there be faith before he returns? Prayer is the answer. When we stop pray-ing, it indicates that we have lost our faith. An atheist or agnostic does not pray because there is no faith in God. Believe in God, and prayer is a natural and normal means of communication with him. Believe in the goodness of God and our prayers will be assured. Faith in the power of God will cause us to pray for the "impossible," because with God all things are possible. It is not therefore a matter of always praying, but of always believing. So we believe, so we pray.

Contemplation

Insights

1. Discouragement. Apparently Jesus knew that people are subject to losing heart, for he urged his Disciples never to become discouraged. (v. 1) Often life is not fair. Injustices abound and there is no relief in sight. The powers of evil are insurmountable and we ask, "Why fight City Hall?" A bad marriage, drug-addicted children, prolonged illness, or unanswered prayer can cause us to lose hope. In this kind of world, we need to persistently pray in the faith that God will help us.

2. Our Only Weapon. Our situation, like the widow's in the parable, may seem hopeless. She was helpless and in utter desperation. As a poor widow, she had no money to bribe the judge. As a woman, she had no clout. As a widow, she had no influential husband or friends to plead her case before the judge. Her last resort was to appeal over and over, until the judge gave in to her cry for justice. By her persistence she bothered him to the point where he gave her what she wanted in order to get rid of her. Her only weapon was persistent prayer. We may find ourselves in the same situation. Our last resort, our only weapon is unceasing prayer.

3. Why Persist? "Don't give up! Keep praying!" Why should we? What makes a person stubbornly persistent? The widow of the parable shows us how to continue in prayer. First, one like her has a desperate, crying need. It is a matter of life and death. Second, she had a good case, a worthy cause. She wanted, needed, and demanded justice. She knew she was one-hundred percent right. Third, faith made her continue. She believed in herself and in her cause. No one, not even a godless and callous judge, can stop a person like that.

4. The Wrong Use of Persistence. Persistence in prayer may be misunderstood and misused. We are not to persevere in our prayers to force God, like the judge, to answer our prayers, but rather to condition us to receive the answer. Again, persistence is not based on the idea that we will be heard by God for our many words, a vain repetition. Moreover, we do not persist in order to persuade God to do our will, but rather for us to bend our wills to conform to his.

5. Religion and Ethics. The judge in the parable is described as one who did not fear God and as one who had no respect for human beings. This accounts for his refusal to hear the case of the widow. He would not even give her the time of day. She was a non-person to him. What did he care if she had no food for her children, that she could not pay her husband's debts, that she could get no employment? He could not have cared less about her situation. The ethical thing for him to do would have been to hear her at once and dispense justice. Why was he so callous? Because he had no fear of God. When there is no fear of God, there is no respect for "man." The brotherhood of "man" depends upon the Fatherhood of God. Ethics is a practical result of religious faith. "Be holy for I am holy," says God. God, not Moses, gave the Decalogue; God gave the moral absolutes through Moses. The answer to our moral corruption today is a total return to faith in and fear of God.

6. God and the Judge. In Jesus' day perhaps many were shocked when, in the parable, Jesus used an unjust judge as a metaphor for God. They could have said, "God is not like that at all!" And they would have been right. Once before Jesus used the same technique when he told of a dishonest steward. But God is more correctly a contrast to the judge. God has respect for humans. He does care about the poor and oppressed. He is not reluctant to help. He does not need to be begged endlessly for his aid. Jesus is teaching that God is the opposite of the judge. He hears the cries of his people and responds speedily. This answers the oft-asked questions: Does God hear when I pray?", "Does God answer prayer?

7. Prayer and Faith. In the opening of the parable, Jesus might have said, "Do not lose faith," instead of "Do not lose heart." We are to keep praying because we do not lose heart. Really, we keep on praying because we keep on believing. As long as we believe, we will have hope. As long as we have hope, we will pray. Prayer is dependent upon faith. Non-believers do not pray. The widow in the parable believed in the rightness of her cause. We will not cease nor desist from clamoring for help and justice as long as we believe in our cause, and believe that God hears and answers prayer. At the end of the parable Jesus asks, "Will the Son of man find faith on the earth when he comes?" Apparently, he saw the connection between prayer and faith.

Homily Hints

1. Keep at It! (Habakkuk 1:1-3; 2:1-4; 2 Timothy 3:14—4:5; Luke 18:1-8) The context of the parable indicates that persistence is not limited to prayer. The three lessons for this Sunday show the need of perseverance in various areas of life.

A. Persist in faithfulness to God despite injustice — Lesson 1.
B. Persist in serving Christ — Lesson 2.
C. Persist in prayer — Gospel.

2. Long-range Praying. (18:1-5) Persistence involves praying over a long period of time until the request is granted. The widow kept coming to the judge. Her "continual coming" brought results. Some things need praying for over the years. What are some of them?

A. Pray for God's Kingdom to come.
B. Pray for justice in our society.
C. Pray for a continued happy marriage.
D. Pray for peace on earth.

3. A Widow's Victory. (18:1-8) The parable is an account of a life situation. A penniless, bereaved woman faces a cruel world of injustice. Her situation appears hopeless. Yet the story has a happy ending.

A. The problem — a desperate situation.
B. Who cares about the problem?
C. The keys to victory — persistent prayer.

4. When All Else Fails. (18:1-8) The widow had only one weapon: persistence in her appeal. She had nothing else; no money, position, influence, or friends. When all else fails, Christians still have —

A. Prayer — "Vindicate me" — v. 3. Prayer must lead to —
B. Persistence — "her continual coming" — v. 5. Persistence results from —
C. Faith — v. 8b.

5. God is Better than That! (18:1-8) Good for the judge for helping the widow! He really deserves no credit, because he acted out of selfishness and his own personal well-being. God is better than that.

A. God respects people — v. 6.
B. God hears the appeal of his people — v. 7.
C. God answers speedily — v. 8a.

6. So We Believe, So We Pray. (18:1, 8b) We pray because we first believe. We continue to pray because we continue to believe. Believers pray. If we stop praying, Jesus will not find faith on earth. Our prayers come out of faith —

A. We believe God is — the existence of God.
B. We believe God is good — the nature of God.
C. We believe God answers prayer — the mercy of God.

Contact

Points of Contact

1. A hostile world. As always, many today can identify with the widow of the parable. She found it was a tough, cruel world filled with injustice, prejudice, and discrimination. She was a victim of injustice. Someone was depriving her of her rights. She had the misfortune of losing her husband. She faced poverty. To top it all, a judge was heartless concerning her problem. Life can be unfair. When we preach on this parable, some will identify with the widow because of a similar problem in the past or present. It is a live and pressing problem. Many are asking today, "Where is justice?" Bad things are happening to good people.

2. Losing heart. Discouragement is a perennial experience. Who never gets discouraged? The ancient Psalmist asked, "Why are you cast down, O my soul?" (Psalm 43:5) In the parable Jesus urged his Disciples not to become discouraged. Stop and count the people in your congregation that are blue and despondent. Because we lose heart, we stop praying. We become weary of well-doing. We stop trying and we no longer want to keep going. We want to quit. Many of us are asking, "What's the use?" This sermon can encourage the congregation and give them new hope. This encouragement is based on the truth that God cares and fulfills his promises. The ultimate cure is "Hope in God."

3. Faithful in faith. Faith is a fragile element. You can have it today and lose it tomorrow. It is not like grace. We cannot fall from grace, for grace is of God and from God. God is ever-faithful and ever-loving. Faith is a human response, and humans are prone to fail. The Disciples once asked for an increase in faith. The risen Lord urged the church to be faithful unto death. The question Jesus asked in the parable, "When the Son of man comes, will he find faith on earth?" was no idle or rhetorical question. We are always one generation away from no faith. Faith to continue until Jesus comes needs to be caught and taught. This is a concern for every member of a congregation.

Points to Ponder

1. Duplication of themes. In preparing a sermon on today's parable, it would be wise to recall that ten weeks ago we dealt with the twin parable of the Friend at Midnight. We want to avoid repetition. There need not be a duplication of theme, because that parable was strictly related to prayer. Today's parable goes beyond persistence in prayer to looking for the Kingdom, the Parousia, and faith.

2. Is God like the judge? The preacher will want to be careful not to give the impression that God is like the judge in the parable. He is the very opposite of the judge. Jesus uses a corrupt judge to show the contrast — if an evil person can help another for a poor reason, a good God will that much more speedily help for the sake of love. By this contrast, we can show people how good, caring, and responsive God is to his people who cry to him for mercy.

3. Petition only. The parable deals with only one aspect of prayer, persistence in petitioning. The average person thinks of prayer as asking for a blessing. A boy was once asked if he prayed every day. He replied, "No, because I don't want something every day." Petition is probably the lowest level of prayer. Higher levels are adoration, praise, thanksgiving, and submission.

4. Does God need to be persuaded? The emphasis in the parable is on the "continual coming" of the widow to the judge, who gives her what she wants in order to get her off his back. In this case, perseverance was the key to getting an answer. Is that true with God? Must he be persuaded to help us? God knows what we need before we ask. He is more ready to give than we are to ask. In the parable Jesus says that God will answer speedily. (v. 8a) If all of this is true, why then do we emphasize persistence in prayer? It is we and not God who needs the persistence. We need it to keep us open and ready to receive the answer, when God decides it is time to give the answer to our prayer.

5. The main character. Who is the main character in the parable, the judge or the widow? If the judge is the chief character, then the message deals with the nature of God in contrast to the judge. If the widow is the main character, the emphasis will be on persistence. The context of the parable seems to indicate that the widow is the main person, even though the text is known as the Parable of th Unjust Judge.

Illustrative Materials

1. The Devil's Chief Weapon. There is a legend that once the Devil put his weapons up for sale. The weapons were displayed and a price sign was at the base of each one. The price varied according to the deadliness of the weapon: hatred, fear, worry, prejudice, jealousy, etc. But there was one weapon that did not have a price sign on it. An inquirer asked what was its price. He was told that it was not for sale at any price because it was the Devil's chief weapon. The name of the weapon was discouragement.

2. Not Yet Begun. In 1779 there was a famous naval battle between the American ship, *Bonhomme Richard* with John Paul Jones as captain, and a British vessel, *Serapis,* captained by Richard Pearson. When the ships were lashed to each other and fierce fighting had continued for some time, until it seemed that the American ship was about to sink, Pearson called to Jones asking if he wanted to surrender. John Paul Jones shouted back with head raised high, "I have — not — yet — begun — to — fight!" John Paul Jones won the battle and the English captain surrendered his sword.

3. Stand and Wait. In the television movie, *Resting Place,* the story was told of a black Viet Nam veteran's childhood in Mississippi. As a boy he had gone to a public library to borrow a book, but the white librarian had told him that the library did not lend books to blacks. Nevertheless, he still wanted to borrow a book. He kept standing at her desk for her to check out the book. He remained standing until closing time, five o'clock. She was so unnerved by his persistent request that she gave him the book he wanted.

4. Keep Praying. Monica, the mother of Saint Augustine, tried to raise her three children in the Christian faith. Augustine was her oldest child. For thirty years she followed her son's wanderings and continually prayed for him and his conversion. For fifteen years he lived with a mistress and had an illegitimate son. Her prayers were answered when Augustine was converted while listening to the sermons of Bishop Ambrose in Milan.

5. Keep on Going. Robert Falcon Scott led an expedition to the South Pole in 1911. For seveny-eight days they walked more than 1600 miles over glaciers in subzero storms. When they reached the South Pole, they found that Amundsen of Norway had preceded them by five weeks. On their return Scott and his party perished in a gale when they were only eleven miles from their home base with its depot of supplies and safety.

6. Six Inches from Gold. A man once bought a gold mine for $300,000. After digging for several years, he did not get enough gold to meet his expenses. He sold the mine and, after only six hours of drilling, the new owner discovered one of the purest pockets of gold ever found in North America. The former owner was only six inches away from the find.

7. Try, Try Again. Cyrus Field got the idea of connecting America and Europe by telephone. He decided to lay a copper wire on the floor of the Atlantic to Europe. When they laid the wire 360 miles out to sea, the wire snapped and Field lost all of his savings. A second try ended the same way. Then his business failed. He tried a third time after saving for nine years to try again. When 1200 miles out to sea, the wire again snapped. Still not discouraged, and determined to succeed, a fourth cable was prepared and this one was successful.

8. Getting to Jesus. In Luke 5:17-26 is an account of some men who were persistent in getting a paralytic to Jesus for healing. It took some effort to carry the man. Then they faced the problem of a crowd so big and tight that they could not get into the house where Jesus was teaching. Determined to get their man to Jesus, they went to the trouble of removing the roof from a man's house, searching for rope, and lowering the man into Jesus' presence for healing. It takes persistence some times to get people to Jesus.

Proper 25 • Pentecost 23 • Ordinary Time 30

Common   Lutheran   Roman Catholic

---

19. Two Men at Prayer

Luke 18:9-14

---

⁹He also told this parable to some who trusted in themselves that they were righteous and despised others: ¹⁰"Two men went up into the temple to pray, one a Pharisee and the other a tax collector. ¹¹The Pharisee stood and prayed thus with himself, 'God, I thank thee that I am not like other men, extortioners, unjust, adulterers, or even like this tax collector. ¹²I fast twice a week, I give tithes of all that I get.' ¹³But the tax collector, standing far off, would not even lift his eyes to heaven, but beat his breast, saying, 'God, be merciful to me a sinner!' ¹⁴I tell you, this man went down to his house justified rather than the other; for every one who exalts himself will be humbled, but he who humbles himself will be exalted."

Let's go to church not to pray but to listen to others' prayers. Maybe we can learn something about praying, what prayers reveal about the prayers, and the results of praying.

The first person we overhear praying is a devout man, a religious leader. He thanks God that he is not a gross sinner like other people, and he tells God that he has shown his devotion to God by fasting and tithing. In one sense, he is the best of men, but he really is the worst because his prayer reveals that he is proud and self-righteous. He gets nothing from his prayer because he asks for nothing. He is pleased with himself and has no need of God.

We go to the back of the church and hear another man praying. He does not have much to say — only seven words. He says more by his body language. He tells us that he feels unworthy to enter God's presence. So he stays in the rear of the church. He is ashamed to look at God. So he keeps his head bowed. He is so sorry for his sinful ways that, in desperation, he beats his chest. In utter earnestness he appeals, "God, be merciful to me a sinner." Then he goes home a man forgiven and at peace with God.

These two men come to us in the Parable of the Pharisee and Publican. With which one do we identify? To whom is Jesus speaking? Luke tells us that he told the parable to those who trusted in themselves and despised others. Is this parable meant for us? Is Jesus speaking to us? To find the answer, check on your prayers. Are they like the Pharisee's or the Publican's?

Context

Context of Luke 18

Luke 18 begins with two parables. Last Sunday we considered the Widow and the Judge. This Sunday we confront the Pharisee and Publican at prayer in the temple. This latter parable ends the special section of Luke. The section is resumed with the account of Zaccheus, chapter 19. Following the Parable of the Pharisee and Publican, we read about the rich young ruler, Jesus' announcement of their going to Jerusalem, and the healing of blind Bartimaeus in Jericho as Jesus proceeds to Jerusalem. The Parable of the Judge and Widow was addressed to the Disciples as a follow-up to his discourse on the coming of the Kingdom. Today's parable is addressed generally to those "who trusted in themselves and despised others," and specifically to Pharisees, who were guilty of that charge.

Context of the Lectionary

The First Lesson. (Zephaniah 3:1-9) God's judgment is coming to the nations.

Before good King Josiah in the Seventh Century made reforms, the prophet, Zephaniah, observed the wicked conditions in Judah as well as in other countries. He pronounced doom upon them, but after the judgment, he promises that they will pray to and obey Yahweh.

This pericope may be related to the parable in the Gospel lesson. Zephaniah says of Jerusalem, "She does not trust in the Lord." The parable was directed to those who trusted in themselves rather than in the Lord. The Word in this pericope is that they who trust in themselves are doomed to destruction.

The Second Lesson. (2 Timothy 4:6-8; 16-18) Paul looks forward to his reward in heaven.

This lesson brings to a close the series of seven lessons from 1 and 2 Timothy. Today's pericope appropriately deals with Paul's preparation for death. Because he has fought the good fight and kept the faith, he is now looking forward to receiving a crown of righteousness in heaven.

This righteousness is connected with today's parable. The Publican went home "justified." (v. 14) To be justified is to be righteous in God's sight. To be righteous is to be rightly related to God. Paul emphasized righteousness by faith in Christ and not by Law. A person like the Publican who throws himself on the mercy of God is justified. On earth this is a partial gift, but the full gift is received in heaven.

Gospel. (Luke 18:9-14) The Parable of the Pharisee and Publican. In prayer a proud man tells God how good he is. A humble man can only beg for mercy. The result is that one remains estranged from God and the other is acceptable to God.

Psalm. (Psalm 3) Like the Publican in the parable, the Psalmist cries "aloud to the Lord, and he answers me . . ." He is a God who delivers and saves those who cry for mercy.

Prayer. We pray for an increase in faith, hope, and love that we may obtain what God promises. His chief promise is mercy and forgiveness. By faith, hope, and love we lay claim to that promise.

Hymn of the Day. "To You, Omniscient Lord of All" The refrain of the hymn echoes the Publican's cry. "O God, be merciful to me."

Getting It All Together. The lessons and propers revolve around the Publican's prayer, "God, be merciful to me a sinner," and his return home as a justified sinner. In the First lesson we learn that those who trust in themselves, as the Pharisee in the parable did, will experience judgment. Paul in the Second lesson is a justified person who claims the crown of righteousness in heaven. His teaching harmonized with the Publican's cry for mercy and was justified by grace. The Gospel teaches us through the parable that we get right with God, not by good works, but by a humble cry for mercy. The Psalmist in Psalm 3 is one like the Publican who cries to the Lord and gets deliverance. In the Prayer we accept by faith God's promise of mercy. The Hymn repeats the prayer of the Publican. The theme of justification by grace through faith comes to us from every angle. This is the predominant truth for this Sunday.

Context of Related Scriptures

> Genesis 4:1-8 — Cain's unacceptable prayer.
> Deuteronomy 14:22-23 — The law of the tithe.
> Psalm 17:3-5 — A prayer similar to the Pharisee's prayer.
> Psalm 34:6, 18 — A prayer similar to the Publican's prayer.
> Psalm 51 — A prayer for mercy.

Luke 14:7-14 — A parable of pride and humility.
Romans 3:27-31 — How we are justified.
Philippians 2:1-11 — Humility ends in exaltation.

Content

Content of the Pericope

The pericope contains the parable of two men at prayer in the temple. Both came to pray, for Jews were expected to pray three times daily, at nine o'clock a.m., twelve noon, and three o'clock p.m. They both came to the best place to pray. The temple was considered God's dwelling place. His presence was symbolized by the ark of the covenant in the holy of holies. Jesus called the temple a house of prayer. The parable shows us that prayers differ in their efficacy. One man gets nothing and the other receives his request. The one got nothing because he asked for nothing. What the other received meant everything to him.

The content raises several questions involved in our understanding of the parable. First, take a look at verse 11. The *Revised Standard Version* translates it, "The Pharisee stood and prayed thus with himself." The *Good News Bible* says, he "stood apart by himself and prayed." In the former case, the Pharisee prayed silently and if so, how do we know what he prayed? Or, if he prayed with himself, it means that he was not talking to God but to himself. If the latter translation is correct, we see the Pharisee standing in the front of the temple, because he considered himself first-rate, better than others such as the Publican. To avoid this impression — is that why a church's front pews are usually empty?

Secondly, there is a difference in the translation of verse 13. In some Bibles the Publican prays, "God, be merciful to me a sinner," while others say, ". . . to me, the sinner." If the Publican says "a sinner," he identifies with all people. If he says, "the sinner," he is comparing himself with the self-righteous Pharisee who stands in front of him. "He is the righteous one; I am the sinner."

Thirdly, a question arises concerning verse 14b. Many New Testament scholars claim that this statement, that every one who exalts himself will be humbled, is an ending added by the early church. If Jesus said it as a part of the parable, it would seem that the point of the parable deals with pride and humility. Many sermons on this text deal with pride and humility because of verse 14b. However, apart from verse 14b, the parable deals with justification. Indeed, pride can be seen in the prayer of the Pharisee and humility in the Publican's prayer, but they are only illustrations of the point that they who trust in themselves are given to pride and despising others. Those who recognize their sin are overcome with humility and unworthiness to the point that they can only beg for mercy. The key to understanding the parable is in verse 9. The parable was told to those who trusted in themselves and despised others. Verse 14a confirms this truth, for the Publican went home "right with God." The good works of the Pharisee led to pride but not to right relations with God, because he trusts in his own moral accomplishments. Because of his confession of sin, his sense of unworthiness to even approach God, and his prayer for mercy, the Publican goes home forgiven and right with God. Before Paul taught the doctrine of Justification, Jesus taught it in this parable.

Precis of the Parable

Jesus told a parable to those who were proud of their goodness and who looked down on others whom they considered less righteous. Two men went to the temple to pray, a Pharisee and a Publican (tax collector). The Pharisee stood and prayed with himself: "God, I thank you I am not like others who are greedy, dishonest, and adulterers, such as the tax collector standing behind me. I fast twice a week and pay tithes of all that I get." In contrast, the tax collector, feeling guilty and unworthy, stood in the back, dared not lift his face to God, and beat his chest saying, "God, be merciful to me a sinner." Jesus continued, "I tell you this man, the Publican, went home being right with God, for his prayer was heard and he was forgiven. For everyone who puffs himself up with pride will be humbled and everyone who humbles himself will be great."

Thesis: Repentant sinners are justified by grace.

Theme: Beggars for mercy are blessed.

Key Words

1. "Trusted." (v. 9) The parable centers in trust. Whom can you trust? In what do you trust? In money? In government? In education? In family? The Pharisee put his trust in himself, in his own goodness to be acceptable to God. The tax collector trusted in God and therefore received mercy. Trust is an element of faith. Thus, the parable teaches that justification is by grace through faith.

2. "Pharisee." (v. 10) The Pharisee is the "good" man of the story. A Pharisee took his religion seriously. He was a devout person and upheld the Law. The Pharisee in this parable was a super-believer. He did more than was expected of a faithful Jew. He lived an exemplary life. He fasted twice a week every week when he was required to fast only one day of the year on the Day of Atonement. Fasting meant neither food nor drink for the entire day. He also paid tithes on everything, even on items for which the tithe had already been paid. Who can fault a man like this? Every pastor would be delighted to have members like him. He would be called the salt of the earth. But, he spoiled it all by his pride. His good words were for finding acceptance with God. Though he said, "I thank thee," he did not really give God the credit for activating and enabling him to do these good works.

3. **"Tax collector."** (v. 10) A tax collector was called a Publican. He is the bad guy in the story. He was a renegade Jew who went to work for the Romans, Israel's hated conquerors. A Publican was a quisling, a traitor, a collaborator and was despised by every patriotic Jew. Moreover, a Publican was a thief, because he exacted for personal profit more taxes than the Romans demanded. As a result society ostracized him and deprived him of civil rights.

The good thing about this "bad" man was that he knows he is rotten, a good-for-nothing person. He stands back in the temple because he feels unworthy of going forward. He is so ashamed of himself that he cannot raise his eyes to heaven when he prays. His remorse is so great that he beats his chest. Then, he offers a seven-word prayer in comparison to the Pharisee's thirty-three word prayer. He throws himself on the mercy of God without offering an excuse for his wicked life. If he could have, he would have sung: "Nothing in my hand I bring. Simply to thy cross I cling."

4. **"I."** (vv. 11, 12) The Pharisee used "I" five times in his prayer of two sentences, whereas "I" is never mentioned in the Lord's Prayer. It indicates that the Pharisee's eye was on himself. He was an egocentric and conceited person. His world revolved around "I" — what I am, what I did. Look at me, Lord! This "I" is the central letter in pr-I-de and also in s-I-n. When the "I" becomes the center of life, the person becomes conceited. He makes an idol of himself.

5. **"Justified."** (v. 14) Of the two men, only the Publican went home with his prayer answered. Of course, the Pharisee made no request and therefore received nothing. He merely reported to God how good he was. His lack of relationship with God did not change. But, the tax collector went home being right with God. He was "justified." It meant "just-as-if-I'd" never sinned. God had mercy and forgave the confessed sinner regardless of how bad he had been. The sin was taken away and he was now in good standing with God. Salvation is based, according to Jesus' teaching here, not on moral attainment but on God's love for the sinner who truly repents and believes. This is the Gospel.

Contemplation

Insights

1. Thank God for everything? Paul advises that we should give thanks in everything. (Philippians 4:6) Thanks for everything? The Pharisee began, "God, I thank thee . . ." He then gave thanks for not being like other people — evil-doers. He was thankful that he fasted and tithed. Is there a limit to our thanksgiving? Can we be thankful for pride, arrogance, and self-righteousness?

2. Is it the prayer or the pray-er? The prayer of the Pharisee was one of thanksgiving. It is one of the elements of true prayer. The Publican had only petition in his prayer. He omitted praise, adoration, thanksgiving, and submission. Yet, his prayer, though imperfect, was heard. The perfect prayer of the Pharisee was not answered. What is the difference? It is not the content of the prayer but the spirit of the pray-er. The spirit of the Pharisee was one of pride. The Publican's attitude was one of unworthiness and humility. Paul in Romans says we need the Spirit to aid us in our prayers.

3. Wanted: a consciousness of sin. In the parable the Pharisee had not one sin to confess, and so he did not ask for mercy. In contrast, the tax collector was overwhelmed with his sin. A realization of his sin made him feel unworthy to be in God's presence and to ask for mercy. The difference between the two is a consciousness of sin. The question is, how can we get our people to feel like the Publican so that they will fall on their knees and beg for mercy? A recent book by a psychiatrist asks, *Whatever Became of Sin?* The daily newspaper with its tabloid of crime should prove that we are marinated in sin.

4. Being Good without being Lost. The Pharisee in the parable was not all bad. We wish our church people would match his ardor. We do need members who do not commit adultery, steal, or lie. We need people who pray, fast, and tithe. All of this is commendable. Our problem is to help our people avoid the pit of pride and self-righteousness. Goodness and character should flow from a grateful heart for all that God does and gives to us. If there is any good in us, and if we have accomplished anything worthwhile, the credit belongs to God alone.

Homily Hints

1. Thank God I Am Like Other Men. (18:9-14) The Pharisee prayed, "Thank God that I am not like other men." It expressed his sense of moral superiority to others. Maybe it would be better to pray, "I thank thee that I am like other men." How can I be like others?

    A. Like others who are sinners?

    B. Like others who cry for mercy?

    C. Like others who are justified?

2. The Dangers of Being Good. (18:9-14) As Christians we need and want to be good. We want clean living, to be helpful to people, to be loyal to God and the Church. We want to even outdo the Pharisee. But, there are dangers to be faced —

    A. The danger of pride for being and doing good.

    B. The danger of guilt for not being good enough.

3. The Best and Worst of People. (18:9-14) In the parable we have the best of men in the Pharisee and the worst in the Publican. We do and we don't want to be like both men.

    A. The best — the Pharisee.

        1. Be like him — moral attainments, devotion to God.

        2. Be not like him — proud, arrogant, self-righteous.

    B. The worst — the Publican.

        1. Be not like him — traitor, thief.

        2. Be like him — repentant, believing.

4. Is Jesus Speaking to Us? (18:9) This parable was addressed not to the Pharisees only, nor the scribes, nor the Disciples. Jesus was telling the story to any who "trusted in themselves and despised others." Could he be speaking to us?

    A. Do we trust only in ourselves?

    B. Do we despise others because of race, religion, morality, education?

5. The Eyes Have it! (18:9-14) When a piece of legislation is passed, the chairperson announces, "The eyes have it." In this parable we have "eyes" and "Is."

    A. Pharisee — had eyes on himself — Pride.

    B. Publican — had eyes on heaven — Humility — v. 13.

    C. God — had eyes on the Publican — Mercy — v. 14a.

Contact

Points of Contact

1. Good works or Gospel? Do church people need the teaching of to-day's parable dealing with justification by grace rather than by works? Are there church members who would stand with the Pharisee and thank God for their goodness and the good they do? Do we really believe in and accept the Gospel that we are saved by grace alone through faith alone in Christ? Many people would rather earn their salvation than receive it as a free gift. It makes them feel important, independent, and self-sufficient. Good deeds give people a sense of satisfaction and accomplishment for which they can feel proud and gain self-esteem. Not many are willing, like the Publican, to beat on their chests and say they are lost and condemned sinners. Today people want to feel good about themselves.

Statistics show that a majority of Christians depend upon works, rather than grace, as the way to heaven. In a 1983 poll of 4371 church members, seventy-two percent indicated their agreement with the statement, "The Gospel is God's rules for right living," and seventy percent agreed that we are saved by good works. In 1986 another poll of church members was taken, and seventy-two percent said they expected to go to heaven because of their goodness and humility. These facts prove that today's parable is greatly needed to persuade church people that a person is justified only when one cries, "God, be merciful to me a sinner."

2. Whatever became of confession? The parable emphasizes the fact of sin. The tax collector confessed his sin, "Be merciful to me a sinner." In contrast, the Pharisee had no confession of sin. The Publican returned home "justified." To be justified was to be made right with God by means of the forgiving mercy of God for sin committed.

To what extent today are Christians confessing their sin: are they praying only for their accomplishments? One protestant denomination discovered, after a survey of worship services, that over eighty percent of their congregations made no provision for the confession of sins in their orders of service. Other denominations now make the confession of sins optional. One of the six most popular television preachers declares that he never mentions sin or humility in his sermons. If there is no confession of sins, there is no awareness of sins. If there is no awareness of sins, there is no need for the Gospel or the Savior. In this case, we are arrogant Pharisees who claim to have no sins, only good works.

Points to Ponder

1. Humility or mercy? As we have seen, this parable can be understood as teaching either humility based on verse 14b, or justification based on verse 14a. If the theme of humility-pride is chosen, we have a duplication of themes with the Parable of the Chief Seats. (Luke 14:7-14) If justification is the theme, there is no repetition. Most New Testament scholars hold that justification is the main teaching of this parable.

2. Justification without the cross? In these parables we have been asking, "Where is the Gospel?" In today's parable we learn of a sinner who, after confessing his sin to God in the temple returns home "justified." Apparently Christ and the cross are not involved in the forgiving act. How could Christ be involved when he gave the parable? Does this mean that forgiveness and salvation can be secured apart from the atoning death on the cross? If so, Jews do not need Christ, for they can pray the same prayer of the Jew-Publican. If so, why then should the church have a program of outreach to non-Christians? Nevertheless, the New Testament repeatedly teaches that Jesus is the Christ (Savior) who expiates, propitiates, and redeems us from sin, death, and hell. In this there is the Gospel. Once again, the parable reminds us that it needs to be interpreted in the light of the entire Bible's teaching.

Illustrative Materials

1. Amazing Grace. In a small, poverty-stricken house in London, there was a hard-working woman. For years she bent over a washtub to make a living for her family. As she worked, she prayed for her teen-age son who had run away to sea. She prayed that her son would give his life to God. After she died, her prayer was answered. Her son became the captain of a slave ship and later a preacher. He wrote a hymn which brought many to Christ. Like the Publican, John Newton could sing: "Amazing grace, how sweet the sound that saved a wretch like me."

2. Grace Alone? William Muehl tells of meeting a Lutheran layman who was a pillar of the church and community because of his wonderful good works. He asked the farmer, "Why is it that you put yourself out so often to serve your neighbors, when you claim to believe that we are saved by grace alone? Is it out of sheer gratitude to God for the gift of unconditional love?" The man replied, after looking around to see if his pastor was within earshot, "Well, I guess that is the official answer, sure. I am saved by grace alone. But, I figure, why take a chance?"

3. The Consequences of Self-centeredness. The newspaper, *Peking Daily*, gave the following interpretation of Liu Yong, who knifed a young woman to death and then electrocuted himself:

> "Liu's outlook was based on self-centeredness, self-design self-struggle, and self-importance. All these lead to self-destruction."

4. Pride Before a Fall. *Time Magazine* gave the following description of the Jim and Tammy Bakker scandal of 1987:

"If Jim Bakker began with holy intentions, he eventually fell victim to his own substantial ego. Bolstered by adoring crowds and flush with donated cash, the evangelist lost sight of the Christian message he preached. The more PTL prospered, the more, apparently, the preacher believed he could do no wrong."

5. "I Love Me." A prisoner asked a magazine editor to print his letter. In the letter he said,

"David Mayson, who is a born-again Christian, very open-minded, and, yes, an all-around nice guy, and a down-to-earth fun-loving gent, with a beautiful sense of humor at age 45, has been incarcerated for twelve long and painful years . . ."

6. Not Like a Pharisee. After a lengthy lesson on the Pharisee and the Publican, a Sunday School teacher said to her class, "Now, children, let us thank God we are not like that nasty Pharisee."

7. Getting into Heaven. There is a legend about a man who was met by an angel at the gates of heaven. He was told that he would need 1000 points of merit in order to enter. The angel asked him if he had earned any good points while on earth. The man said he had joined the church. The angel said that that was worth ten points. He had worshiped regularly. That was worth five points. He had gone to Sunday church school. Another five points. He had given generously to the church. That gave him a few more points. Finally the angel asked, "Do you think you will ever get into heaven?"

The man replied, "Only by the grace of God will I make it." The angel then opened the gates and said, "Enter."